W9-BKA-127

Po 78355

11-6-01

Bull
Run

Bull Run

Wall Street,

the Democrats,

and the New Politics

of Personal Finance

Daniel Gross

 PublicAffairs

New York

Printed in the United States of America

Book design and composition by Mark McGarry,
Texas Type & Book Works.

Library of Congress Cataloging-in-Publication Data
Gross, Daniel
Bull Run : Wall Street, the democrats, and the new politics of personal finance / Daniel Gross.
p. cm.
Includes index.
ISBN 1–891620–29–0
1. Wall Street. 2. Stock exchanges—United States. 3. Business and politics—United States. 4. Democratic Party (U.S.). 5. Finance, Public—United States. I. Title.
HG4572.G76 2000
332'.0973—dc21
99–086752

FIRST EDITION
10 9 8 7 6 5 4 3 2 1

For my parents, Barry and Sandra Gross

Contents

Bull
Run

1

The Democratization of Money

*U*sing a cab driver as a straw man is one of the oldest journalistic tricks in the book. For decades, writers parachuting into new territory with the intent of reporting on a certain individual, a sports team, or a trend have used a conversation with a hack driver as a dramatic device. Aside from sparing the writer the effort of having to seek out and interview an authentic working-class individual, talking shop with a cabbie lends a certain blue-collar authenticity to even the most elitist reporter. If the salt-of-the-earth cab drivers are talking about a topic, the logic goes, it must merit our attention—no matter what the subject matter.

For example, writer James Atlas traveled to Washington in 1989 to do some reporting for a *New York Times Magazine* article about the middlebrow intellectuals' topic du jour, the assertion by political theorist Francis Fukuyama that "History Had Ended." In the piece, Atlas reported on his casual conversation with a Washington cab driver about Fukuyama's neo-Hegelian thesis—which goes to show that some clichés are endlessly elastic. Thus it is with some trepidation that I kick off this book with an anecdote about an encounter with . . . a cab driver.

In early April 1998, I flew into Boston on one of those perfect spring days that make you realize why the Puritan settlers chose to disembark there 370 years ago. Brilliant sunshine sparkled on the Charles River, where crew teams knifed their boats through the water. The air, infused with the slightest essence of salt, was warm but crisp. As I climbed into a cab at Logan Airport, I noticed that the driver—a slightly disheveled man with heavy black-rimmed glasses and sparse, yellowed teeth—was perusing a document whose distinctive rectangular shape and green tint I recognized as a statement from Fidelity Investments.

Spotting a fellow Fidelity Investments account holder—one of the 12 million in the country—I made small talk. "Checking your investments?" I asked snarkily. Over the next half hour, I would come to regret the question and wonder why I didn't instead bury my nose in the *Boston Globe*.

The cabbie's name was Sheldon Appel, and he had one of those inordinately heavy Beantown accents you hear only on Boston-area talk radio or in the Fenway Park bleachers. "Let me aaahsk you a few questions," he said, launching into a routine he'd obviously performed before on unsuspecting passengers. He proceeded to aaahsk me if I worked in a field related to finance (yes), what my income was (none of his business), and if I was married (yes). Then he made me look silly. In rapid sequence, he fired off a series of complicated questions about personal finance: What's the difference between a Keogh and a SEP-IRA plan, and how much money can a person legitimately stow in each annually? What's the level of income for a child that triggers the kiddie tax? To whom is the alternative minimum tax applicable? What's the maximum allowable home mortgage deduction? Each time, I mulled the question, fumfered for a few seconds, and mumbled an incorrect response. Peeking into the rearview mirror to check out the dull look on my face, he then ripped off the answers with an air of bemused satisfaction.

Appearances to the contrary, Mr. Appel was apparently a savvy and experienced investor. He kept the Fidelity statements in his car, he said, because he didn't want his current girlfriend, with whom he shared an apartment, to know how much money he had. (Appel was smarting from a prior divorce.) He described his condo in Florida, and told of his ability to get in on hot initial public offerings managed by Merrill Lynch, where his girlfriend worked. As traffic backed up on Storrow Drive, and as my destination loomed achingly far in the distance, Appel began to spin tales about the IRS's efforts to get him. While I listened, my mind sporadically flashed back to *Conspiracy Theory*, the Mel Gibson–Julia Roberts vehicle in which Gibson played a deranged but well-meaning cab driver. When Appel mentioned the CIA in a muted voice, I checked to make sure the doors weren't locked. I began to wish I had saved $20 and taken the "T."

But just as I was beginning to doubt my driver's sanity, he passed his statements over the front seat. One, from Fidelity, showed a balance of more than $100,000. Another, from Merrill Lynch, detailed holdings in the low six figures. Stocks, bonds, mutual funds—in all a nicely balanced portfolio. So here I was, relaxing in the backseat of a beat-up Ford, having alighted from a Delta shuttle where my fellow passengers included former White House counsel Bernard Nussbaum, wearing my one decent suit, clutching a newly leased Dell laptop, feeling rather professional. And I was being chauffeured to Harvard Square by a cabbie with a net worth in the mid-six figures—several times the size of my meager portfolio.

So what business does our friendly cab driver have being the leadoff character in a book about the markets, the Democratic party, and the new politics of personal finance? Answer: everything.

AMONG the many astonishing developments of the past decade has been a phenomenon I've dubbed the "democratization of money." The democratization of money has several different meanings and distinct manifestations. Some of them, like the millions of Americans who now trade stocks with abandon on the Internet, are glaringly obvious. Others, like the growth and power of pension plans representing public employees, are latent. But whether advertised in neon or bubbling sub rosa, the democratization of money was one of the dominating and distinguishing marks of the 1990s. After the crash of 1987, the entire American financial system, from underwriters to mutual fund companies, from commercial banks to the financial news media, retooled and restructured to serve people like Appel and the 84 million other Americans who own stocks, to ply them with information and services, and to make them feel as if they are insiders in one of the greatest and longest-running confidence games around: the 1990s bull market.

In 2000, with our brief memory spans and even shorter news cycles, it's difficult to conceive that the financial world once was quite different. But in terms of money and the markets, the events of the past decade have been simply astonishing. For much of the twentieth century, the percentage of American households owning stock hovered between 10 percent and 20 percent. As late as 1990, fewer than a quarter of adult Americans owned stock or mutual funds. But as equity values soared in the 1990s, individual investors flooded into the markets like Christmas shoppers in pursuit of Furby dolls. Since 1990, the percentage of Americans owning stocks and mutual funds has doubled, from 23 percent to 46 percent. Factor in the millions whose pension funds are invested in the markets, and for the first time in American history, a majority of citizens have a stake in the public equity and debt markets.

In the 1990s, investing evolved from the exclusive privilege of the rich into a do-it-yourself hobby for the vast middle and upper-middle class. Along with the explosion of the Internet, this trend may prove to be one of the decade's more important and far-reaching developments. Today, more people own stocks than surf the Internet, watch the hit TV show *ER*, or vote—and by large margins. In November 1995, mutual fund assets, at about $2.6 trillion, first exceeded deposits in the commercial banking system. In other words, Americans for the past five years have felt more comfortable stowing their cash in the volatile markets than in federally insured bank accounts. Indeed, people are investing in stocks to the exclusion of other, more traditional instruments. The percentage of individual wealth tied up in equities soared to 28 percent from 12 percent in 1992. Meanwhile, money management firms have stumbled over themselves to pitch new offerings to small investors. Today, there are some 7,400 mutual funds, up from 3,086 in 1990. That's pretty stunning, considering there are only about 7,000 stocks traded on the principal U.S. exchanges. In addition, brokerages ranging from established behemoths like Merrill Lynch to upstarts like E-Trade (whose customer base has grown from zero in 1992 to 1.5 million today) have paved the way for even the most humble investor to play the game with the big boys. In 1996, it cost $60 to trade a stock with Fidelity; today, a Fidelity Internet trade costs under $20. Such equalizing shifts may explain why PaineWebber CEO Richard Marron dubbed the 1990s "the decade of the little guy."

The little guys—like me and my friendly taxi driver—thrive on a steady and nutritious diet of financial media. When the market crashed in 1987, there was one failing financial news network, the unimaginatively named Financial News Network. Like many other creatures of the 1980s boom, it filed for Chapter 11 bankruptcy protection soon after the October 1987 drubbing. Today, however, no fewer than three financial television networks cover the markets with all the intensity, fanfare, and overkill the media bring to bear on sporting events.

CNBC, the leading financial news network, was for several years after its birth in 1989 a mere blip on the Nielsen meters. In 1992 it posted a meager 0.3 rating, meaning no more than 50,000 viewers were tuning in at any given time. In the mid-1990s, CNBC was transformed from a laggard into a global, profitable brand name by an unlikely force of democratization: Roger Ailes. The paunchy media adviser to both Ronald Reagan and George Bush and one-time producer of Rush Limbaugh's television show took CNBC's helm in 1993. As the bull market continued to rage throughout the 1990s, Ailes's revamped lineup of news and talk attracted more and more viewers. By 1995, CNBC reached 55 million U.S. homes and raked in a $40 million profit. Capitalizing on the ever-globalizing economy, the network spawned CNBC Asia and CNBC Europe. Today, the networks collectively reach about 147 million homes in 70 countries. CNBC has even created its own stable of stars, including Maria Bartiromo, aka the "Money Honey." The gorgeous thirty-two-year-old market reporter, who loses her Bay Ridge, Brooklyn, accent when the klieg lights go on, is an object of devotion among the troglodytes who roam the floor of the New York Stock Exchange. The Christiane Amanpour of Wall Street, she shouts out the latest developments—relayed to her by producers—while being jostled by floor traders.

Jealous of CNBC's profits and ubiquity in the mid-1990s, other news organizations hastened to start rivals. Ted Turner's CNNfn debuted in 1996. The same year, Dow Jones & Co., long a bit player in TV land, joined forces with ITT to buy a television station from New York City for more than $100 million, and dubbed it WBIS+. In retrospect, it should have been called WBUST. It disappeared within a year, as ITT sold its interest in the station. (Dow Jones later struck an alliance with CNBC to get more of its reporters on air.) WBIS+ was replaced on New York's cable systems by Bloomberg Television, a venture of information mogul Michael Bloomberg. The three networks—

CNBC, CNNfn, and Bloomberg Television—have become a part of the American public landscape, airing silently in restaurants, hotel lobbies, and airports. In November 1999, CNBC's daytime Nielsen ratings topped those of CNN.

The growth in financial television has been mimicked by a boom in print media. The 1990s started with one mass-circulation personal finance magazine, Time Warner's *Money*. In 1992 two new entrants came along. The first was *Worth*, a glossy lifestyle monthly backed by the venture-capital arm of Fidelity Investments. The second was *Smart Money*, backed by Dow Jones: It proved the rare instance in which the venerable company—working with Hearst Publications—successfully leveraged its heritage of journalistic excellence into a profitable sideline. *Smart Money* was run by Steven Swartz, a thirty-year-old wunderkind. Just seven years out of Harvard, the short, boyish-looking journalist had shared a Pulitzer Prize for covering the 1987 market crash as an editor and writer on the *Wall Street Journal*'s page-one staff. Assembling a staff from the *Journal*, including fellow Pulitzer winner James Stewart, Swartz started a mass-circulation magazine from scratch. Chockablock with stock and mutual fund recommendations, as well as tips on how to get the most out of credit cards, *Smart Money* became a huge success, winning not only a National Magazine Award but proving a profitable addition to Dow Jones's bottom line. Its circulation grew from about 396,000 in 1993 to 760,000 in 1999. For its part, *Worth* sports a circulation of 534,000.

The most successful purveyor of financial information in the 1990s was Michael Bloomberg. His multimedia empire now includes a global wire service with dozens of bureaus, a radio station, a television network, two magazines, and a best-selling book entitled, naturally, *Bloomberg by Bloomberg*. With his billboard trucks, rapidly expanding empire, political aspirations, and propensity for putting his name on everything from magazines to the napkins in the in-house snack bar, Bloomberg is the William Randolph Hearst of the 1990s. But whereas Hearst's late-nineteenth-century readers thirsted for details of the latest Spanish outrage in Cuba or of public corruption, Bloomberg's manifold info-con-sumers thirst for the progress of the Standard & Poor's (S&P) 500 and the performance of the latest initial public offering (IPO).

The growth of the financial media has helped contribute to a grow-ing sense of the markets as a shared public space, one that has room for investors large and small, and in which those with the time to monitor and plot their own investments can deal on equal terms with large insti-tutions. Stock ownership has even trickled down to the working and lower classes to a degree. I say this not just because my friendly cab driver—a working-class, Northeastern, urban ethnic; in other words, a prototypical Democrat—has a six-figure portfolio. Rather, in the 1990s, more and more members of traditional Democratic constituencies became moneyed—in the sense that their holdings in stocks, bonds, and mutual funds soared along with the Dow. These individuals include the millions of government workers, schoolteachers, and unionized manufacturing laborers, all of whom own stocks indirectly through their active and powerful pension funds. And there are more of these folks than might be expected. Despite the antigovernment nos-trums of the Reagan era and President Clinton's 1995 declaration that the "era of big government is over," total government employment in the United States rose from 15.8 million in 1982 to 20.0 million in 1998. Since 1992, in fact, the public sector has employed more Americans than the manufacturing sector. Because the vast majority of public employees are covered by pensions, and because the public sector is growing and aging, public pension plans have found themselves with ever-larger piles of cash to invest. Equity holdings of public employee pension funds rose from $120 billion in 1985 to $1.325 trillion in 1998, making them among the largest and most aggressive owners of equities in the nation. The California Public Employees Retirement System (CALPERS), for example, owns some $105 billion in stocks.

Many of the people who run such large pension funds are popularly elected, like Carl McCall, the ambitious New York state comptroller. McCall was the only New York Democrat elected at the state level in 1994, and was easily reelected in 1998. A former banker, and the first black to hold statewide office in New York, McCall runs the state's Common Retirement Fund—a role that gives him far more juice than the traditional comptroller's duties of auditing state agencies and local governments. New York's $115 billion portfolio is larger than Fidelity's Magellan Fund, the world's largest mutual fund.

McCall's situation is not as unique as it seems. Take a simple question: Who owns the largest portfolio of stocks today? If you guessed Warren Buffett or even Bill Gates, you're wrong. In fact, the largest single portfolio of stocks is held in escrow for a class of people whose collective attitude toward Wall Street is indifferent at best, and ideologically hostile at worst. TIAA-CREF, whose net assets top $273 billion, invests the money of some two million college professors, researchers, and employees of 9,000 nonprofit organizations. From its Manhattan headquarters, TIAA-CREF's investment officers manage a portfolio whose worth is greater than the combined market capitalizations of General Motors, Ford, and Daimler-Chrysler. In the past decade, intellectuals have frequently complained about corporate incursions into the once-protected grounds of universities. Irony of ironies, the intellectuals have been making greater inroads into publicly held corporations.

The expanding shareholder population, the boom in the financial media, and the growing financial heft of surrogates for nontraditional investors have helped contribute to a sense that the markets as a *cultural* phenomenon are more democratic. After all, when critics—journalists, politicians, intellectuals—talked about money in the 1980s, they were signifying a certain group of attributes: greed, selfishness, and, almost inevitably, corruption. Rent Oliver Stone's *Wall Street,* or peruse the titles of the classic books on 1980s Wall Street culture: *Barbarians at the Gate, Den of Thieves, Predators' Ball*. These works present an almost

uniformly unsavory gaggle of grasping, salivating financiers who are dis-
loyal friends and lovers to boot.

It was easy to be critical of Wall Street back then because it was not
representative of what politicians like to call the "real America." In the
1980s, stock investing was still restricted to a small minority of the population. Furthermore, the action seemed to be taking place in private,
behind the glittering glass walls of office buildings in lower Manhattan,
not on the bustling floor of the New York Stock Exchange. Even the
language employed to describe the most notorious activities of the
decade had dark, undemocratic shadings. The most prominent and
written-about financial development of the 1980s was the leveraged
buyout (LBO), a tactic through which investors took a company *private*
by buying out the public shareholders, then restructured the company
and resold it for a huge profit. The intent, of course, was to cut the public shareholders out of the wealth creation. The practitioners and
enablers of this black art—Henry Kravis, T. Boone Pickens, Ron Perelman, Michael Milken, among others—were the most exalted and
envied financial figures of the 1980s. How different the prevailing attitude of the democratic 1990s, when the ultimate goal of any private
financier is to take a company *public*, to let the public in on ownership
and watch the shares take off like a wind-up toy. Between 1996 and 1998
alone, there were 1,141 initial public offerings, or more than one a day.

So democratized did the markets become in the 1990s that the conventional wisdom is that one doesn't have to be a sophisticated LBO
artist to succeed on Wall Street. Quite the contrary. The Motley Fool—
a Web site that spawned a half dozen investment and personal finance
books—holds out as its premise that a fool could invest safely in the
market. The authors, brothers David and Tom Gardner, appear on the
cover of their books wearing jesters' hats. A slightly different message
was conveyed by the ladies of the Beardstown Investment Club, who
picked stocks from their little ol' hamlet (population 6,000) 225 miles
southwest of Chicago. Their first book, *The Beardstown Ladies Com-*

mon Sense Investment Guide, featured on its cover a picture of sixteen heavy-set middle-aged women in floral prints holding fans of dollar bills. The group, formed in 1983, claimed 23.4 percent annual returns on the stocks they picked. In the era of democratized money, the Beardstown Ladies seemed to say, every man and woman could be his or her own stock picker. Their bubble was punctured in 1998, when a reporter from *Chicago* magazine ran their numbers. It turned out the Beardstown Ladies' records were considerably more modest than their ghostwriter, former *Time* writer Leslie Whitaker, suggested. Instead of notching 23.4 percent annual returns, they instead returned about 9 percent. The unmasking of the Beardstown Ladies proves to be yet another example of the democratization of money. In the 1990s, you don't have to be a slick, wealthy insider to get rich by pulling the wool over the eyes of the investing public.

The contrast between the financial icons of the two decades is similarly revealing. To be sure, the men who captured the most headlines in the 1980s—Henry Kravis, Carl Icahn, and Michael Milken—are still with us, though in somewhat altered form. Kravis, perhaps sensing a shift in the zeitgeist, divorced his 1980s wife, socialite/fashion designer Carolyn Roehm, and married a serious-minded Canadian economist; Milken is active in educational ventures, raises funds for prostate cancer research, and has authored a macrobiotic cookbook. But Kravis, Milken, and the rest of the 1980s Masters of the Universe have been surpassed in the popular imagination by a group of men who make money not solely for themselves or for their private backers and lenders but for public shareholders. In the age of democratized money, after all, shareholder value is the ultimate measuring stick of an executive's worth. So businessmen like Warren Buffett, Bill Gates, Jeff Bezos of Amazon.com, Michael Dell, the founder of Dell Computers, Bernard Marcus and Arthur Blank of Home Depot, and mutual fund manager Michael Price have been lionized in the press. Each became a billionaire, or near billionaire, in the 1990s. But they didn't get into the ten-figure club merely by having their chums on the board of directors grant them huge options stakes at ridiculously low prices. Rather, their wealth rose as the stock they owned in the companies they founded or bought rose exponentially—at almost exactly the same rate as stock held by their common shareholders. Over the course of the 1990s, a retiree who socked away 200 shares of Microsoft in his 401(K) reaped the same percentage return on cash invested as Bill Gates did—7,723 percent.

The leading moneymen of the 1990s differ from their 1980s counterparts not only in their more wholesome attitudes but also in their conduct. As Connie Bruck so deftly portrayed it in her eponymous book, the defining event of 1980s money culture was the Predators' Ball, Drexel Burnham Lambert's annual Beverly Hills junk-bond conference. Glitzy, over-the-top, and intensely private, it featured gorgeous prostitutes and performances by the likes of Frank Sinatra and Diana Ross. But Drexel, which once occupied 55 Broad Street and 60 Broad Street in downtown Manhattan, is gone. Fifty-five Broad—now dubbed the New York Information and Technology Center—has been transformed by the Rudin real estate family into a playground for cyber-entrepreneurs. It features a cozy playroom called the Hearth, with foosball and pool tables. Across the street, 60 Broad is being converted into loft apartments.

The defining event of today's money culture, by contrast, is the annual meeting of Berkshire-Hathaway, Warren Buffett's publicly held investment vehicle. Each May, the second-wealthiest man in America invites all stockholders to plebeian Omaha, Nebraska, for a weekend. There, hotshot money managers rub shoulders with retirees who scraped together the $2,200 necessary to buy a share of the company's Class B stock. The homespun value stock investor neatly embodies the principles of the democratization of money. Here's a multibillionaire based in the heartland, making sound long-term investments in blue-chip companies like Coca-Cola, the Washington Post Co., and GEICO, sharing his wisdom and profits with adoring shareholders, and operating with a sense of openness and inclusion. How middle American, how family-friendly, how wholesome, how . . . democratic.

But what does the democratization of money mean? Embarrassing encounters between writers and cab drivers? Higher ratings for CNBC? A wider range of mutual funds from which to choose? Yes, yes, and yes. But none of these developments are as important as what I would argue is the larger meaning: its effect on politics.

These developments, combined with secular trends in the two-party system, have altered the relationship between money and politics.* And that interaction has gone practically unnoticed in this decade of unexpected developments and revolutions. Think about all that's transpired in the 1990s. A Democrat won two presidential elections for the first time since 1936; the annual federal budget swung from a $292 billion deficit in 1992 to a $77 billion annual surplus in 1999. Republicans gained control of the House of Representatives for the first time since 1952; Newt Gingrich rose from the backbenches to the podium of the House, only to resign in frustration; and the Republican majority put a president on trial for impeachment for the first time since 1869. Each of these phenomena has been the subject of relentless media overkill. But one of the more interesting upheavals has gone underreported. Specifically, I mean the reorientation of the Democratic party, through the Clinton administration, toward Wall Street, and the coincident alienation of many Republicans from one of their historical bases. These shifts, too, are an important and far-reaching manifestation of the democratization of money.

In the 1980s, it almost goes without saying, big money was identified

---

*I'm not talking about campaign money here. The Supreme Court's 1976 ruling in *Buckley v. Valeo* held that political money is tantamount to speech, thus putting Archer Daniels Midland on the same elevated moral and constitutional footing as Thomas Paine. That premise, as much as the bipartisan addiction to campaign cash, mitigates against any substantive changes in financing campaigns.

as Republican. Haynes Johnson opened his great book on the 1980s, *Sleepwalking Through History*, with an anecdote about private jets lining up on the tarmac at National Airport for Reagan's first inaugural. From that moment on, a series of political and cultural developments—the tax cuts, the stock boom, the LBO craze, Michael J. Fox's junior-Reaganite character on *Family Ties*, *Dynasty*—seemed to reinforce the historical identification between the financial upper crust and the party of Lincoln. The major financiers of the decade were, almost to a man, Republicans. So were many of the more notorious figures in the savings and loan crisis, from Charles Keating to David Paul. The biggest corporate merger of the 1980s was the $44 billion marriage of R. J. Reynolds (RJR) and Nabisco, which was Republican to its very core—quite apart from the fact that it involved an industry (tobacco) that had increasingly come to be identified with the Republican party. The cast of characters included the Forstmann brothers (Ted and Nick), Henry Kravis, American Express chairman and CEO James Robinson and his publicist wife, Linda—active Republicans all. One of the pivotal scenes in HBO's cinematic treatment *Barbarians at the Gate* was set at a Bush-Quayle 1988 fundraiser.

Flash forward to the biggest serious financial services deal of the 1990s, the 1998 merger between Citibank and Travelers, to form Citicorp. The deal had a Democratic tinge to it. Both merger partners, after all, were technology-savvy, internationalist financial services companies, intent on marketing their products to a broad public, and run by Democratic executives: veteran banker John Reed and Sanford Weill, a Brooklyn-born son of immigrants. At the press conference announcing the merger, a reporter asked about potential antitrust problems. Reed remarked, "Sandy will call up his friend, the president." The following year, they recruited Clinton's treasury secretary, Robert Rubin, to join them at the helm of the nation's largest financial institution.

Weill and Reed aren't the only prominent Wall Streeters of the 1990s who are Democrats. In fact, a new group of moneymen surfaced in the 1990s. Fueled by the information age, the resurgence of New York City, the soaring markets, and the broader consumer interest in financial services, they have supplanted the financial icons of the 1980s. Members of this group—I call them the "New Moneycrats"—include the aforementioned Bloomberg, Weill, and John Reed but also James Cramer, the hyperactive hedge-fund manager and founder of TheStreet.com; venture capitalist Alan Patricof, who hosted Clinton's visit to the Hamptons in summer 1998; Lazard Freres investment banker Steven Rattner; Jamie Dimon, formerly with Travelers; Boston buyout king Thomas Lee; former Goldman Sachs cohead Jon Corzine; investment banker Roger Altman; and former Bankers Trust CEO Frank Newman. These men have made huge donations to Clinton's campaigns, hosted administration officials at their homes, and, in the case of Altman and Newman, served in the Clinton administration.

The New Moneycrats are not necessarily a clique, although many of them know and do business with one another. Rather, they're a class. They share a common background. Most are self-made products of the Northeastern meritocratic machine, graduates of Ivy League or comparable schools, residents of Manhattan, socially moderate, and philanthropic. They frequent the same vacation spots—namely, the Hamptons and Martha's Vineyard—and golf at the same clubs. They also share a political worldview that is equal parts inheritance from their parents' New Deal liberalism, a product of their education, and the pragmatic, broad-minded worldview required of anyone involved with big business and high finance today.

Of course, there have always been Wall Streeters who were active Democrats, from Bernard Baruch, who helped Woodrow Wilson finance World War I, to Felix Rohatyn, ambassador to France and éminence grise of Lazard Freres, who helped New York City restructure its finances in the 1970s. Historically, many Wall Streeters chose the Democratic party because, as Jews, they didn't feel particularly welcome in the Republican party. But the tilt toward the Democrats has become more pronounced in the 1990s. In an odd time-delayed reaction, the Democratic party became yuppified in the 1990s, a decade later than the rest of the country. It's more hip to be a Democrat if you're loaded than it was in the 1980s. And it's more hip to be loaded if you're a Democrat.

Wealthy financiers have been attracted to what they perceive to be a "new" Democratic party, one that is more comfortable with the very idea of money. This was the great hope of the self-professed New Democrats who coalesced in the early 1990s around the Democratic Leadership Council (DLC), the probusiness, moderate wing of the party that critics like Jesse Jackson dubbed the "White Boys Caucus" or "Democrats for the Leisure Class." And just as the DLC's attitude toward trade and welfare reform became ascendant in the national party in the 1990s, so did its attitude toward money and the markets.

When Clinton first appeared on the national scene in 1992, he didn't seem likely to initiate a love affair with the markets. Clinton based his 1992 presidential campaign in no small part on class warfare, a posture best personified by consultant James Carville, a rabidly populist Wall Street basher who openly exulted in market plunges. The "putting people first" strategy he devised successfully painted George Bush as someone more concerned with capital gains than with expanding health care coverage, an out-of-touch millionaire incapable of understanding the suffering of middle-class Americans. But as so often proved the case with Clinton, there was a flip side. Aside from relying on Carville, who at times seemed to have just walked off the set of *Deliverance*, Clinton actively sought the counsel of a group of Wall Street insiders. Chief among them was Robert Rubin, the unassuming cochairman of Goldman Sachs, who chaired the host committee for the 1992 Democratic convention.

After he won the election, Clinton instantly became invested in the market—not personally but politically. After all, approval ratings generally follow markets, at least downward, and it fell to Rubin to manage the markets for Clinton. As head of the National Economic Council and, later, as treasury secretary, Rubin served two important purposes. He provided insight and advice to the oddly naive Clintonites on how not to roil the markets, and he provided the markets with a reassuring face in Washington. In a sharp departure from previous Democratic administrations, the Clintonites based nearly every crucial budget decision in part on the anticipated reaction of the bond and stock markets. The strategy worked. In Clinton's first term, of course, the market turned in one of the great four-year performances in American history—rising nearly 100 percent. (Even Carville grew to love the market, although he lamented to me in early 1996 that he pulled out too early.) In fact, the market's strength probably was a key contributor to Clinton's reelection, since the continuing rise of the market and the massive growth in trading volume helped generate huge and unexpected capital-gains taxes, which in turn helped lower the annual budget deficits beyond the administration's wildest expectations. Clinton used these lower deficits as a shield to fend off the Republicans' radical budget assaults. Without the market's performance, it's fair to say, Clinton's first term would not have been as successful.

Indeed, in many ways the most important decision of Clinton's presidency wasn't to press ahead with the 1993 budget deal but to reappoint Alan Greenspan to head the Federal Reserve Board. Greenspan, a one-time jazz saxophonist and Ayn Rand devotee, is yet another of the unlikely financial icons of the 1990s. And he, too, has been Democratized—that is to say, embraced both by Democrats and by the broader public. For most of the century, central bankers have labored in obscurity. But with the onset of the democratization of money, the man who controls the direction of interest rates, and hence the health of the stock market, occupies a much more prominent role. At first, it was unclear whether this hard-core economic conservative would find common cause with the New Democrats in the White House. But Greenspan likes access and the proximity to power as much as the next

guy in Washington. He frequently plays tennis with White House officials, and he married Andrea Mitchell, NBC's White House corre-
spondent. Like many of Washington's alpha males, he's prone to vanity
and concerned with his image. While sitting behind him once on the
Delta shuttle from LaGuardia to Washington, I peeked through the
crack between seats to get a glimpse at what he was reading. The
latest numbers from the Dallas Federal Reserve Board? A chart on the
labor employment cost index, one of his favorite indicators? No. The
world's most powerful economist was poring through—what else?—
The Economist.

Of course, there was never any real doubt but that Clinton would
reappoint him, and that Greenspan would accept. To be sure, he occasionally incurred the wrath of prairie populists like Sen. Byron Dorgan
and Sen. Tom Harkin, and of right-wing supply-siders, who agitate for
lower interest rates with the single-mindedness of out-of-touch zealots.
But by and large, he has been immensely popular among both
Democrats and Republicans in Congress. When he treks to Capitol
Hill to deliver the biannual Humphrey-Hawkins testimony,
Greenspan is greeted with equally unctuous huzzahs from Democrats
and Republicans.

In 1998, Steven Glass, the former *New Republic* staffer whose serial
fabrications went unchecked for an embarrassingly long time, penned
a fictitious article in which he described New York–based bond traders
who erected a small shrine to the Fed chief and celebrated his birthday.
In retrospect, Glass managed to get the story 100 percent wrong and 95
percent right. Greenspan does have a cultlike following on Wall Street.
Traders hang on his every public and private utterance, desperate for
any clue that could signal a move upward or downward in interest rates.
Wall Street economists sift through transcripts of meetings of the Fed's
policymaking body—the Federal Open Market Committee—much as
Roman priests once examined chicken entrails in search of omens.
Greenspan is a man as much listened to as President Clinton is

ignored. Whereas Clinton ladles out his words in huge servings, Greenspan serves his parsimoniously, in carefully measured dollops. After public speeches, packs of journalists scurry around the lobbies of hotels and convention centers, trying to figure out where he will exit and hoping he'll respond to furtively shouted questions. (I'm ashamed to admit I once was one of them.)

Indeed, it was the reaction to one such public appearance by Greenspan—the 1996 event at which he injected the term "irrational exuberance" into our lingua franca—that set this book in motion. On Thursday, December 5, 1996, Greenspan was the marquee speaker at the American Enterprise Institute's $400-per-head, black-tie annual dinner and Francis Boyer Lecture at the Washington Hilton. After discussing the evolving role of the U.S. central bank, Greenspan expressed concern about the astonishing rise of the U.S. stock markets. That day, the Dow Jones industrial average closed above 6,400; it had soared nearly 25 percent in the first eleven months of 1996, and that on the heels of a 33 percent gain in 1995. The fact that stocks traded at high multiples to earnings greatly concerned the central banker, a monomaniac when it comes to inflation. "How do we know when irrational exuberance has unduly escalated asset values, which then become subject to unexpected and prolonged contractions as they have in Japan over the past decade?" he asked rhetorically. "And how do we factor that assessment into monetary policy?"

To any listener versed in "Fedspeak"—the arcane symbolic language spoken by Greenspan and his cohort—this seemingly innocuous musing was a lightning bolt. Greenspan, this speech made clear, believed that stock markets—particularly the U.S. market—were dangerously overvalued, and that stock prices should fall. If the market's invisible hand didn't correct itself soon, Greenspan would correct them with his very visible hand, by raising interest rates. The immediate import of the remarks was largely lost on the guests, whose number included Health and Human Services Secretary Donna Shalala and

Supreme Court Justice Antonin Scalia, as they dined contentedly on lobster bisque, rock cornish game hen in pear peppercorn sauce, and mocha puffs. But the reaction overseas was swift and furious. As Friday unfolded westward, from time zone to time zone, markets swooned as if in some time-delayed bit of choreography. Tokyo's, Hong Kong's, and Sydney's key indices fell 3 percent on the day. The European markets took the news even harder. Amsterdam's bourse nose-dived nearly 6.2 percent off the opening bell, with Paris's slumping 4.9 percent and London's falling 4.2 percent. In New York, the Dow plunged 145 points, or more than 2 percent, in the first thirty minutes of trading. Throughout the trading day, Greenspan's speech was the subject of much head-scratching in Washington, New York, and anywhere else investors watched the markets. Within a full revolution of the news cycle, the phrase "irrational exuberance" entered America's elastic pop-culture lingo—just as surely as had the fabled line from the movie *Jerry Maguire*, "Show me the money."

That speech, and the reaction to it, first got me thinking about the democratization of money as a phenomenon. But my focus wasn't prompted so much by the catchy phrase "irrational exuberance"— which was practically buried in the 4,317-word address—as by the way Greenspan chose to begin the speech: The venerable free-market economist opened with a quote from a venerable free-market antago-nist—William Jennings Bryan. Bryan rose from obscurity and poverty on the plains of Nebraska to become an agitated voice for farmers as a congressman in the 1890s. Bryan was the Democrats' presidential nom-inee in 1896, when there was a huge rift in the Democratic party, and the country at large, between advocates of a tight monetary policy— that is, sticking to the gold standard—and those who favored the free coinage of silver. Bryan favored expanding the money supply through the free coinage of silver, which would boost prices paid to farmers for their goods and enable them to pay off debts to "moneyed interests" on the East Coast with cheaper currency. At the Democratic convention in Chicago, Bryan, making the case for free silver, concluded by thundering, "You shall not crucify mankind upon a cross of gold."

Greenspan used the quote to show how the issue of monetary policy and central banking had been divisive throughout American history. Of course, as Greenspan noted, Bryan's point was about the gold standard, rather than the notion of gold qua money. But Bryan's chilling metaphor has gained great resonance as it has echoed through the decades. As the years passed, Bryan became an icon among Democrats—joining Alfred Smith, Adlai Stevenson, Hubert Humphrey, and others in a long line of admirable losers. (Had he not slipped into revanchist buffoonery by taking the side of God at the Scopes "monkey trial," Bryan would rank as one of the giants of U.S. political history.) Just so, the "cross of gold" evolved into an all-purpose weapon of Democratic class warfare. After all, one would be hard-pressed to devise a better metaphor. It mingles the image of Christ on the one hand and Mammon on the other; humanity pinned by the demands of the material world; the merciful golden rule against the merciless rule of gold; the unvirtuous moneyed (in Bryan's case, Eastern bankers) against the virtuous unmoneyed (in Bryan's case, the farmers of the plains).

The figures of William Jennings Bryan and William Jefferson Clinton, who rose to the national stage one hundred years apart at the head of the same party, make neat bookends—and not just because of the similarity of their names. Rather, Bryan's enduring legacy was as an antagonist of the "moneyed interests," a dogma to which the Democratic party held firm for nearly a hundred years. By contrast, one of Clinton's most enduring legacies may be his party's accommodation to those same interests. Of course, the moneyed interests of the 1990s— the mass of individual investors—are far less sinister than their counterparts were in the age of the robber barons; it's easier to sympathize with a taxi driver than with John D. Rockefeller. Still, the changes in the markets in the 1990s, the rise of new figures in finance, and the shifting fortunes of the Democratic party have combined to change the way many Democrats think about money and the markets.

Furthermore, this accommodation didn't merely dictate where Clinton chose to take his summer vacations, or who received invitations to the White House coffees. Rather, it has wrought serious policy changes that affect all investors and taxpayers, and that may affect future generations as well. The Securities and Exchange Commission (SEC), for example, has been completely remade under the leadership of Arthur Levitt Jr., one of the best-pedigreed of all the New Moneycrats. Since taking over in 1993, Levitt, the son of legendary New York State comptroller Arthur Levitt and president of the American Stock Exchange from 1978 to 1989, has transformed the SEC into a vital consumer protection agency, and has overseen the launch of EDGAR, the online repository of information that has helped fuel the democratization of money. As such, he's perhaps the least appreciated and most successful Clinton appointee.

There have been other, more far-reaching policy implications of the Democrats' accommodation to money. In an action that would have been shocking to any Democrat as late as, say, 1994, Clinton in 1997 signed into law a capital-gains tax cut—essentially giving up the one wedge issue that had consistently worked in favor of the Democrats in the 1980s and 1990s. The reduction of the capital-gains tax has been followed by the shockingly rapid mainstreaming of the notion of putting Social Security funds in the stock market. In 1996, only Steve Forbes dared to suggest such an absurd notion. In his 1999 state-of-the-union address, President Clinton proposed investing 25 percent of the anticipated budget surplus in the markets.

The Democrats' entente with Wall Street is as much a function of their success as it is of the Republicans' failures. In short, the Republican party has essentially been taken over by what used to be Southern Democrats, and many of today's top congressional Republicans exhibit the same prejudices as their Dixiecrat forebears: a hostility toward the center of capital (New York), a deep antipathy toward the Northeastern elite, and an essentially reactionary opposition to modernism. The vicious tide of reaction that began among disaffected Southern Democrats like Tom Watson and "Pitchfork" Ben Tillman in the 1890s and pulsed through a series of similarly disaffected Democrats throughout the century, from Strom Thurmond to George Wallace, now runs squarely through the Southern Republican party. Senate Majority Leader Trent Lott, in fact, is a sort of blow-dried reincarnation of Tillman. Lott, from Mississippi, would feel about as comfortable at a dinner party in the Hamptons as most Hamptonites would feel at a catfish fry in Pascagoula. Which is to say, not very.

Many Wall Streeters are naturally put off by the crude cultural conservatism of Lott and his Southern Republican colleagues. This alienation has been exacerbated by the increasingly shrill anti-big-business tone expressed by the Republican party's growing populist wing. In both 1992 and 1996, Patrick Buchanan scored substantial success in Republican presidential primaries by fulminating against free-trade agreements like NAFTA (North American Free Trade Agreement) and GATT (General Agreement on Tariffs and Trade). Among a growing portion of the Republicans' core constituency, there is a general hostility toward internationalism, trade liberalization, social liberalism, and non-Christians—in other words, opposition to a number of premises and ways of life that are commonly accepted and practiced on Wall Street. Meanwhile, the GOP's genteel, moderate, establishment-oriented big-business-friendly members are fading from public view as rapidly as Christian consultant Ralph Reed's clients. The most powerful businessman in the House of Representatives today is Tom DeLay, a former small-time Texas exterminator who has condemned the theory of evolution in the well of the House.

The reversal, of course, is not complete. The Democrats are now no more the party of the satisfied rich than the Republicans are the standard-bearers of the resentful poor. (With apologies to Marx, it may turn out that the working class isn't the only group laboring under the veil of false consciousness.) Rather, we're in the midst of a transition, perhaps even a realignment, whose manifestations are cropping up here and there: Clinton carried the wealthy suburbs of Westchester County, New York, twice; Loretta Sanchez, a Hispanic Democrat, represents ur-Republican territory Orange County in Congress; the Democrats raised $123 million in soft money in the 1996 campaign cycle, nearly as much as the Republicans' $138 million; New Yorkers in the highest income brackets voted overwhelmingly for Democrat Charles Schumer over Republican Al D'Amato in the 1998 Senate race. In the first half of 1999, business donations were split evenly between Democrats and Republicans.

Still, the Democrats' accommodation to the moneyed interests is far from a fait accompli. A rump of the Democratic party is still hanging back from the Wall Street group hug. The resistance comes chiefly from leaders of the party's shrinking left wing, who view themselves as tribunes of the disenfranchised and those who have otherwise not benefited from the wonders of the new economy. In the 2000 presidential primary, some of the battle lines were drawn around precisely the issues posed by the democratization of money, such as the wisdom of capital-gains tax cuts and putting Social Security funds in the markets. And they are sure to reappear in the general election this fall.

The chapters that follow constitute an effort to describe how the party of Franklin D. Roosevelt and Lyndon Johnson has become, to a degree, the party of Dow and Jones, and why that isn't necessarily a bad thing. Given the democratization of money, the Democrats can be the party of Wall Street *and* Main Street, of the rich *and* the poor, of Orange County *and* East Los Angeles. To paraphrase Nixon's embrace of deficit spending, we're all stockholders now. Democrats who run for any office—president, senator, governor, representative—can make great use of the developments of the past decade and run squarely on the Clinton administration's record of managing the markets and improving life for investors.

Just as investing personal capital in the markets does, investing political capital in the markets carries equal measures of risk and reward, of upside and downside. In the past decade, Democrats, like the broadening investing public, have reaped far more profits than losses from their ventures. The candidates who understand these slowly emerging truths and make the best use of the leverage they can provide will have the most success in the first election of the new millennium.

2

Public Employee Pension Funds

*I*n November 1864, if General William Tecumseh Sherman had taken a *right* turn after torching Atlanta and headed toward Montgomery, Alabama, the original capital of the Confederacy, he would have tramped through the same terrain over which Interstate 85 courses today: gently rolling hills covered with pines and farmland. Today, drivers crossing the border from Georgia into Alabama set their watches back an hour as they enter the central time zone. But when I pulled into the parking lot of the Alabama Visitors Center, which then-Governor George Wallace christened in 1977, the time lag seemed more like a few decades. Outside the building stands a small cement marker etched with the state's motto, adopted in 1939: "Alabama. We Dare Defend Our Rights."

This noble sentiment wears thin considering that the locals once numbered among these rights owning other human beings and prohibiting blacks from attending public colleges. And quick pit stops a few miles down the road reveal the fallacy—and endurance—of the ancient doctrine of "separate but equal." To the south of I-85, a few miles off the road at exit 38, sits the proud but shabby campus of historically black Tuskegee University. Behind a soaring modern chapel, somewhat incongruously planted amid cracked sidewalks and patchy grass, sit the modest graves of Tuskegee's leading lights, George Washington Carver and Booker T. Washington. The chapel is one of the few buildings on the state-supported campus whose masonwork isn't crumbling. By contrast, Auburn University, a few miles north of I-85 at exit 51, is the epitome of a well-tended land-grant university, all green lawns and handsome brick buildings; its most distinguishing feature is the massive Jordan Hare football stadium.

North of Auburn, Route 280 quickly gives way to countryside. A right turn onto a two-lane road took me past low-slung cottage-style homes, their driveways fronted with twin brick posts. Another right, and I was on a meandering two-lane parkway, separated by a grassy median. Driving for about two miles without encountering signs of human habitation, I feared I'd trespassed on a local magnate's private spread. Then I saw the welcoming gate marked "Grand National Golf Course," and, sitting atop a rise, the course's clubhouse. Built in the style of a plantation house, it has a colonnaded front porch stocked with rocking chairs and a cock weathervane on its roof. Located in Opelika, Grand National seems like the archetypal southern country club—exclusive, discreet, well-heeled, lily white. But there are some subtle differences. The signpost out front reads "Public Welcome." And the parking lot is filled with sport utility vehicles, pickup trucks, and vans, all of U.S. origin. BMWs and Mercedes are few and far between.

Pete Rouillard, a stocky redhead from South Carolina who runs the place, showed me around the three eighteen-hole courses that wind around 645-acre Lake Saugahatchee. In a cart equipped with a global positioning satellite unit, we rambled through thick pine woods laden with wild turkey, deer, armadillos, and the occasional gray fox. Magnolias and the ubiquitous longleaf pine trees, which shed their lower branches as they grow skyward, frame the winter-parched fairways. On a steely February day, the Lake Course, which has hosted the LPGA Tournament of Champions and a Nike Tour event, was sparsely populated—and not by doctors on their day off. On the third hole, an elderly woman knocked a tee shot about thirty feet; squawking geese expressed their disapproval. Two young women huddled in a cart while their boyfriends hacked away from the fairway of the fourth hole. "Here, we don't discourage anybody, boyfriends, husbands, wives, significant others, from coming along, even if they don't play," said Rouillard, who chirped out greetings to every golfer he saw (as per course policy.) It's a democratic golf course. There is no dress code. There are no caddies. And patrons are not required to rent carts to play any of the three eighteen-hole courses. "What we try not to do is discriminate based on who can pay," says Rouillard.

Such a sentiment is out of sync with the ethos of southern golf cathedrals like Augusta National, which prides itself on rigid devotion to antediluvian strictures of class, wealth, and race. But it's par for the course at Opelika and the seven other installations of the 378-hole Robert Trent Jones Golf Trail. Designed by the legendary golf course architect, this network of public links represents a flowering of democratic intentions in a state to which real democracy came only in the late 1960s. And it isn't only the putting greens that are democratic: The investors who built the course are middle- and lower-middle-class teachers and public employees in one of the poorer states in the union. A plaque commemorating Grand National's 1992 dedication reads: "Dr. David G. Bronner's investment philosophy, 'the stronger the

retirement systems can make Alabama, the stronger the retirement systems of Alabama will be' was instrumental in him conceiving of the
idea of a series of championship public golf complexes on spectacular
sites in Alabama. The golf complexes will be paramount in recruiting
industry, expanding tourism, and attracting retirees, thus strengthening
the state while improving quality of life for all Alabamians."

Dr. David D. Bronner, a Minnesota native, is the veteran chief
executive officer of the Retirement Systems of Alabama (RSA), a $22.4
billion collection of funds that invests on behalf of some 285,000 teachers and civil servants. Not since Sherman's enervating rural renewal
project has a Yankee done so much to alter the Confederate landscape.
Aside from building the golf courses, Bronner has financed the construction of a dozen-odd factories all over the state, erected a half dozen
buildings in downtown Montgomery, including a twenty-four-story
office tower, and then acquired companies to populate them.

Bronner leads the single largest financial entity in the state. And he
acts the part. He pads around a spacious corner office lined with tomb-
stones and framed political cartoons documenting his many battles
with George Wallace and his successors: Fob James, Guy Hunt, and
Jim Folsom. A Bloomberg machine is tucked behind the desk, and a
television silently broadcasts CNBC in the background. The most
attractive young woman I saw in three days in Montgomery was one of
his assistants. Sitting for an interview, he rocked back in a leather chair,
pulled out a drawer, opened a cigar box, and lit up, though he was careful not to let ashes fall on his pinstriped suit. He sported a full head of
blond hair—the tint was somewhat implausible for a fifty-four-year-old
man—that would do Donald Trump proud. Cracking open a door, he
surveyed a trading floor where his assistants sat, monitoring their portfolios. "Today, we're doing $200 million a month in an international
index trade and a domestic S&P trade of about $150 million." He makes
$240,000 a year—merely walking-around money for most big fund
managers—but Bronner is Alabama's unrivaled master of high finance
and arguably the most powerful man in the state.

Bronner's range of activities and tenure—he's held this job since 1973—make him unusual among the universe of largely colorless public employee pension fund managers. But the ballooning of the assets he manages, from $500 million in 1973 to $22.4 billion today, is representative of the way such funds have grown. His activities illustrate how the money of a class of people not typically thought of as investors has come to speak volumes in today's money culture. Today, public employee pension funds cover 15 million state, municipal, and educational workers—in every corner of the United States—and collectively have an estimated $3 trillion in assets.

Like many underpinnings of America's financial stability—for example, the Securities and Exchange Commission and the Federal Deposit Insurance Corporation—public pension funds trace their roots to the reputedly anticapitalist New Deal. In the 1930s, retirement programs were set up for teachers in many southern states, including the Alabama Teachers Retirement System in 1939. Next came pension funds for other civil servants. Alabama's, founded in 1945, now covers the workers of 900 cities, counties, and municipalities. Together, they constitute the Retirement Systems of Alabama. RSA is internally managed, meaning the manager, in this case Bronner, appointed by two boards, makes investment decisions rather than parceling out the task to outside managers.

Today, about half the nation's state funds are similarly managed. Funded by a continuing stream of contributions from employees and their public employers, and by investment income, these defined-benefit programs pay out fixed benefits at a fixed point in time, according to an employee's time served. Historically, most funds confined their investments largely to conservative, fixed-income assets such as bonds. Today, however, such funds invest their humble capital in everything from exotic securities to leveraged buyout funds.

These massive pools of capital are endowed with attributes that have made them prime drivers behind the democratization of money: political accountability, liberal constituents, and a mandate to seek out investments with social value. They are Democratic politically because their investors—government workers and teachers—are two of the most reliably Democratic voting blocs. And they are democratic socially and culturally because they act as surrogates for people who traditionally have been excluded from or uninterested in the markets and high finance.

The career of David Bronner, whose childhood could have served as a model for a Sherwood Anderson novel, epitomizes the potential of these funds. Bronner grew up in Austin, Minnesota, home to a Hormel Meat Company packing plant, where he once saw union workers beating up scabs. His father, who had never attended high school, ran a pool hall, where young David worked for a dime an hour. When Bronner was in ninth grade, a counselor told his mother he wasn't smart enough to attend college. But he hit the books, and did well enough to be accepted to the University of Iowa. After a fire destroyed his fraternity house, Bronner transferred to Mankato State University, in Minnesota. He worked his way through college by digging graves and pulling overtime shifts as a brakeman on the Rock Island Railroad.

An intense, natively keen student, he took a master's in finance, and considered applying to the University of Chicago law school. But one of his professors had just accepted a senior post at the University of Alabama and encouraged Bronner to follow him south. When he checked into Tuscaloosa's Moonwink Hotel in August 1968, Bronner turned on the television and saw *Hee-Haw* for the first time. He called his girlfriend back north: "I think I have taken a wrong turn and fallen off the edge of the world." But Bronner stayed, sensing opportunities in a state where ambitious young men with advanced degrees and well-connected mentors were few and far between. In three years, he earned both a law degree and a Ph.D. in management from the University of Alabama, the alma mater of George Wallace and virtually every other member of the state's political and business elite. Immediately upon his graduation, he was named assistant dean of the law school.

In 1973, the Teachers Retirement System and the Public Employees

Retirement System were looking for a new manager. With the respective boards unable to agree, Bronner was nominated as a compromise choice. He moved to Montgomery and took over the operations, housed in a dingy brick building at 312 Montgomery Street. Just twenty-eight years old and with virtually no experience in the private sector, Bronner may have seemed an odd choice to run a $500 million retirement fund. But the pension funds weren't exactly a sophisticated operation. "We were relying on a one-day-old *Wall Street Journal*" for investment intelligence, he recalled. The half dozen accountants stashed incoming checks in a drawer until they confirmed they had received the correct sum. "They literally had millions and millions of dollars of checks stuffed in the drawers out here," said Bronner.

The investment decisions were even more suspect. The fund had parked a large chunk of its assets in ancient utility bonds that yielded a meager 3 percent. Worse, the funds had bought locally issued municipal bonds as favors to politicians, and then either held them or tried to peddle them to other funds. (Because public pension funds aren't subject to taxation, they receive none of the tax benefits that offset the lower interest rates offered by municipal bonds.) Soon after arriving, Bronner encountered an RSA employee who complained of having to tote loads of bonds. It turned out she was carrying a six-inch-thick book of bearer bonds—bonds issued by banks in $1,000 chunks that could be redeemed by any individual bearing them. "I found out the treasurer's office had about $87 million worth of bearer bonds in it for which there was no security," Bronner recalled.

Bronner was most distressed to learn that the funds had only twenty-five cents of hard assets for every dollar they would theoretically owe. By 1975, some 116,000 people were working in the system, and almost 18,000 were already retired—a good ratio. But the state's politicians, and especially Governor George Wallace, had a long history of tendering ever-higher retirement benefits in lieu of raises—so much so that by the mid-1970s the National Education Association rated Alabama's teachers' benefits within the top three of the fifty states. Although the system was funded by a 4 percent salary deduction, interest, and state contributions, the state frequently failed to pay its promised contributions. By February 1974, the state owed $170 million to the public employees retirement system alone, which had $200 million in assets.

Like many people who had dealings with George Wallace, Bronner was drawn by the man's charisma but burned by his relentless slips into demagoguery. In the early 1970s, Bronner convinced Wallace to speak to a teachers convention he was hosting. "He started talking about pointy-headed bureaucrats and the intellectuals who carried their lunch in their briefcase to a room that was full of Ph.D.'s," Bronner recalled, shaking his head at the memory. Bronner did little to endear himself to Wallace, as he lobbied for greater funding and cut off an extra $836,000 in pensions paid to some fifty-seven supernumerary judges and other court staffers, most of them political allies of the governor.

Acting essentially alone, Bronner began searching for higher yields and ways to put money to work in Alabama. He bought federally guaranteed mortgages and loans held by state residents, and made a point of snapping up bonds issued by local companies like Alabama Bancorp, Alabama Gas, and Alabama Power. Then he began making loans directly to companies that had Alabama operations. In February 1977, he loaned $10 million to a unit of International Paper Corporation, which employed many state residents. With the state unable to sell bonds to expand office space, Bronner in November 1974 bought land on Union Street, around the corner from the capitol, and spent $3.5 million building an 80,000-square-foot facility that, upon its completion, would house RSA and other state agencies. By 1978, he had increased the percentage of the funds' assets invested locally from 15 percent to 46 percent.

Throughout the 1970s, less than 3 percent of the funds' assets were in common stocks. Emboldened, Bronner, assisted by three Auburn students, began playing the stock market, building a portfolio of about thirty stocks. In April 1977, he snapped up 80,000 shares of Phillips Petroleum, after one of its wells blew out, for $2 million. In the ensuing fourteen months, they rose 47 percent. He also scored big with a bet on 3M (Minnesota Mining and Manufacturing). When his portfolio out-performed the Dow Jones industrial average by about 400 percent in the first half of 1978, that success earned him a laurel from *Business Week* as a "fund manager on a hot streak." (In those dark pre-Internet days, quadrupling the Dow was noteworthy.)

In early 1979, Fob James, who had succeeded Wallace in 1978, tapped the financial whiz kid to be his finance director. Bronner agreed to take on the additional responsibilities, and immediately earned the sobriquet "the Ayatollah of the James administration" for his fanatical intolerance of unseemly behavior and untidy practices. He purged his own department, opened an investigation that led to the conviction of a State Building Commission official on kickback charges, barred bill collectors and solicitors from buildings in the state capitol complex, and, bizarrely, prohibited state employees from eating at their desks. (He thought crumbs would damage typewriters.) By the end of 1979, the courts ruled he had to choose between RSA and the finance job. Bronner chose RSA, figuring he would have more autonomy in his own little empire.

Although he was widely regarded as the second-most powerful man in Montgomery, Bronner continued to mark himself as something of an outsider. He openly bragged about his market value — "Wall Street has offered me double what I get with Retirement" ($49,000 in 1979) — and ill-manneredly allowed his 1980 divorce from first wife Patricia Powers Bronner to become public as they challenged each other's mental fitness. He further violated Alabama's enduring sense of chivalry by telling State Treasurer Annie Laurie Gunter in a 1980 memo, "Your financial ability is exceeded only by your lack of intelli-gence." And in an act that bordered on professional suicide, he took on the most revered man in the state — University of Alabama football

coach Paul "Bear" Bryant. Having won six national championships at
'Bama, Bryant occupied a niche just below Jesus in the state's pan-
theon. In 1981, when Bryant was sixty-eight, the state legislature passed
a law that would have let him continue to coach, at his $100,000 salary,
past the mandatory state retirement age of seventy. The RSA filed suit
to overturn the law, for Bronner deemed the exception unfair to other
sixty-eight-year-old state workers who would be forced to retire in two
years. State judges, virtually all of them University of Alabama alumni
reluctant to depose the high priest of the Crimson Tide cult, threw out
the case three times. Bronner persisted, however. Yet another judge
threatened to throw him out of court again. "You can do that, but I'll be
back," Bronner told him. The judge responded: "You don't understand.
I'm the *only* judge on the court that graduated from [Alabama archri-
val] Auburn University."

The courts ultimately ruled in Bronner's favor, and Bryant retired
after the 1982 season as the winningest coach in college football history.
Bronner was simply too valuable and too powerful, both as guarantor of
the retirement for 180,000 state citizens and as lord of a $2.1 billion pool
of capital. Indeed, by the early 1980s, if the state wanted to get an economic development deal done, it had to turn to Bronner. For example,
in 1983 he loaned $25 million to a United Technologies subsidiary to
build a factory and office building in Huntsville, and another $75 mil-
lion to U.S. Steel, which built a pipe mill at Fairfield. Aside from scor-
ing political points, these loans produced income. The U.S. Steel loan
carried a 12.25 percent interest rate—a decent return, to be sure. Nevertheless, in the early and mid 1980s, many public pension funds were
beginning to lift the limits on investments in riskier instruments like
equities. And some began to invest small chunks of their portfolio into
high-wire ventures that would make those returns seem piddling by
comparison: leveraged buyout funds.

In the late 1970s, Henry Kravis and his colleagues at Kohlberg,
Kravis & Roberts (KKR) tapped wealthy individuals to back their first

leveraged buyouts. But in the early 1980s, as the size of their acquisitions began to grow, they turned to institutional investors, including public employee pension funds. In 1981, when KKR tried to acquire Fred Meyer, a chain of grocery stores based in Oregon, partner George Roberts convinced Roger Meier, chairman of the Oregon Public Employees Retirement System, to supply $178 million of the $533 million financing required.

The next year, when KKR raised a $300 million fund, Meier agreed to invest $25 million. Armed with Meier's imprimatur, KKR convinced the managers of public pension funds in Washington and Michigan to invest as well. The rest, of course, is financial history. As the 1980s wore on, these unlikely partners set the business world aflame. KKR's funds grew exponentially larger: $980 million in 1984, $1.8 billion in 1986, and $5.6 billion in 1987. Each was stocked with contributions from the public employee pension funds; Oregon alone entrusted more than $1 billion to KKR over the course of the decade, providing about 10 percent of the funds Kravis and his colleagues used to make runs at dozens of companies. (Bronner received his share of visits from the buyout barons, but turned them down because "their fees were usually outrageous" and he didn't relish simply turning over money to third parties. Michael Milken even called upon him, for ninety minutes. "While I was impressed with Mr. Milken, his associates reminded me of rich pool hall sharks," Bronner later wrote.

Throughout the 1980s, a steady stream of investment bankers landed their private jets on airstrips in Sacramento, Madison, and Helena and endured poor service at what the locals considered luxury hotels. None was more adept at enlisting the fund managers in their cause than KKR. The firm invited fund managers to conferences at fancy hotels in New York and San Francisco. Roger Meier even joined the board of one of KKR's acquisitions, Norris Industries. "By allying themselves with KKR, the Walter Mitty types who ran big state pension funds could feel that they were players too," as George Anders put it in *Merchants of Debt*.

One of the more unnoticed ironies is that the orgy of debt and specula-
tion that climaxed with the $33 billion RJR-Nabisco deal in 1989 was
fueled by the money of social workers in Eugene, Oregon.

As the 1980s bull market raged, managers looking for greater returns
began to plow more cash into equities. By the fall of 1987, Missouri's
fund was 61 percent invested in stocks, and Florida's fund had plunged
half its assets into equities. Bronner, however, maintained a mere 10
percent position in stocks, and when the market crashed 25 percent in
October 1987, his caution made him look even smarter. After the crash,
he snapped up about $100 million in equities, which rose quickly in
value. His reputation, burnished by such moves, grew to such an extent
that by 1989 Bronner was described by *Newsweek* as one of "Wall
Street's New Musclemen." But in the next decade, he and other pension fund managers would begin to exercise that muscle by engaging in
the kind of activities favored by the moguls whose buyout funds he had
spurned: building golf courses, buying trophy office buildings, and
acquiring television stations.

Bronner had long been distressed by the derelict state of downtown
Montgomery, and by the equally dirty bargains that inhibited development. The state paid huge amounts of rent to local real estate barons—
$3 million a year in the 1980s—whom Bronner accused of maintaining
their lock on the state's business by paying off a succession of governors
with campaign contributions. One building owner, early Wallace sup-
porter Aaron Aronov, was collecting $1.85 million a year in rent from
eighteen separate state units in 1989. Most of the offices were housed in
shabby, ill-kept buildings lining Dexter Avenue, the historic broad
boulevard that dead-ends at the foot of the imperious, shimmering state
capitol.

Just as he aimed to cleanse the temples of state government by
expelling bill collectors, Bronner set about sprucing up downtown
Montgomery by replacing the rent collectors' red-brick buildings with
gleaming white showpieces. In 1989 he paid top dollar—$2.6 million—

for two parcels of land in the downtown area. On one plot, adjacent to the original RSA building, he erected RSA Plaza, a six-story, 150,000-square-foot structure that houses the Department of Aeronautics, the Commission on Aging, lobbyists, the Alabama Trial Lawyers, and interested corporations like Norfolk Southern. Its roof features a catering facility modeled on New York City's Tavern on the Green. On the other plot, down Adams Avenue, he built the Alabama Center for Commerce (ACC), a $25 million office building that houses economic development agencies, the Department of Tourism and Travel, and offices of the state universities. Bronner frequently lunches at the ACC's Commerce Café, a small institutional cafeteria where workers dish out fried okra. The Four Seasons, it's not.

The buildings were completed in 1991. But Bronner was just getting started. In addition to busting up the cozy relationship between landlords and government officials he viewed as corrupt, Bronner believed his building program would provide Montgomery with the amenities a downtown needed to attract private-sector development. Next came the ten-story RSA Union, completed in 1995. Near it, on Monroe Avenue, he put up two smaller buildings. One, the Helen Hunt Early Learning Center—named after the wife of Governor Guy Hunt, not the *Mad About You* star—is the only professional day care center catering to workers in downtown Montgomery. The second, the Alabama Activity Center and Plaza, a low-slung brick building, hosts continuing education and community meetings. Bronner also provided about $20 million in financing for the Embassy Suites hotel, on Talapoosa Street, in 1995. Riding the glass elevator up the hotel's eight-story atrium, I could have been in a hotel in Chicago or Atlanta. At least until the doors opened and I was jostled by several middle-aged white farmers with flaming red jackets and thick accents—members of the Alabama Cattlemen's Association—in town for a convention.

The pièce de résistance of Bronner's *grande travaux* is the RSA Tower, completed in 1997. With twenty-four stories and 750,000 square

feet of office space, it was the tallest building in the state. Amsouth Bancorp has several suites of offices here and has planted its name atop the
building. The twenty-second floor contains lavish guest rooms to house
dignitaries for whom the Embassy Suites is not sufficiently upscale, and
the Capitol City Club. Aside from giving state employees better accom-
modations, Bronner's public works program has also rendered more
power unto RSA; Bronner is, in effect, the landlord of a substantial part
of the state government.

Montgomery is full of public monuments and memorials to the two
epochs when the city was vital to the nation's destiny. The state capitol,
with its massive set of marble steps—on which George Wallace
famously declaimed, "Segregation now, segregation tomorrow, segregation forever"—sits amid a profusion of trees and bushes, including a
sycamore transplanted from a Virginia Civil War battlefield. Practically
in its shadow sits the Dexter Avenue Baptist Church, Martin Luther
King Jr.'s historic pulpit. Bronner's buildings constitute a third, race-
neutral set of monuments—to himself and to the teachers and workers
of Alabama. The development efforts have given the management
Ph.D. an outlet to express his theories about the interrelationships
between business and education, between commerce and knowledge.
Embedded in the north side of the Alabama Center for Commerce are
gears of industry and a lamp of education, a motif that reappears in
other RSA buildings. Bronner commissioned two life-size bronze sculp-
tures that stand in a park between the RSA Tower and the RSA reflect-
ing pool: *Commerce* portrays a man in a suit and tie holding a
newspaper, representing management, with his arm around a lunch
box–toting laborer. *Education* shows three life-size figures, a teacher, a
girl, and a boy. On Tuskegee's campus is a famous statue of George
Washington Carver, lifting a veil from a barefoot slave, who is holding
books. It bears the inscription: "He lifted the veil of ignorance from his
people and pointed the way to progress through education and industry." Clearly, the manager of a public pension fund in a state that lags

the rest of the country in many crucial areas views himself in much the same light.

The officials who run many public pension funds are popularly elected controllers, comptrollers, or treasurers. As a rule, the jobs of controllers are utterly mind-numbing. Auditing the operations of state agencies is a post more suited to accountants than aspiring politicos. And historically, the post was a political dead end, but that has changed. For example, New York City Comptroller Alan Hevesi is an odds-on early favorite to succeed Rudolph Giuliani as mayor in 2001, and New York State Controller Carl McCall, the Democratic party's Great Black Hope, is regarded as a potential candidate for governor or senator. Their promise doesn't stem from their ability to shed light on the finances of the New York City Department of Housing or the State Dormitory Authority. Rather, both men derive their substantial influence from the funds they manage. Hevesi runs some $90 billion in assets. And since 1993, McCall has been the sole trustee of the second-largest public pension fund in America, the New York State Common Retirement Fund (NYSCRF), which counts more than one million active and retired members, and assets of more than $115 billion.

A shining star in the constellation of the East Coast meritocratic elite, McCall was born and raised in Boston, the eldest of six children. The family was on welfare for a period after his father left. McCall attended Roxbury Memorial High School, then Dartmouth, graduating in 1958. After studying at the University of Edinburgh and at Andover-Newton Theological School in Maine, McCall was ordained as a minister in the United Church of Christ in 1961. Instead of seeking a pulpit, however, he moved to New York, finding work as a social worker at a YMCA in Bedford-Stuyvesant. He later worked in Mayor John Lindsay's administration and became head of the New York City Council Against Poverty, a training ground for many black officials. A Republican in college, McCall became an active Democrat and helped register voters with future mayor David Dinkins in the 1960s.

In 1974, McCall was elected to represent the Upper West Side in the state Senate. After two terms, he was named by Jimmy Carter as deputy ambassador to the United Nations. He ran unsuccessfully for lieutenant governor in 1982 and went to work at Citibank. From 1985 to 1993, he managed much of the giant bank's retail business in New York City and was responsible for state and local government relations. In 1991, his occasional tennis partner, David Dinkins, by then mayor, appointed him president of the New York City School Board. Governor Mario Cuomo tabbed him as comptroller to replace Republican Edward Regan in 1993. The following year, McCall was the only Democrat to win a statewide race. More significant, he became the first African American ever elected to statewide office. "I've been telling people across the state, this is not a campaign, it's a crusade," he said at countless campaign stops. Aided by a large black turnout, he won 52 percent of the vote against Herbert London, who ran a truly vile campaign.

Like Bronner, McCall has been able to play a conspicuous role in economic development, providing funding for affordable housing programs and financing home loans. But because of his fund's size, its location in New York—and because of the color of his skin—McCall is an important investor in public companies. At the time of his appointment, no African American controlled more assets. And the ordained minister has used his massive stock portfolio to draw attention while acting as a responsible shareholder. In 1996, a major fracas exploded at Texaco, a company not known for its efforts to manage diversity, when disgruntled executive Richard Lundwall leaked tapes on which senior executives could be heard referring to Kwanzaa and minority workers in derogatory terms. A chorus of predictable voices rushed to condemn Texaco, from Jesse Jackson to Al Sharpton. But the most important black response may have come from Carl McCall, who controlled about 1.2 million shares of Texaco, worth about $114 million. In November 1996, he sent a letter to Texaco's chairman and CEO, Peter I. Bijur, demanding a response to the "outrageous racial slurs and improper actions" reportedly made by Texaco executives.

CEOs of big companies have long made a practice of ignoring Sharpton and Jackson. But it's more difficult to dismiss the concerns of large shareholders. Texaco acted quickly, settling the lawsuit for $156 million and naming Deval Patrick, the former head of the Justice Department's Civil Rights Division, to chair a task force on equality and fairness. As further penance, Texaco agreed to purchase $1 billion of goods and services from women- and minority-owned suppliers over the next five years. (Texaco ultimately named Patrick general counsel in late 1998, making him one of the few African American general counsels at a Fortune 500 company.)

Another aspect of McCall's job has contributed to the growing sense that big money is a Democratic and democratic ball game. After all, McCall and his team decide which buyout funds receive state retirement investments. In 1997, for example, McCall committed $250 million and $50 million to funds raised by Thomas Lee Co. and Lazard Freres, respectively. The leading lights of these highly reputable firms—Thomas Lee and Steve Rattner, respectively—were well-heeled Wall Streeters who happened to be active Democrats, though that party affiliation is not why they received the funding. (Indeed, McCall kicked in $300 million to the 1996 fund of the ur-Republican KKR.) But only in today's democratized money culture do billionaires show up in Albany, hat in hand, asking a former state senator from the Upper West Side to entrust them with the retirement money of Department of Motor Vehicle clerks. More important, these activities have given McCall a vast network of grateful, potential donors, a base that will make him a formidable primary favorite should he decide to run for a higher office.

McCall raised $3.6 million for his 1994 campaign, much of it from Wall Street. Between 1995 and 1998, he raised another $5.2 million. Of that, some 32 percent, or more than $1.8 million, came from individuals and companies that did business with the New York Public Employees Retirement System (NYPERS). About 40 percent of the donors were from out of state. The *New York Times* charged that McCall has "repeatedly awarded contracts and other work for the $100 billion pension fund to businesses that have given sizable sums to his re-election campaign." But McCall is simply playing by the rules laid down by his colleagues and predecessors. Indeed, Edward Regan had been the subject of inquiries by federal and state prosecutors in the late 1980s, when memos released by staffers included choice phrases such as "Those who give will get."

McCall can also exercise another form of patronage that illustrates how such pension funds contribute to the democratized culture of investing. Given its membership and its location in one of the more liberal and ethnically diverse states in the country, NYPERS not suprisingly has made significant efforts to involve minority- and woman-owned brokerage firms in managing assets and conducting transactions. Indeed, by doling out pieces of the asset management pie to such firms—for example, Blaylock & Partners, Utendahl Capital Partners, Muriel Siebert & Co., Samuel A. Ramirez & Co.—McCall and his predecessors have given many of these tiny firms a boost. It's a two-way street, of course, for McCall has raised campaign cash from these firms' executives.

David Bronner, unlike Carl McCall, is not a political liberal. Yet he too has a powerful incentive to pursue the types of socially useful local investments that purely private investment funds would shun. The most constructive project Alabama undertook in the 1990s may be the Robert Trent Jones Golf Trail. As with virtually every other social activity—voting, education, swimming—the history of golf in Alabama is inextricably bound up with race. In 1990, when the PGA was planning to hold its championship at the Shoal Creek Country Club, a Jack Nicklaus–designed course outside Birmingham, the city's seven major country clubs had a grand total of two black members. Neither of them belonged to Shoal Creek. In June 1990, a reporter for the *Birmingham Post Herald* asked Shoal Creek founder Hall Thompson, sixty-seven, for his reaction to the demand by a black city councilman that the city withdraw $1,500 earmarked for an advertisement in the tournament program. Thompson, who had kept blacks out of the Birmingham Rotary Club in the early 1980s, responded: "I think we've said that we don't discriminate in every other area except the blacks." An outcry quickly ensued. IBM and several other advertisers refused to buy time on the ABC telecast, and Toyota recommended that its paid endorsers not wear the company logo during the tourney. Shoal Creek quickly brought in Louis J. Willie, president of the Booker T. Washington Insurance Company, as an honorary member, and the tournament went on as scheduled. In August 1990, the PGA announced it would not hold tournaments at country clubs that discriminated. At the time, seventeen of its thirty-nine tour courses were at private clubs that had no black members. Fortunately for the PGA, Augusta National, home of the hallowed Masters, hastened to admit its first black member.

Bronner and his colleagues sensed an opportunity amid the embarrassment. Alabama economic development officials had long noted that many residents of Tennessee, Kentucky, and states to the north drove through Alabama to play golf in Florida. In either a stroke of brilliance or a fit of grandiose self-delusion, Bronner decided to build a network of high-class public golf courses throughout the state. "I was going to build something that would forever change the image of Alabama," he said. In 1991, he committed $300 million of the $18 billion fund to build what would become an eight-location, 378-hole network of courses. He hired Sunbelt Golf Corporation, which coaxed Robert Trent Jones out of retirement, to design the courses.

Building seven of the eight sites simultaneously, Sunbelt and RSA rolled out the golf trail over nine months in 1992 and 1993. Today, golf enthusiasts can spend several weeks in the state, traveling from multi-course installations at Huntsville and Birmingham in the north, to

Opelika and Prattsville in the middle of the state, to Magnolia Grove in the south. An instant success, the trail has recorded more than one million rounds while generating revenues of $950 million since 1993. As an income producer, it's not very prolific. "This year [1999] I'll get a whole $3 million out of it, which is a lousy investment on its face," said Bronner. But the trail has done wonders for Alabama's image, generating more than 3,000 articles in newspapers and magazines around the world. Out-of-state golfers flock to the courses—at Opelika, about 80 percent of the players are non-Alabamians. And tourism spending in Alabama has exploded from $2.5 billion in 1992 to more than $5 billion today.

If the RSA could build golf courses, make huge loans to companies, and construct office buildings, Bronner reasoned, why couldn't it simply buy existing companies? Just such an opportunity appeared when Park Communications, a collection of radio and television stations and newspapers, came on the block in early 1994 after the death of its founder, Roy Park. Bronner enlisted two of his buddies—South Carolina real estate developer Donald Tomlin and Gary Knapp, a Kentucky securities dealer—to form a company and bid on part of the Park properties. Armed with $573 million in cash from RSA—4 percent of its total funds—Tomlin and Knapp outbid established players like Paxson Communications and Heritage Media Corporation. In 1995, when the Federal Communications Commission relaxed rules on the concentration of ownership of radio stations, the newly acquired radio stations became hot properties. Knapp and Tomlin sold Park's twenty-two radio stations for $230 million. In January 1997, they sold the remaining ten television stations and more than 100 newspapers to Media General for $710 million. Because of the way the deal had been structured, Bronner and the RSA incurred a $17 million penalty for early loan repayment. But Knapp and Tomlin, who had put up peanuts for their stake in the company, pocketed $108 million each. The experience left Bronner feeling burned, and looking like a rube.

Chastened—to the extent the headstrong Bronner could be chastened—he took extra precautions engineering his next media deal. In 1996, he helped found Raycom, a company that quickly acquired several television station companies. It first bought Ellis Communications, based in Atlanta, with twelve stations, for $732 million. In June 1996, it bought Federal Enterprises in Michigan, which owned eight stations, for about $166 million. Then Bronner asked one of his former protégés, Joe Smith, the chief investment officer of Georgia-based AFLAC, if the insurer wanted to sell its seven television stations. Raycom bought them for $485 million. In each instance, RSA provided the cash for the deal, in the form of a loan. But RSA also retained warrants on 80 percent of the company that could be converted to equity in the case of a sale or public offering. "It protects me from the problem I had with Park," said Bronner. In addition, the golf trail and the Huntsville Space Camp would receive $2 million a month in free advertising on Raycom stations like KNDO, the NBC affiliate in Yakima, Washington, and KTVO, the ABC affiliate in Kirksville, Missouri. Bronner also moved Raycom's headquarters to the RSA Tower in Montgomery.

Raycom has provided Bronner with a platform for engaging in derring-do with the giants of the buyout field. In the summer of 1997, Hicks, Muse, Tate & Furst, a Dallas-based buyout firm, bid $47.50 a share for the eight television stations belonging to LIN Television, or nearly $1.64 billion. Spurred by Bronner, Raycom a few weeks later upped the ante with a $52.50 per share bid, because, Bronner says knowingly, "we could see that they were stealing it." That move forced the Hicks, Muse group to jack up its bid to $55 a share, or $1.9 billion—16 percent higher than the original offer. "What the little old RSA did made more than $225 million for stockholders of LIN," Bronner crowed. Soon after the LIN bidding, John Muse came to Montgomery to pay a courtesy call on Bronner. "He was interested in meeting the SOB who cost him an extra $200 million," Bronner says, repeating an oft-told anecdote that he punctuates with a nasal, high-pitched giggle.

Bronner was attracted to television stations because they produce steady cash flows and have monopolistic characteristics. Believing small-town newspapers had similar attributes, Bronner in 1997 decided to bankroll a start-up company, run by former Park Communications executive Ralph Martin, to acquire such papers. In less than three years, Bronner has lent the company, Community Newspapers Holdings, Inc., more than $1 billion to acquire 200-plus newspapers, most in tiny towns like Gallipolis, Ohio, Poteau, Oklahoma, and Cherokee, Iowa. As with Raycom, RSA holds warrants on the company and will profit from any sale. In addition, Community Newspapers has moved its headquarters to Birmingham, and various state tourism attractions receive about $4 million in free advertising annually.

By starting companies and moving them to Alabama, Bronner has personally added to the state's corporate base. And he's not alone in his tactics. In the 1990s, investing close to home has become a commonplace of public pension funds, even in states with large, healthy economies, like California. CALPERS, the California Public Employees Retirement System, the largest public pension system in the nation, has more than $155 billion in assets, or about what Coca-Cola is worth. Headquartered in Sacramento, it provides retirement and health benefits to more than one million state and local public employees, retirees, and their families. By its own estimation, CALPERS has pumped more than $20 billion into the state's economy. It owns $8.9 billion in stocks of companies based in California, and has provided $4.2 billion in mortgages to nearly 33,000 California families. In March 1996, it teamed with basketball-star-turned-entrepreneur Earvin "Magic" Johnson and a real estate investor to pump $51.5 million into California urban areas.

But CALPERS has had a broader impact on the democratization of money *outside* California. Prodded by its activist board—rather than by an individual manager operating with wide autonomy—it has become the leading voice in demanding improved corporate governance and protection for public shareholders. In theory, shareholders of publicly owned firms vote every year on the election of directors and approve executive compensation plans. In reality, insiders control the voting stock at many companies, and at most others stock is so widely diffused among institutions and individuals that the CEO and board of directors are largely left to their own devices. But with increasing frequency and volume, CALPERS, NYPERS, and funds like the State of Wisconsin Investment Board (SWIB) have tried to breathe life into the concept of shareholder democracy by using their substantial stakes as bully pulpits from which to shame errant executives.

Each year, CALPERS publishes a list of the top underperforming companies in its massive portfolio. Then it proceeds to seek meetings with board members and executives, and if it finds the companies insufficiently responsive, it threatens proxy battles. Typically, CALPERS's moves garner headlines and instill a little fear in the hearts of arrogant executives. In the spring of 1998, for example, CALPERS sought to meet with board members of Electronic Data Systems (EDS), the information technology consulting firm in which it owned 2.4 million shares, to discuss the company's poor performance. Rebuffed, CALPERS launched a proxy campaign to remove EDS Chairman Richard Brown. CALPERS convinced 21 percent of shareholders to support its motion—an impressive figure considering shareholders' general quiescence.

Almost as a rule, such efforts don't succeed. CALPERS has yet to topple a board of directors or a chief executive officer at a poorly performing company. But the efforts have a larger meaning. The in-your-face style and the willingness of public employee funds to challenge entrenched management have substantially altered the dynamic between shareholders and management. CALPERS's stakes are magnified when it joins forces with other public employee pension funds. These funds' activism has laid the groundwork for other large investors with social agendas—namely, union pension funds and TIAA-CREF—to wage war on unresponsive management. Frequently, public funds enlist in campaigns orchestrated by union pension funds to embarrass managers and change corporate behavior.

Whereas institutions like CALPERS and SWIB have adopted a national scope, Bronner remains focused almost solely on the state of Alabama and continues to take a direct hand in its economic development. One of Alabama's greatest triumphs of the 1990s was its successful effort to convince Mercedes-Benz to build a plant in Vance in 1995 by promising about $300 million in various tax breaks. In typical fashion, the state's politicos miscalculated and earmarked funds originally intended for the school system to build a Mercedes training facility. Outraged, the Alabama Educational Association threatened to sue. Bronner stepped in, offering the state a $98 million line of credit to build the training center. Of course, he did so at a rate substantially higher than the 7 percent at which the state generally borrowed. "I did get criticized for the onerous rate," said Bronner, but "that's my job."

Bronner has adopted southern ways. He remarried, to Mary Lynn Marman, a Georgia native who had worked for RSA and later started her own investment management business. His children attend the (virtually all-white) Montgomery Academy. And yet he marks himself an outsider by publicly discussing topics deemed to be impolitic and impolite. He uses his monthly newsletter *The Adviser*—which has a circulation greater than that of the *New Republic* and *Weekly Standard* combined (and is frequently a livelier read than either)—to spread the Gospel According to Bronner. He continually harps that Alabama ranks last in the nation in the percentage of adults over age twenty-five who have completed high school. He ascribes Alabama's lack of progress to the fact that the elites like the status quo and the rest of the citizenry is too passive to do anything about it. In 1992, Bronner warned that Alabama could become "the Mexico of the United States" because of its dearth of educated adults.

In Manhattan, such comments would mark Bronner as a player worthy of a *New York* magazine cover story; in Montgomery, they mark him as somehow uncivilized. "It's not Southern, and it's not good manners to be as egotistical as David is," said a former state senator, Mac Parsons. And it's a measure of Alabama's insularity that after nearly thirty years of public service, Bronner is still viewed as an interloper, a "modern-day carpetbagger in the Cradle of the Confederacy," as the *Huntsville Times* memorably put it in 1992.

And yet Bronner is also a source of great local pride, in part because he has partially reversed Alabama's long-standing subservience to the northern centers of capital and industry. None of Bronner's out-of-state investments inspires as much pride as 55 Water Street, a fifty-three-story, 3.6-million-square-foot hulk that looms over the East River at the edge of Manhattan. Built in the early 1970s, the glass-and-steel giant trails only the World Trade Center towers in heft. The Reichmann family acquired it in the 1970s and sold mortgage bonds on the property to finance their other ventures, including the ruinous Canary Wharf in London. Bronner bought $100 million of the bonds. In 1992, as the Reichmanns were forced to declare Chapter 11 bankruptcy in the United States, holders of some $548 million in debt on the asbestos-plagued building were eager to disentangle themselves. Bronner offered to buy out his fellow bondholders at twenty-nine cents on the dollar, and took control of the building.

One of the challenges Bronner faced after acquiring 55 Water Street was the high cost of waste removal—$1.2 million a year—which was artificially inflated by a long-standing cartel. Manhattan District Attorney Robert Morgenthau had been investigating the mob-influenced industry for years but had difficulty gaining the cooperation of New York building managers. Bronner agreed to let an agent pose as a building manager. In 1994, the agent accepted a $15,000 bribe from Vincent Ponte, son of cartel ringleader Angelo Ponte. In 1997, Ponte *père et fils* pleaded guilty and went to jail. "It took the Retirement Systems of Alabama to stand up and do the right thing," said Morgenthau. Bronner wasn't above a little preening. "We ain't exactly idiots in the sticks,"

he said. "We decided to fix it up and knew we had run into bad boys."
Back in the sticks, the *Birmingham Post-Herald* paid tribute to
"Alabama's mob-busting version of Elliott Ness." And Browning-Ferris
agreed to haul 55 Water's trash for a mere $120,000 a year.

The building has paid other dividends. RSA spruced up 55 Water
with $156 million, sheathing the elevators and lobby in marble, satin-
wood, stainless steel, and aluminum-leaf and installing an extra twenty
megawatts of electrical power capacity on the roof. By the end of 1997,
the Tower of Power, as it was redubbed, had signed up tenants for the 44
percent of vacant space. These now include blue-chip Wall Street
names: Standard & Poor's, Chase Manhattan, and Depository Trust,
the clearing operation of the New York Stock Exchange. Today, about
11,000 people work there. Ed Kulick, who manages the building for
Bronner, estimates it could now sell for about $850 million.

Although he's responsible for $22 billion — a sum greater than the
Fidelity Asset Manager mutual fund — Bronner earns about what an
undistinguished fifth-year associate at a large Manhattan law firm takes
home. Bronner doesn't seem to mind. "I know as many wealthy people
as anybody in the country. I have done deals with many of them and
many other are trying to get our money. I don't find wealthy people to
be a helluva lot happier than me." He stays in Alabama for the power,
not the money. "This is as close to Deadwood, South Dakota, in the
1860s as I could find. I mean, we shoot 'em on the streets. Cross me,
come on, it's the OK Corral," he says. In early 1998, Bronner made
noises about running for governor on the Republican ticket, but he
eventually decided against it. Quite apart from his reputation, Bronner
would have to contend with two potentially debilitating political disad-
vantages: his accent (or lack thereof) and the fact that he's a divorced
Catholic. Besides, at the RSA, he doesn't have to deal as much with a
calcified political system poisoned by race, partisanship, and ancient
personal feuds. And he can act without the annoying and exhausting
mandate of building consensus. If he had it to do all over again, Bron-

ner said, he would have liked to have been an LBO artist. Had he grown up on the East Coast and attended Williams College or the University of Pennsylvania instead of Mankato State and the University of Alabama, it's likely his wish would have been fulfilled.

Dr. David Bronner is extraordinary in the public pension world, to a large degree. Few managers, if any, operate with such independence, flair, and longevity (he's run the funds for twenty-six years). But his record of achievement is testimony to how the manager of retirement savings for humble civil servants in Montgomery, Alabama, can match wits with just about anybody. Over the years, chicken-fried southern politicians, from Tom Watson to Fob James, have found it easy to stir up resentment because locals rightly believed they were powerless to contend against multinational banks and the Northeastern commercial elite. Many people in Alabama may still feel that way, but the truth is more complicated. The members of RSA hold about $11 billion in stocks—enough to buy the Washington Post and Times-Mirror companies. Each month, Chase Manhattan Bank, Standard & Poor's, and the other tenants of 55 Water pay rent to the teachers of Eufaula. And when a busload of well-heeled Japanese tourists rolls into Grand National for a few rounds of *gorufu*, the greens fees line the pockets of the secretaries at the State Department of Health.

By virtue of their size and the moral authority with which they speak, public pension funds like the RSA and CALPERS cannot be ignored. And because of the democratized climate to which they have contributed, they *will* not be ignored. In coming years, as the number of retirees grows and the number of active members will likely decline, such defined-benefit plans may find themselves paying out more than they take in. As a result, pension fund managers may engage in some of the unorthodox high-wire techniques favored by Bronner in an effort to boost returns. That's a risky approach, but not necessarily a bad one, because when pension fund managers buy companies or buildings, or construct golf courses for their own account, the recipients of the heightened reward that comes with heightened risk will be the civil servants—not the partners of an LBO firm in Manhattan.

The activities of fund managers like Bronner and McCall should change the way we think about big-money investing. Their growth and clout have contributed to the expansion of what economist Lawrence Kudlow has dubbed "the investor class." But public school teachers and state bureaucrats aren't the only hard-core Democrats to have joined the masses of stockholders in the past few decades. Indeed, two of the Democrats' other most crucial constituencies have amassed vast stockholdings. Ironically, these groups, labor and intellectuals, have been among the most vehement critics of the capital markets and the values they represent. In the past decade, however, their surrogates—labor union pension funds and the massive TIAA-CREF complex—have begun to make their presence felt, in part by making common cause with public employee funds.

3

Labor
and Intellectuals

Franklin Roosevelt's vaunted New Deal coalition, composed of urban ethnics, southern whites, blacks, intellectuals, labor, and government workers, has been buried time and again since 1968, when political scientist Theodore Lowi famously proclaimed its demise in *The End of Liberalism.* This snippet of conventional wisdom has been the subject of countless drearily earnest roundtable discussions in Washington and Cambridge and in points in between. But over the past thirty years, as the Solid South became *terra Republicana,* big labor, government workers, blacks, and intellectuals have primarily stuck with Democrats. Largely overlooked have been the ways these constituents of the die-hard New Deal coalition have helped to transform the money culture. In his smart 1994 book *A Piece of the Action*, Joseph Nocera described the 1970s and 1980s as a period when the middle class began to join the moneyed class. In the 1990s, I'd argue, some elements of the working class have done the same.

Labor union pension funds have generally kept a lower profile than public employee funds. In part that's due to their smaller size. So-called Taft-Hartley funds (named after the 1947 legislation that established the first significant regulations for union pension funds) have about $450 billion in assets among them, compared with about $3 trillion for public employee funds. Management-controlled pension funds, like the General Motors pension fund, control about $3 trillion in assets. But the comparative inconspicuousness of labor funds is also partly due to their spotty history. In the years after 1955, when the International Brotherhood of Teamsters Central States and Southern Sections signed contracts calling for employers to contribute to pension funds, James Hoffa used them as a personal kitty. By 1963, Hoffa oversaw a $200 million honey pot and made investment decisions himself. As Hoffa biographer Arthur A. Sloane put it, "Many hotels in booming Las Vegas—Caesar's Palace, the Circus Circus, the Sands, the Stardust, and the Desert Inn, among others—were indebted either exclusively or primarily to Central State Pension Funds loans for their establishment." (Of course, many of these hotels were owned by people with mob affiliations.) Hoffa was accused repeatedly of misusing pension funds.

Like public employee funds, labor funds through the 1970s and the 1980s were rather conservative and passive, confining their legitimate investments to bonds and other fixed-income assets. Concerned with inflation and capital appreciation, they began buying stocks out of financial and economic prudence. In the 1980s and early 1990s, as companies like Northwest Airlines ran into trouble and restructured, union members found themselves with substantial stakes in public companies where they worked. And as other union pension funds continued to amass stockholdings, the labor movement came to realize that it held significant equity stakes in the means of production. The Teamsters, whose pension funds include 1.4 million members and 400,000 retirees, now control about $60 billion in pension assets in some 173 different funds. On average, Hoffa's heirs own about 0.5 percent of any company in the United States. (Fidelity Investments, the massive mutual fund complex, owns about 1 percent of any given company.)

Paradoxically, unions have found their stockholdings swell even as their membership rolls dwindle. After tremendous gains during World War II, labor's workforce presence fluctuated between 22 and 25 percent until the mid-1970s. But in each of the fifteen years after 1983, when 20.1 percent of the workforce was unionized, the percentage of American workers belonging to unions either held steady or fell, according to the U.S. Bureau of Labor Statistics. By 1998, union penetration stood at 13.9 percent. In absolute numbers, employees belonging to unions fell from 17.6 million in 1983 to 16.2 million in 1998, even as millions of new jobs were created. Each year, labor loses about 300,000 members, merely through attrition and death.

As companies have devised increasingly ingenious methods to combat organizing, the graying and beleaguered labor movement has come to realize that stockholdings, and the stock markets generally, can be a crucial point of leverage. Activists have realized that the most important elections may no longer be those the National Labor Relations Board (NLRB) sanctions for union recognition but rather public companies' proxy elections that the Securities and Exchange Commission (SEC) sanctions. And because of their generally more militant attitudes, union pension funds have often had more success in proxy contests than their public employee counterparts.

The thrust for workers to embrace their status as owners of the means of production got a boost with the ascension of John Sweeney to the presidency of the AFL-CIO in October 1995. Sweeney, who got his start with the International Ladies' Garment Workers' Union (ILGWU), served as president of the Service Employees International Union for fifteen years. During his tenure, SEIU's membership soared from 625,000 to 1.1 million. Aside from offering the usual boilerplate on aggressive organizing and bargaining, Sweeney promised to raise the financial power of union investments. He followed through by creating an office of investment, and hired as its manager Bill Patterson, a veteran of the Teamsters and the Amalgamated Clothing and Textile Workers Union.

Patterson and his team have acted as a sort of clearinghouse and encouraged affiliated unions to take to the warpath, wielding shares as a blunt instrument. For example, in February 1998, Matthew Walker, the director of research and education at the 300,000-member Hotel Employees and Restaurant Employees International Union (HERE), was reviewing a routine proxy form filed by Marriott International Inc. on the SEC's EDGAR database. The hotel company, founded by J. Willard Marriott in 1927 as a Washington root-beer stand and still controlled by members of the Marriott family, was seeking shareholder approval for its proposed merger with French catering company Sodexho Alliance SA. Marriott planned to meld Sodexho into its food services unit and spin off the firm into a new unit called Sodexho Marriott Services, laden with 87 percent of the company's $1.6 billion debt. The action would leave the rump company, Marriott International, as an independent, debt-free entity engaged in managing hotels and senior living facilities.

But some provisions in the proxy filing set off alarm bells. The company proposed to replace the existing common shares of Marriott International with two classes of common stock. New Class A shares would bear ten votes, and existing common shares would carry one vote; each existing shareholder of Marriott would receive one of each. The move was an obvious attempt by the Marriott family, which already held about 20 percent of the company's outstanding stock, to lock up control for generations. The proposal would have permitted the Marriotts to sell all their one-vote stocks, or half their holdings, while relinquishing only a fraction of their voting control. Further, the company bundled the two measures, trying to sugarcoat the bitter pill of reduced voting power with the attractive Sodexho transaction.

Walker, a slim 1984 Yale graduate with little round glasses and a distinctly un-unionly accent, swung into action. From headquarters in a quaint former school building on the western edge of Georgetown, he and other HERE staff members tried to rally the 80 percent of Marriott stockholders not related to management to reject the proposed merger and stock plan at the March 17 vote. The union's pension funds owned a few shares of Marriott stock through their index investments. But the union was primarily concerned with the fate of its 6,000 members who worked at Marriott. It saw the measure as a means of giving a frequently hostile management a freer hand.

Union staffers identified the top 200 institutional holders—mutual funds and pension funds that owned about 40 percent of Marriott's stock—and asked them to vote against the measure. It also hired Kissel-Blake, a New York–based proxy solicitation firm, to solicit votes. The biggest holders of Marriott stock were massive fund complexes like Putnam Investments and Fidelity, which had 5 million and 2.2 million shares, respectively. As is usual in such campaigns, most mutual fund managers, unwilling to betray fellow members of the corporate ruling class, declined the request.

HERE found a more enthusiastic response among smaller investors. Seeking to enlist grassroots support, the union mailed literature to individuals holding more than 5,000 shares and set up an anti-Marriott Web site, www.unbundle.com. It also appealed directly to like-minded public employee pension funds. From Albany, Carl McCall on March 9 announced his intention to vote New York's 452,100 shares against the proposal, couching his opposition in civil rights lingo. "Dual classification violates the fundamental principle of 'one share, one vote,'" he said. Three days later, CALPERS, which owned 569,000 shares, or about 0.5 percent, climbed aboard. And officials at those funds helped the union marshal opposition from their counterparts in other states. Within days of the announcement, the Council of Institutional Investors, an umbrella group for large public and private pension funds, sought its members' opinion of the proposal. Each of the nineteen responses was negative.

Fearing it couldn't garner the two-thirds majority needed to pass the measure, Marriott on March 16 offered the institutions a deal: If they voted to approve the merger—and hence the stock plan—in March, Marriott would let them vote again on the share plan by itself at the May 20 annual meeting. The union assented, and the merger was approved on Friday, March 20. In the next two months, the campaign continued. Marriott's executives fought the union's onslaught as if they were in a 1980s takeover battle. (This time, however, the grasping raiders were the company's existing management.) With 20 percent of the vote locked up, Bill Marriott traveled around the country in the firm's jet to rally institutions. The company flooded shareholders' mailboxes with overnight packages and personal pleas. The Marriotts complained that the union opposed the plan "to advance its own agenda," and was acting out of anger at Marriott's tactics in a labor dispute at the Marriott Moscone Center in San Francisco. Marriott also pressured large asset managers that in March had indicated a willingness to vote against the proposal, including American Express's IDS asset management unit.

Meantime, the union forces fought sub rosa, reaching out to shareholders with 500-plus shares, working phone banks on both coasts, and erecting yet another Web site, www.singleclass.com. And they began to make headway with large institutions. Walker convinced John Serhant, chair of the investment committee at State Street Global Advisers (asset manager of $470 billion), which had 1.6 million Marriott shares, to oppose the Marriott offer. Meanwhile, Institutional Shareholder Services (ISS), a proxy voting service that votes on behalf of about $25 billion in labor assets and issues advisory opinions for other institutions, weighed in against the measure.

The Marriott family, which has had difficulty adjusting to an era in which shareholders expect managers to take their interests seriously, overplayed its hand. On May 20, at the company's annual meeting, held at the Crystal Gateway Marriott Hotel in Arlington, Virginia, 53 percent voted against the management proposal. The vote marked the first time a union-proposed countersolicitation had blocked such an initiative. For Walker and his colleagues at the union across the Potomac, the vote represented not merely a temporary triumph of labor over management but a tectonic shift in the dynamics of industrial relations. "People assume that there is a division between labor and capital," he told the *Wall Street Journal*. "The fact is that we demonstrated an ability to identify with our fellow shareholders in Marriott and to build an alliance with shareholders."

In each of the past four years, labor funds have sponsored over 100 resolutions on issues such as director independence, executive compensation, and poison pills (a corporate device, discussed later, designed to make attempted hostile takeovers unattractive propositions). Shareholder resolutions have become popular in part because they are the simplest and least expensive means of taking on management. HERE's successful effort at challenging Marriott cost less than $50,000. But they are only one means through which shareholders can breathe life into the theory of corporate democracy, through which unions can take formal legal steps to ensure that their money isn't used against them. "All the assets, whenever they vote on a proxy, should use guidelines that are appropriate for labor funds in that they promote greater corporate democracy," said Richard Ferlauto, a former staffer at the AFL-CIO who is now managing director of proxy services at ISS.

It is almost beside the point that such resolutions are often nonbinding, and that management is prone to ignore them. Shareholder activism gives labor an opportunity to engage companies in an arena other than a picket line. Furthermore, union leaders find that their arguments about shareholder value resonate better with the broad investing public than do their demands for overtime and better benefits. Of course, they take great relish in tweaking their nemeses. Between 1996 and 1998, when the Teamsters issued its annual list of "least valuable directors," the item was invariably picked up by CNBC. And the union's complaints about Dow Jones Co.'s overpaid and underperforming board members, like Vernon Jordan, were resoundingly amplified by celebrity hedge-fund managers like James Cramer. In April 1997, the AFL-CIO launched a Web site called Executive Pay-Watch that listed compensation figures for 393 U.S. chief executive officers, including Jack Welch of General Electric and Robert Allen of AT&T. Those with excessive compensation were listed on a page called the OverBoard Room.

Beyond the external validation these efforts bring, unions find they also have a salutary effect on the morale of union workers. After all, annual meetings are one of the few arenas in which rank and filers can meet their bosses with the roles theoretically reversed. Of course, management often finds such give-and-take difficult to stomach, as if the peasants showed up at the castle and demanded tribute. Indeed, when the Teamsters expressed their intention to appear at a mid-1990s annual meeting of Consolidated Freightways, the company issued pointed decorum rules: Attendees were explicitly discouraged from spitting and personal criticism. In a sign of how quickly things can change, Consolidated Freightways in July 1997 announced it would divide about 4.5 percent of its stock among its 21,500 full-time employees. About two-thirds of that stock went to members of the union that had loudly crashed the previous year's annual meeting.

The tactics have occasionally goaded preternaturally arrogant CEOs and business leaders into acts of self-destructive contempt. In 1997, Thomas Donohue, president of the U.S. Chamber of Commerce, foolishly referred to union shareholder activists as "thugs in blue suits." At the General Electric annual meeting in spring 1997, the Teamsters introduced a resolution to limit CEO Jack Welch's pay. His $27.6 million in compensation, charged a labor group called United for a Fair Economy, was 1,003 times greater than that of the average U.S. factory worker. Welch responded, "I'm one of the fat cats." In both 1996 and 1997, the Teamsters pension fund, which owned about sixty-five shares of food wholesaler Fleming Companies, filed proposals to eliminate the firm's poison pill. The company's stock had dived from $40 in the early 1990s to the mid-teens in 1997, as sales slumped and the company fought legal charges that it had overcharged customers. CEO Robert Stauth tried to exclude the fund officials' proposal, sneering, "They don't own enough shares to be a concerned pension-fund shareholder." Nonetheless, the Teamsters convinced 60 percent of shareholders to back resolutions forcing the company to discard its poison pill. In the summer of 1998, Stauth himself was cashiered.

That unions are interested in revoking poison pills is ironic. In the 1980s, poison pills were frequently adopted as defenses against corporate raiders. When an unwanted investor starts acquiring a large amount of shares, poison pills give existing shareholders options to buy huge amounts of additional shares at lower prices, or sell additional shares at higher ones. The goal is to make the acquisition of more shares so economically unattractive to the raider that suitors either retreat or sue for peace. In the 1990s, however, unions have come to view the poison pill as a fundamentally undemocratic means of inhibiting the realization of maximum shareholder value. They believe that entrenched management is likely to be less responsive to the interest of both shareholders and workers. And just as laborers have been affected and buffeted by the winds of competition, so the reasoning goes, management officials should not be unduly insulated from market pressures if their performance lags.

Aside from raising its voice as a shareholder, the AFL-CIO has flexed its muscle as a consumer of asset management services. Most union funds parcel out their assets to outside investment managers. The Las Vegas hotel union's $1.5 billion fund, for example, is managed by Wall Street aristocrats like Lazard Freres and Weiss, Peck & Greer— yet another example of the extent to which the center of capital and some of its fiercest critics make common cause.

On October 1, 1996, the United Steelworkers of America struck eight of Wheeling-Pittsburgh Steel Corporation's plants after negotiations on (surprise!) pension plans broke down. When the company was in bankruptcy in the 1980s, the union agreed to suspend the pension plan if management would reinstate it ten years later. Ronald LaBow, the chief executive officer of Wheeling-Pittsburgh's parent company, WHX Corporation—a real thug in a blue suit—failed to keep his end of the bargain. As the strike wore on into December and January, the AFL-CIO began to take its case to companies that held WHX shares on behalf of clients. Union members protested outside offices of Merrill Lynch and Mellon Bank, and officials applied pressure to other asset managers. Dewey Square, a subsidiary of United Asset Management (UAM), con- trolled a large chunk of WHX, and the AFL-CIO believed Dewey Square was encouraging management to prolong the lockout. Another UAM subsidiary, Fidelity Management Association, relied on union funds for about two-thirds of its business. Patterson's AFL-CIO investments office made it clear that it didn't make sense for unions to employ asset man- agers who took antilabor positions. After discussions with union officials, Dennis Smith, a senior vice president of Fidelity Management, wrote a letter to Dewey Square in support of the union. In August 1997, the par- ties reached a tentative settlement, ending the ten-month strike.

Today, the nexus of pension funds, union offices, and shareholder activists in and around Washington, D.C., constitutes an alternative center of capital. And in an odd inversion, some companies now attempt to legitimize their strategic actions by seeking the imprimatur of Washington-area union-friendly investor groups. In February 1999,

WHX Corporation made an unsolicited bid for Global Industrial Technologies. When Global Industrial invoked its poison pill, WHX filed proxy materials to have board members elected to repeal the pill. In May 1999, it announced, with glee, that Institutional Shareholder Services had recommended that its clients, including pension funds under the AFL-CIO umbrella, support WHX's platform.

Of course, their role in the continuing drama of the democratization of money has left unions somewhat conflicted. On the one hand, labor relishes the fact that the ritualized choreography of shareholder activism—the solicitations, the proxy fights, the annual meetings—plays out on a public stage. Unions seldom get press so positive as when they take up the cudgels on behalf of shareholders. Yet the union moneymen are reticent when the topic turns to the size and breadth of their holdings. Even as they use their stock portfolios as platforms, they are reluctant to acknowledge that the workers are indeed shareholders, and pretty big ones; that they are participants in the market, not merely its victims. To a large degree, union pension funds have internalized the logic of shareholding, which pushes companies to take actions that boost share prices but may not always be friendly to labor. As such, unions are no less spared from the agony of shareholding than are the rest of us. They suffer from a sort of double consciousness: the heady rush of possessing and using capital, and the guilt over benefiting from its more pernicious tendencies.

Intellectuals, another group not traditionally thought of as big-time investors, exhibit a similarly conflicted attitude toward money. Intellectuals have long combined a taste for expensive finery with a studied distaste for the pursuit of money. One of my conventionally liberal professors at Cornell tooled around campus in a vanity-plated German import. A professor at Harvard invited his class out to his suburban Boston spread for tea on fine china and a game of tennis on his court. The dichotomy came into clearer focus in the early 1990s, when I attended a lecture by Stanley Fish, the Duke University deconstructionist, whose topic was "Why Academics Like Volvos." Fish believed academics' affinity for Volvos was really a metaphor for their ambivalence toward the material world. Volvos represent safety, and hence are utilitarian. And yet, as moderately expensive foreign cars, they are status symbols. These intentionally ugly products of Swedish design, he continued, represent desire and sublimated desire, style and antistyle. The talk was typical of Fish's academic discourse—obscure, self-satisfied, and occasionally offensive. My fellow graduate students and I were subsisting in Cambridge on $10,000 a year, far less than a new Volvo cost, and I could barely afford to keep my 1977 Toyota Celica running. Besides, Fish was subverting his own discourse. About the same time, he was seen driving a Jaguar convertible around the leafy environs of Durham, North Carolina.

Even in the 1990s it seemed strange for an avowed Marxist such as Fish to discuss—and desire—cars as status symbols. But in fact when it came to money, intellectuals had long been laboring under a false consciousness. Most intellectuals are college professors. And college professors—tenured ones, at least—have been some of the most unwitting beneficiaries of the bull market of the past thirty years. That's because virtually all of them are members of the largest and most powerful investor in the market today: TIAA-CREF.

When Andrew Carnegie, the self-made steel magnate, was appointed to Cornell University's board of trustees in 1890, he was appalled to learn that professors received compensation roughly equal to that of office clerks. (Were he alive today, Carnegie would likely be appalled to find that frequently is still the case.) Concerned that his fellow senior citizens would have to subsist on meager savings, Carnegie in 1901 started a pension fund for employees of Carnegie Steel. Mindful of teachers' limited financial prospects, Carnegie in 1905 established the $10 million Carnegie Foundation, which offered generous pensions for college teachers: $400 plus half salary annually for life upon retirement. At its inception, 2,653 teachers from 112 institutions joined; their average salary was $1,800.

Because the fund was open-ended, and the foundation intended to pay out interest from Carnegie's original donation, the admirable system was an actuarial time bomb. The fund's trustees realized they needed to switch to a scheme that would be funded by contributions from employers and employees. So in 1918 the Carnegie Foundation morphed into the Teachers Insurance Annuity Assurance Company (TIAA), a stock insurance company. Thirty institutions joined the new contributory retirement system in its first year, ranging from large state universities like the University of Michigan to smaller private schools like Yale and Bryn Mawr. The nest eggs were also to be portable, so that a professor who moved from, say, Purdue University to the University of Georgia could take the pension with him.

TIAA sold life insurance and annuities to its members and invested the premiums in bonds. In the early 1950s, when inflation threatened bond returns, TIAA began to invest in stocks. In July 1952, it set up a separate unit, the College Retirement Equities Fund (CREF), which began offering a variable annuity that would provide lifetime pensions from income generated by the appreciation and dividends of common stocks. It allowed participants at 613 institutions to roll small amounts every month into stocks.

As more and more professors entered the system and enjoyed long careers, CREF swelled with new premium inflows. It poured the money into stocks, which continued to rise. The appreciation was such that $1 invested in CREF in 1952 was worth $36.74 in 1988. By May 1999, CREF was up 17,308 percent, or 173 times—$1 invested in 1952 was worth $173. As of October 30, 1999, TIAA-CREF had assets of $273 billion, spread among 2 million participants at 9,000 participating institutions. The thirtieth-largest U.S. company ranked by assets, and the third-largest life insurance company, TIAA-CREF is the largest pension plan in the United States—bigger than that of General Electric or General Motors or IBM. It controls a portfolio of stocks bigger than Fidelity's Magellan Fund and the entire Janus family of funds, worth more than Bill Gates and Warren Buffett combined.

TIAA-CREF has turned many intellectuals into unwitting million-aires, including the ones I know best: my parents. In many ways, they are representative of CREF's unlikely stockholders. My father was born in the Bronx in 1938, the only child of older parents who had survived the depression working as bank tellers. Dad grew up in a one-bedroom apartment in the halcyon postwar Bronx, when the nearby Yankees were great, the Grand Concourse still lived up to its name, and the city's public schools were the envy of the nation. After attending the Bronx High School of Science and the City College of New York, and having gotten it into his head that he could be an English professor, he went off to Cornell. There, he met my mother, an undergraduate English major from Great Neck.

They married and quickly began having children. After obtaining his Ph.D. from Ohio State University, my father took a job at Michigan State University in 1966. Andrew Carnegie likely would have been shocked at his starting salary, about $9,000—or just five times the aver-age salary of participants in TIAA-CREF in 1905. Over the years, as he gained tenure and took on administrative posts, the salary climbed into the mid-five figures. In a middle-class college town, this marked us as solidly middle class. Not well off, to be sure, but solidly middle class.

I never recall that money and investing were topics of discussion in our household. It's doubtful the *Wall Street Journal* ever passed our threshold. I never once caught my dad poring over the stock tables or comparing mutual funds over the backyard fence with a neighbor. My mother did not participate in an investment club. Other households received popular magazines like *Money* or *Kiplinger's*; I grew up think-ing *Commentary* was a mass-circulation magazine. If anything, the pre-vailing ethos toward money and the markets in the Gross household was a utilitarian indifference. Money was needed for the necessities of life, but not to be pursued as an end. My mother had grown up haute bourgeoise in Great Neck. So rooted was her family in the immigrant retailing ethos that when one of my brothers told a distant uncle he was pursuing a doctorate in philosophy at the University of Chicago, the response was "So what are you going into, wholesale or retail?" (Ultimately, he did go into wholesale. He's an institutional options strategist at Salomon Smith Barney.)

As my brothers and I grew up, my parents scraped, denied themselves, and borrowed so their three sons could go off to college and, ultimately, graduate school. In thirty years they bought exactly one new car—a 1987 Chevrolet Nova. And they waited until we left home to make some needed upgrades in the house. They never opened a brokerage account and didn't consult a financial planner until their mid-fifties. But all those years, my parents were quietly putting a small percentage of their income into the market. From the day he began working at Michigan State, my father began contributing to a pension plan, invested on his behalf by TIAA-CREF. Each year he put in 5 percent of his salary, and his employers, the taxpayers of Michigan, kicked in 10 percent. TIAA-CREF, in turn, plowed this money into its massive stock and bond funds, month after month, year after year. This pattern continued for some thirty-three years, a period in which, fortuitously, the market rose steadily. As a result, my dad retired in 1999 at age sixty-one, sitting on a cool million in liquid assets.

My parents owe their good fortune to TIAA-CREF. So do their colleagues and neighbors in the bucolic college town of East Lansing, Michigan, as do celebrity professors like Henry Louis Gates of Harvard, unreconstructed leftists like Howard Zinn and Stanley Fish, and the entire inscrutable comparative literature department at Duke University, among other hard-core critics of capitalism. As a class, intellectuals have never been great fans of corporate America. Campus causes— from the South Africa divestment fad of the 1980s to the more contemporary cause célèbre of sweatshop-produced college apparel— frequently obsess on the ravages of global capitalism. Except in isolated pockets like Michigan's Hillsdale College, Pepperdine University, and certain departments at the University of Chicago, most professors regard multinational corporations with the sort of disdain they reserve for holding office hours. But even professors less militantly anticapitalist than, say, Noam Chomsky would be shocked to learn of their vast stockholdings. In 1999, CREF's stock account contained 26.3 million shares of AT&T, worth some $1.5 billion.

TIAA-CREF is easily overlooked in large part because of its understated style. Its CEO, John Biggs, former vice chancellor of administration and finance at Washington University in St. Louis, doesn't talk shop with Willow Bay on CNN's *Moneyline Newshour*. Nor does TIAA-CREF sponsor golf or tennis tournaments, as do other large investment managers. Indeed, the demeanor of the quiet, modest giant is best exemplified by Douglas Dial, manager of the CREF stock account. Dial has an unremarkable corner office on the tenth floor of TIAA-CREF's unremarkable headquarters, a twenty-seven-story office building at 730 Third Avenue in midtown Manhattan. Balding, wearing khaki pants and a red-striped shirt on casual Friday, he resembles the eminently sensible Vermont Senator Patrick Leahy.

For the past twenty years, the CREF stock account—the largest single managed equity fund in the world—has combined indexing and active management. Today, about 75 percent of the funds are invested in indices—it owns all the stocks in the Russell 3,000 index, for example. About 20 percent of the funds are in overseas indices. The remaining part, about $30 billion, is managed actively. Dial, a former analyst and research director at Dean Witter and C. J. Lawrence, has a team of about thirty analysts, who are responsible for industry or geographic sectors, and a dozen-odd quantitative experts. Together, they assemble a portfolio composed of a few hundred stocks, with fifty or sixty very large positions, and several packages of smaller companies in a particular sector or industry that it wishes to give extra weight. TIAA-CREF avoids speculation. Indeed, its equity trading floor more closely resembles a small provincial day-trading operation than the nerve center of the largest single stock fund in the world. There's a lone television, set to CNBC, its plug hanging from the wall outlet, and about a dozen-odd people sitting quietly at their desks. It's seven miles north and a world away from the chaotic football-field-sized trading floors of Wall Street.

At root, TIAA-CREF is rather similar to other large institutional investors: cautious, colorless, quick to take advantage of its scale and scope. And its scale and scope are tremendous: In 1997, for example, the CREF Stock Account became the first and only fund to reach the $100 billion mark. "In terms of how we approach the investment process, be it in stocks or fixed income, there's very little difference between us and Fidelity," said Dial. But TIAA-CREF's particular constitution—a nonprofit serving people with a generally liberal social agenda—is unique. And because it takes its role as a representative of its constituents seriously, TIAA-CREF has contributed to the democratization of money, in both senses.

No other institution, for example, has done as much to promote diversity among investment managers. Despite their lip service, the vast majority of investment banks and mutual fund companies are bastions of uniformity. When it went public, Goldman, Sachs had one African American partner, Garland Wood. TIAA-CREF, by contrast, was politically correct (PC) when PC wasn't cool. In the 1950s and 1960s, it backed the construction in Columbia, Maryland, of James Rouse's planned community designed for middle-income, integrated housing. It appointed the first woman to its board, Radcliffe College President Ada Comstock Notestein, in 1940. TIAA-CREF named its first black board member, Tuskegee Institute President Dr. Luther Foster, in 1957, five years before James Meredith enrolled at Ole Miss. When Clifton R. Wharton Jr. was named chief executive officer in 1987, he became the first black to lead an organization whose financial assets would rank it among the Fortune 500. He served until 1993.

TIAA-CREF was also the professional home for four years to the one African American who now oversees more assets than Carl McCall: Tom Jones. Jones's life has taken almost as many odd twists and turns as the eponymous Henry Fielding novel. His father was a Presbyterian minister and nuclear physicist who designed missiles for the Defense Department. Growing up in Queens, the precocious child entered high school at age twelve and went to Cornell as a sixteen-year-old freshman. There, he was elected freshman class president and joined a white fraternity. But by the fall of 1969, Jones had become radicalized. Black students, upset with the university's failure to establish a black studies program and enraged by a cross-burning episode on campus, were primed for action.

In the early morning of Saturday, April 19, 1969, Jones and 100 other students, most members of the Afro-American Society, took over the student union, Willard Straight Hall, and locked themselves in. That night, having repulsed an attempt by fraternity jocks to boot them out, the students armed themselves with seventeen rifles and shotguns. It marked the first introduction of weaponry into a campus conflict. Thirty-four hours later, on April 20, they agreed to leave the building after the university essentially acceded to their demands. Jones was the last to leave, a rifle in one arm, a raised clenched fist in the other, his Afro rising to the arch of heaven. (Zachary Carter, who went on to become U.S. Attorney for the Eastern District of New York, was one of the other ringleaders.) Later that night, Jones engaged in fiery rhetoric. "In the past it has been the black people who have done all the dying. Now the time has come when the pigs are going to die too . . . when the faculty are going to be dealt with. . . . Cornell has until 9 o'clock to live. It is now 3 minutes after 8." The tension eventually eased, but the university was never the same. President James Perkins was forced to resign in disgrace a month later.

Jones stuck around Cornell to earn a master's degree in 1970 and took a job as a consultant at the Arthur Young accounting firm, which put him through night MBA courses at Boston University. In 1982, he went to work for John Hancock Mutual Life Insurance Company, where he quickly rose to the post of treasurer. In 1989, Wharton hired him to become chief financial officer at TIAA-CREF. Jones boosted the organization's credit rating and oversaw the launch of four new highly rated funds, including its Money Market Fund and Social Choice Account. The man who twenty years before had threatened to "deal with" Cornell's faculty was now responsible for their retirement savings.

As a prominent executive in the investment and education field, and as an African American, Jones was a natural choice for a position on Cornell's Board of Trustees, to which he was (controversially) appointed in 1993. (In 1995, he endowed a $5,000 prize in honor of Perkins, given to people who foster "interracial understanding and harmony.") At meetings and trustee weekends, Jones got to know another Cornell graduate who had risen to prominence on Wall Street: Sanford Weill, the chief executive officer of the Travelers Group. In 1993, Weill hired Jones to run his asset management business. Weill took Jones with him when he acquired Citigroup. As vice chairman, Jones now runs the asset management business of the nation's largest bank. From Black Panther to blue-chipper, it's been a long, strange trip—and it would not have been possible were it not for TIAA-CREF.

As a conscientious investor, TIAA-CREF had always voted its shares. Given its buy-and-hold philosophy, TIAA-CREF believed it should hold onto rather than simply sell out of losing positions. It started filing proxy proposals as early as 1970, and in 1985 began to file proxies, asking companies to divest holdings in South Africa. Typically, though, TIAA-CREF has favored a less confrontational style than that found in public employee funds. Nor does TIAA-CREF target companies in a geographic or industrial area, as unions have. Rather, it has developed a quasi-scientific approach that would make MIT economists proud. Between 1993 and 1995, TIAA-CREF created a database on twenty-five separate governance issues, such as board independence, the makeup of a company's compensation committee, and consulting arrangements with board members. Firms in the 1,700-company portfolio that fall short on an inordinate number of issues receive letters and visits from a TIAA-CREF staffer or consultant. Since 1995, TIAA-CREF has retained as part-time consultants Kenneth West and Dolph Bridgewater, the former CEOs of Harris Trust and the Brown Group, respectively, who meet with executives to express their concern.

If the talks fail to yield results, TIAA-CREF then files proxy resolutions. But unlike union pension funds, it does not identify publicly the companies with which it files resolutions. "We found that when we came to an agreement we had to work with them on a face-saving public statement. Then another phenomenon started to occur—they preferred to resolve matters quietly," said Peter Clapman, the Harvard-educated lawyer who runs TIAA-CREF's corporate governance unit. Between 1992 and 1996, according to a study by three University of Arizona professors, CREF obtained governance concessions from forty-two of forty-five targeted companies. Thirty-two of them negotiated without issues actually coming to a vote.

Still, TIAA-CREF has been increasingly aggressive. In 1998, it became owner of about 17.7 percent of the stock of Furr's/Bishop's, the struggling cafeteria company based in Lubbock, Texas, after the company defaulted on debt issued to TIAA in a private placement. The stock, which began trading in 1996 at about $2, had fallen to about $0.81. Displeased with the existing management—board chairman Kevin Lewis had recently dumped all his shares and had been largely unresponsive to CREF's concerns—TIAA-CREF in May 1998 nominated a full slate of seven candidates for the board of directors to challenge the management slate. "Finally, we felt the only alternative for us was to run an independent slate," Clapman recalled. It included two former Furr's directors who had resigned to run on TIAA-CREF's slate. In its proxy, TIAA-CREF charged that "there is something fundamentally wrong at the company and that the company has been operated for far too long for the benefit of a few rather than all the stockholders." TIAA-CREF convinced 80 percent of the votes cast to topple the incumbent board. After the election, CEO Theodore Papit resigned and was replaced by Suzanne Hopgood, a hotel industry executive and former Furr's director who ran on the dissident slate. That event marked the first time institutional investors had managed to throw out an entire board.

TIAA-CREF also doesn't shrink from confronting head-on the largest of companies. Disney is an example. For over a decade, after ascending to his lofty post in 1984, Disney's CEO, Michael Eisner, was known as a master of corporate feel-good shtick. But in recent years, his act has worn thin. Like a spoiled child in a sandbox, Eisner has been unwilling to share his corporate toys, and top executives and erstwhile friends like Jeffrey Katzenberg and Michael Ovitz have fled. Eisner has also made a number of risky moves, including the $19 billion acquisition of ABC in 1996, at a time when the network business was beginning to tank. Since that acquisition, Disney's stock has performed about as well as some of ABC's insipid sitcoms, lagging the market badly. Nonetheless, the directors on Disney's compensation committee, among them Eisner's personal lawyer, saw fit to award Eisner twenty-four million stock options worth more than $195 million on top of his $750,000 salary and $7.9 million bonus.

In 1997, Eisner's massive proposed compensation package required a shareholder vote. TIAA-CREF, which owned 6.9 million shares of Disney worth about $700 million, or about 1 percent of the company, sprang into action. "We looked at the board membership and compensation committee that had approved what was a salary package totally out of balance," said Clapman. It asked Disney to restructure its board of directors so that a majority would be independent of the company. The board, after all, was stocked with former executives and worthies who have done business with the company, including actor Sidney Poitier, architect Robert A.M. Stern, who designed a Disney animation studio, and former Senate majority leader George Mitchell, who has consulted for Disney. It further urged that Disney's audit, compensation, and nominating committees be composed entirely of directors who were clearly independent of management.

A few conversations got nowhere. "It was 'We've got a great board, we're great, what's your problem,'" said Clapman. Rebuffed, TIAA-CREF in February 1998 presented its first shareholder resolution urging greater director independence. The company fought it hard, with Eisner taking to the phones to lobby shareholders. The measure failed, but it garnered 35.5 percent of the shares voted, more than double the average recorded for such resolutions in the previous year. Considering Eisner's self-image as a benevolent genius, the vote was something of a slap in the face. Since then, Disney has agreed to make changes. All board members stand for election every year, and two insiders were replaced by independent directors. Also, Eisner's 1998 bonus was cut in half, from $9.9 million to $5 million, and he received no more stock option grants.

TIAA-CREF has also taken the lead in campaigning against "dead-hand" poison pills—measures that can be removed only by incumbent directors *before* a proxy fight. "This organization is really out to extinguish deadhand poison pills," said Clapman. In the 1998 proxy season, TIAA-CREF filed anti-deadhand resolutions with ten companies. Seven revoked the offending measure before it came to a vote. At two of the resisters, Cleveland-based lubricants company Lubrizol Corporation and pharmaceutical giant Bergen Brunswig, TIAA-CREF took its case to the investors. At both of these companies' April 1999 annual meetings, the measures passed, with 68 percent and 74 percent majorities, respectively. In general, TIAA-CREF finds it easier to enlist other institutional shareholders than do union funds. "Being an investor gives us a certain cachet in the world out there," said Clapman. "When we're upset with particular company practices, we're doing it for reasons related to investment."

Indeed, TIAA-CREF has distinguished itself as an investor. In keeping with its democratic ethos, TIAA-CREF's expenses are substantially less than industry averages. In 1998, the annual expense fee for CREF was 31 basis points—meaning it spent only .31 cent for every dollar under management. That compares with about 2 cents per dollar for the average comparable fund rated by Morningstar. In turn, the lower fee translates directly into greater returns for investors. TIAA-CREF also saves money by indexing and by performing functions like record-keeping in-house. But the main reason TIAA-CREF undercuts its peers on costs is its bare-bones approach to marketing. Unlike Fidelity, it doesn't run expensive advertising campaigns or purchase full-page advertisements in the *Wall Street Journal* and *New York Times*. As one might expect for an outfit that views towns like Madison, Wisconsin, as a core market, it does sponsor National Public Radio's *All Things Considered*. But it does not offer incentives to financial advisers and brokers who sell its services. After all, it's marketing to a somewhat captive audience. (Professors and college administrators can usually choose from other plans but have remained loyal to TIAA-CREF.)

In the past few years, as rivals such as Fidelity and Vanguard tried to encroach on its turf, TIAA-CREF has responded by expanding services. In 1997, Congress, acting at the behest of financial services rivals, revoked TIAA-CREF's tax exemption. But the move, which forces TIAA-CREF to pay taxes on certain funds generated from operations, also freed the institution to offer new services to its vast customer base and to new groups of potential customers. In a move once unthinkable to 1960s-era graduate students, TIAA-CREF offers trust services to its wealthier members. Since the fall of 1997, CREF has offered six no-load mutual funds to its members and the general public. The funds, which include the likes of TIAA-CREF Growth Equity and Bond Plus Mutual Funds, bear the institution's trademark low operating funds. Each requires an initial investment of a mere $250 and allows investors to roll in cash in $25 monthly dollops. All six beat the industry averages in their first year. By late 1999, the barely marketed mutual funds had attracted $2 billion.

Even as it expands into new areas, TIAA-CREF remains a democratic institution with primarily Democratic investors. And it displays some of the internal conflicts of the democratization of money. CREF's indexing strategy largely spares the managers and members from complicity in distasteful endeavors such as picking winners and participating in the frequently disastrous money flows in and out of emerging markets. Still, at those moments when they have been asked to choose between returns and conscience, TIAA-CREF's holders have energetically voted their pocketbooks. Given the number and political leanings of its members, CREF receives surprisingly few requests to change its investment strategies or to divest from one sector or another. In 1988, TIAA-CREF opened the Social Choice Account, which screens out tobacco, alcohol, and defense stocks. In over a decade, it has attracted only $4 billion. TIAA-CREF members have proposed internal proxies urging CREF, for example, to divest tobacco stocks. But in the fall of 1998, the proposal was defeated for the third straight year by a healthy margin of 68 percent to 25 percent.

The vote could signify that most intellectuals still agree with Cornell French professor Richard Klein, who entitled his 1997 book *Cigarettes Are Sublime*. Or it could simply be that CREF's satisfied investors are reluctant to mix social agendas with investment strategies. Indeed, intellectual investors, it turns out, are much like nonintellectual investors. "Word has gotten out that they better provide for themselves, and they do not see a personal conflict between their ideals and having their money work successfully for them," said Peter Clapman.

Through its penny-pinching, shrewd management, and activism, TIAA-CREF has made its members, including my parents, financially secure while enabling them to pursue careers and lifestyles that are to a large degree insulated from the markets. Their membership in the cooperative allows academics simultaneously to rail against the ravages of insidious global markets while reaping their benefits. As David Lodge, the academic turned satirical novelist, might say, "Nice work!"

SINCE the early decades of the twentieth century, labor and intellectuals, the bastions of the Democratic party's left wing, have agitated for a greater socialization of the economy. Now, through the vast expansion of pension plans that run workers' money, and through the growth of mutual funds, it's finally happening. But something tells me this isn't quite what Marx had in mind. In 1975, Peter Drucker wrote a remarkably prescient book, *The Unseen Revolution: How Pension Fund Socialism Came to America*. He argued that if one defined socialism as ownership of the means of production by workers, then the United States was the first truly socialist country, because at the time, by Drucker's calculations, pension funds of all types owned about a quarter of the nation's equity capital. In the mid-1970s, the largest 1,000 private pension funds had $115 billion, whereas union funds had $35 billion, and nonbusiness pension funds had $50 billion. He concluded that "the employees own American business; but they do not know it, do not perceive it, do not experience it. Indeed, under the present systems it is very difficult for them to do so."

Drucker was largely right. But institutions like public employee and union funds and TIAA-CREF are laboring to provide a means through which employees can experience their ownership. If anything, the trends Drucker noticed in the mid-1970s have picked up pace. TIAA-CREF alone has greater assets than all the pension funds counted by Drucker back in 1975. Of course, in these years, U.S.-style capitalism didn't give way to European-style socialism. It turns out, capitalism hasn't collapsed under the tremendous weight of its own internal contradictions. Rather, socialism has. Indeed, the last serious socialist in American politics left a legacy that is more financial than political.

Henry Wallace, the son of an Iowa State College dairying professor, rose from the cornfields to become a New Deal secretary of agriculture and Roosevelt's wartime vice president before being dumped in favor of Harry Truman in 1944. Booted from his post as commerce secretary in 1946 for appearing soft on communism, Wallace ran on the Progressive party ticket in 1948, garnering more than one million votes. His political career quickly petered out. Fortunately for his heirs, Wallace also had a mind for commerce. In 1926, Wallace founded a seed company to help farmers plant more efficiently. That firm, Hi-Bred Pioneer, went public, and as it grew into an agribusiness giant, the Wallace family retained at least 15 percent of it. In 1999, Hi-Bred was sold to DuPont for $7.7 billion. Through their holdings in a public company, the descendants of the man who in 1942 rejected Henry Luce's "American Century" and proclaimed "the century of the common man" have become billionaires.

Such developments, and the existence of millionaire sociologists and shareholding stevedores, have upset many of our most cherished notions about money, the stock market, and wealth. To a large degree, their presence overturns some of the most hoary 1980s money clichés. The age of the Masters of the Universe has given way to an era in which the masters—the CEOs—are increasingly being forced to answer to the servants, and in which the fiercest critics of capitalism clip bond coupons and collect dividends. The place of money and stockholding in politics has undergone a similar shift in the 1990s: The precinct of money, traditionally rock-ribbed Republican, has become one in which Democrats are more comfortable. In many ways, the democratization of money has led to the Democratization of money. As the 1990s wore on, Democrats, and, in particular, the Clinton administration, grew not only to tolerate and appreciate the markets but even to love and embrace them.

4

Bill Clinton and Money

On Friday, January 15, 1999, the House prosecutors took to the Senate floor to argue, once again, for the impeachment of President William Jefferson Clinton. (Why the newscasters felt compelled to intone his three names during this period, when plain old "Bill" sufficed in other times, is still a mystery.) That morning, Clinton headed to New York City to attend a gathering at Windows on the World, the ultraexpensive restaurant on the 107th floor of One World Trade Center. But the event wasn't one of the innumerable fundraisers the president had held in and around Wall Street in the previous eight years. Rather, it was a conference hosted by Jesse Jackson's Wall Street Project, an organization founded in January 1997 to instruct the financial services industry on the glories of diversity and on ways to help minorities play a greater role in the realm of money.

Clinton, late as per usual, entered the room to the strains of "Hail to the Chief" and a whooping chorus of cheers, punctuated by cries of "We love you, Mr. President." In the front row, Jack Kemp sat between Ron Burkle, the grocery store magnate and Clinton fundraiser, and AFL-CIO head John Sweeney. Donald Trump was also in attendance. Jackson, who had arranged a series of brief testimonials to the embattled president, introduced Richard Grasso, the gaunt, birdlike chairman of the New York Stock Exchange, as "one of our able allies in this struggle," and gave the diminutive stockbroker a podium to stand on. ("That's a Dukakis thing here," Jackson joked.) Grasso, summoning up the ghosts of the civil rights movement, declared with certainty that Martin Luther King would have approved of the Wall Street Project. "I know Dr. King is smiling down today because of the progress but most importantly because of the unwavering commitment of our president," he said. Grasso, who had donated $1,000 to Clinton's reelection campaign, noted that the Dow had tripled during Clinton's tenure. But, he said, "my little corner of Manhattan is not what the U.S. financial markets are about." Between individual shareholders and pension beneficiaries, "two hundred million Americans have benefited over these last six years from your unwavering commitment."

Michael Armstrong, the chairman of AT&T, recalled the dark days of 1993 in Southern California when "we had something more than a recession." But the straight-talking engineer credited Clinton with making the unpopular choices to reduce the deficit and lower interest rates. "You made those tough decisions, and because of that a lot of us in our businesses look awfully smart." After announcing that AT&T's $1 billion bond offering would be comanaged by a minority-owned firm, he concluded: "So, Mr. President, my message is, you had the courage to get it started, and we all were along for the most wonderful economic ride in the history of this country."

Finally, Jackson introduced Clinton. Reviewing his tenure and obliquely mentioning his late travails, the preacher chose some remarkably inapt metaphors: "How do you judge Bill Clinton? How do you judge Babe Ruth? How do you judge Hank Aaron? How do you judge Michael Jordan? . . . You judge them by their cumulative box score." Sure, Clinton had his share of clashes, but, Jackson noted, "the only people at the end of the game whose uniforms are clean are those who do not have enough confidence in them by the coach to make it to the field. . . . Those who play have stains on their uniforms . . . those who play, those who play . . . have stains."

Clinton, clearly touched by the support, returned the compliments. "How can any American, of any station in life, not be proud of the financial markets we have built, and, as Mr. Grasso said, of the fact that now 200 million of our 260 million people actually benefit from it. We are beginning to share the wealth," he said. "That's why Jack Kemp's here, and why I always liked him." (As if on cue, Kemp piped up, in his husky voice, "I like you too, Mr. President.") Acknowledging that government has a role to play in spreading the wealth even further, Clinton pledged to "stay with the strategy that's got us this far." Much as he would like to propose new investment programs, he recognized the need "to keep the budget balanced to keep the interest rates low and the confidence high." Clinton endorsed the goals of the conference and pledged to help "build a bridge between Wall Street and our greatest untapped markets"—low-income inner-city areas—by extending new tax credits.

A gathering high above Wall Street organized by Jesse Jackson, whose audience included a supply-side guru, a 1980s icon, and corporate executives, perhaps seemed a peculiar refuge for the beleaguered president. After all, Clinton shot out of Arkansas in 1991 slamming the failure of trickle-down economics; condemning the Trumpesque values of the 1980s, the habitués of the New York Stock Exchange, and soulless multinational corporations like AT&T; and taking great pains to distance himself from Jackson. But his participation in Jackson's conference is a logical fit, given the many tacking and evasive maneuvers the president took over the course of his eight-year tenure. During Clinton's two tumultuous terms, the markets proved time and again to be his rock and redeemer—and he theirs.

The typical narrative of the domestic side of the Clinton presidency goes as follows. At first, Clinton tried to govern from the left, proposing to raise taxes, initiate new spending programs, let gays serve openly in the military, and nationalize health care. Such liberal overreaching led to the 1994 Republican takeover of Congress. Dominated by Newt Gingrich and a group of radicalized House freshmen, the new Republican majority overplayed its hand, shutting down the government when Clinton and the Democrats refused to go along with their radical program. As Clinton heeded the advice of political consultant Dick Morris and triangulated—playing off both the Republicans and the Democrats in Congress—he notched significant popular accomplishments such as welfare reform. These actions disarmed the Republicans so effectively that in 1996, carried along by a growing economy and a booming stock market, Clinton easily won reelection. In his second term, Clinton fell victim to his own obstinacy and depravity in the Lewinsky affair but was rescued by the obsessive overreaching of independent prosecutor Kenneth Starr. Hell-bent on unseating Clinton and consumed by hatred, the Republicans lost steam in the 1998 elections and continued to pursue the unsuccessful impeachment effort. The American public, though disgusted with the president's behavior, approved of how he was doing his job. Thus Clinton will go down in history as a deeply flawed individual and occasionally brilliant politician who presided over an era of prosperity and progress.

There is, however, an alternative narrative, one that takes into account the role of money and the markets. For Clinton was aided by an alignment of economic stars that appear about as often as Halley's comet courses through the heavens. And that development, more than his supple political ability, may have been the key to his survival.

When Clinton announced his candidacy from the steps of the Old

State House in Little Rock on October 3, 1991, the air was redolent with the stench of rot, like Bourbon Street the week after Mardi Gras. The good feelings generated by the Gulf War had dissipated. With the parades over and the reservists safely home, the nation was free to focus on its flagging economy. Wall Street was at one of its periodic lows in public esteem. A recession loomed, the savings-and-loan bailout was in full swing, the Dow lingered at about 3,000 — just 20 percent above its 1987 peak — and a continuing skein of scandals grabbed headlines. A few months earlier, Salomon Brothers had fired Paul Mozer, the head of its government bond trading desk, for illegally bidding in a series of Treasury auctions. *Den of Thieves*, the book by James Stewart that documented the malfeasance and moral vacancy of several leading 1980s financial figures, was flying off the shelves and about to hit the *New York Times* best-seller list. Michael Milken was serving his 36–40 month sentence at the federal penitentiary in Pleasanton, California.

Clinton wasted no time in announcing his intention to run against the decade of greed. "Do you know that in the 1980s, while middle-class income went down, charitable giving by working people went up?" he asked. "And while rich people's incomes went up, charitable giving by the wealthy went down?" Clinton charged that the chief executives of big companies "raised their own pay in the last decade by four times the percentage their workers' pay went up." The combative candidate was quick to name names and charge President George Bush as complicit with the evils of Wall Street: "When Salomon Brothers abused the Treasury markets, the president was silent. When the rip-off artists looted our S&Ls, the president was silent. In a Clinton administration, when people sell their companies and their workers and their country down the river, they'll get called on the carpet." In a speech several weeks later at Georgetown University, Clinton offered the wounded nation a "New Covenant for economic change that empowers people, rewards work, and organizes our country to compete and win again." Its centerpiece: a middle-class tax cut paid for by a tax increase on the rich.

In tarring Bush as a wealthy Republican uninterested in the plight of real Americans, Clinton was merely carrying on a grand Democratic tradition: class warfare. Since the 1930s, Democrats have deployed class-warfare tactics with varying degrees of success. Franklin D. Roosevelt's first inaugural address is remembered chiefly for the line "the only thing we have to fear is fear itself." But it contained a far more politically potent warning about the perfidy of the denizens of lower Manhattan. "The money-changers have fled from the temple of our civilization," Roosevelt thundered. "There must be an end to conduct in banking and business which too often has given to a sacred trust the likeness of callous and selfish wrongdoing."

In 1992, George Bush, with his preppie background, old-money airs, and four names, wore his inherited wealth like an albatross around his neck. Iowa Senator Tom Harkin, the political heir of Henry Wallace, barnstormed out of Iowa as if in a colorized 1930s newsreel and relished taunting the Yalie. "I'm here to tell you that George Herbert Walker Bush has got feet of clay, and I intend to take a hammer to them," Harkin roared when announcing his candidacy for president. Bush's aloofness and waspish devotion to cutting the capital-gains tax— widely seen as a sop to the rich—didn't help Bush's cause any. In 1991 and 1992, as the economy contracted and unemployment spiked to levels not seen since 1984, Bush refused to declare a fiscal emergency, which would release extra unemployment funds. Instead, he called for a capital-gains tax cut as the best way to "create jobs almost instantly."

As the primary season got under way, Clinton distanced himself from the left wing by talking about welfare reform and by lashing out at rapper Sister Souljah. But he was also careful to come down on the left side of the money debate, and found a perfect foil in Paul Tsongas, who larded a declinist message with substantial doses of economic nationalism. Calling himself a "probusiness Democrat" and dubbing his supporters "economic patriots," Tsongas supported free trade and opposed strikebreaker replacement legislation. One of the more startlingly incorrect assessments in recent memory was Tsongas's assertion that Germany and Japan, with their then-robust economies, were the true victors of the Cold War.

Tsongas, whom James Carville accused of having "the cultural agenda of Boston and the economic agenda of Wall Street," carried New Hampshire. But when the campaign turned to the South, Clinton staked out the good-ol'-boy turf, tagging Tsongas as a chardonnay-swilling proto-Republican, a "soulless economic mechanic" who would be "on the side of the big CEOs and against the rights of shareholders." When Tsongas labeled Clinton a "Pander Bear" for scaring the elderly about Social Security, Clinton bristled. "You want to talk about pandering," Clinton said. "It wasn't me that went to New York and said I'd be the best friend Wall Street ever had." (Clinton, of course, won the New York primary with 41 percent of the vote and turned out to be the best friend Wall Street ever had.) In Florida, Clinton ran a damaging TV spot that accused Tsongas of proposing "another capital-gains tax cut for the rich."

As the primary season closed and Clinton began to train his rhetorical guns on Bush, class warfare came to the fore. At the Democratic convention, on July 16, 1992, Clinton assailed Bush: "He has raised taxes on the people driving pickup trucks, and lowered taxes on people riding in limousines." Ridiculing Bush for promising 15 million jobs back in 1988, and being "over fourteen million short," Clinton spelled out a vision of America "in which the wealthiest few—those making over $200,000 a year—are asked to pay their fair share." Clinton's attitudes toward money and the markets were more fully expressed in his campaign manifesto, *Putting People First*. The book was an alphabetized compendium of interest-group liberalism chestnuts. Chapter headings included Agriculture, AIDS, Arms Control, Arts, Campaign Finance Reform, Cities, Civil Rights, Corporate Responsibility, and so on. But between the earnest policy proposals lay clarion cries of class warfare. The rich, he argued, had essentially cheated in the past decade. "While the rich got richer, the forgotten middle class—the people who work hard and play by the rules—took it on the chin." Referring to the "corrupt do-nothing values of the 1980s," Clinton proclaimed that "never again should Washington reward those who speculate in paper, instead of those who put people first." To rein in runaway executive pay, he argued that companies should not be allowed to deduct more than $1 million of CEOs' salaries from their taxable income, and that shareholders be allowed to determine the compensation of top executives.

As the campaign wore on, Bush was ultimately crippled by his identification with wealth. At the debate in Richmond, Virginia, twenty-five-year-old Marisa Hall asked the candidates: "How has the national debt personally affected each of your lives? And if it hasn't, how can you honestly find a cure for the economic problems of the common people if you haven't experienced what's ailing them?" Bush struggled with his answer. "Are you suggesting that if somebody has means, that the national debt doesn't affect them? . . . I'm not sure I get—help me with the question and I'll try to answer it." The woman responded that she knew people who couldn't make their mortgage or car payments. Of course, Bush didn't know anybody who faced such quotidian difficulties. But Clinton practically pounced off his stool. He asked the woman how the deficit had affected her, described the way the federal deficit impacted his work as governor, and blamed the persistent red ink on trickle-down economics, "a failed economic theory." Just then, a television camera caught Bush looking at his watch. This infelicitous time-check instantly became one of those defining campaign moments, as were Nixon's sweating during the 1960 Kennedy debate, Muskie's tears in 1972, and Reagan's "there you go again" applause line in 1980. From then on, Clinton's election seemed a fait accompli.

Clinton could run against the markets because they were far from the phenomenon they are today. In late 1992, the Dow was hovering at close to its summer 1990 level. About 25.8 million American households held mutual funds, up only 11 percent from 1990. CNBC was an obscure signal coursing through the ether, and Jeffrey Bezos, the founder of Amazon.com, was an investment banking associate at Merrill Lynch. As a practical matter, Clinton had little to gain by aligning himself with the markets. To be sure, he did have the support of many Wall Street Democrats, foremost among them Robert Rubin, the co-head of Goldman, Sachs. But given Clinton's penchant for class-warfare rhetoric, and the supposed environmental radicalism of his running mate, Wall Streeters and the stock markets had little reason to jump aboard the Clinton-Gore band-bus. Still, although most market participants had viewed Clinton with suspicion, they quickly become resigned to his victory. In the fall of 1992, Wall Street analysts began to recommend so-called Clinton portfolios, stocks of infrastructure companies and managed health care firms that would benefit from the presumed victor's proposals to stimulate the economy through public works and reform of health care.

During the transition, Clinton's domestic policy appointments—remember the tortured search for a double-X-chromosome attorney general?—received the most attention. But the economic appointments ultimately proved more important. After Robert Rubin turned down an offer to become treasury secretary, he agreed to run the National Economic Council (NEC). "Clinton wanted someone who knew Wall Street and the bond market close to him in the White House," as Bob Woodward put it. Another Wall Streeter, fellow Georgetown alumnus Roger Altman, was named deputy to Treasury Secretary Lloyd Bentsen. Altman, vice chairman of the Blackstone Group, earned more than $3 million in 1992 and listed his net worth as greater than $20 million. (In those pre-Internet days, $20 million was real money.)

The Wall Streeters' main contribution, at first, was to help Clinton understand the necessity of working with Federal Reserve Chairman Alan Greenspan. Relations between Greenspan and the Bush administration had deteriorated throughout 1992 as officials continually cajoled the Fed chief to cut interest rates. (Never mind that by the summer of 1992, the Fed had made twenty-three discrete easing steps in three years and had reduced the discount rate from 7 percent to 4 percent.) In the midst of the campaign, communications all but ceased between Greenspan and Treasury Secretary Nicholas Brady. But Clinton took steps to repair the breach. At a meeting in Little Rock in December 1992, he allowed Greenspan to school him about the virtuous circle. Deficit reduction would reduce interest rates, thus making bonds less attractive as investments and encouraging people to put money into stocks, Greenspan said. That would be good for the economy. In addition, lower interest rates would free up cash from refinancing and lower debt costs, thus reducing the deficit further. The key, of course, would be for Clinton to present a deficit reduction plan that bond investors would regard as credible.

This mandate would prove difficult, for during the transition, the Clintonites learned the projected annual deficit was some $60 billion larger than previously expected. Clinton also was getting contradictory advice from some of his oldest friends, namely, that what was good for Wall Street was bad for the American people. Robert Reich viewed his colleague Lloyd Bentsen as "a free-trader and a deficit hawk with close ties to business and Wall Street," and hence a two-time loser uninterested in the plight of the working class. At a January 7 meeting of the NEC, when the discussion turned to how the bond market would respond to the new administration's agenda, Clinton famously exploded with a venom he would later reserve for Ken Starr. "You mean to tell me that the success of the program and my reelection hinges on the Federal Reserve and a bunch of fucking bond traders?"

Meanwhile, congressional Democrats were raging against Greenspan. Moderate senators like Tennessee's Jim Sasser lambasted the economist at one of his congressional appearances for keeping interest rates too high. "Over the past three years, the Federal Reserve Board wore its monetary policy like a hair shirt," he charged. House Banking

Chairman Henry Gonzalez was pushing legislation calling for the Senate to confirm regional Fed bank presidents. But the Clintonites didn't let their hostility toward the bond market and the Federal Reserve Board spill into the open—easy and convenient as that would have been. Instead, Bentsen schmoozed Greenspan, having breakfast with him every week and joining him for periodic rounds of geriatric tennis.

By February 1993, just three weeks into his term, Clinton had already rationalized a change in strategy. "All the folks that I ran to help would be more hurt by a slow economy than they would be helped by a marginal extra investment program," he said. On February 15, he used an address from the Oval Office to break the news that he couldn't cut middle-class taxes. "I had hoped to invest in your future by creating jobs, expanding education, reforming health care and reducing the debt without asking more of you," Clinton said, striking that sincere tone of regret with which the American public would become all too familiar. "But I can't—because the deficit has increased so much beyond my earlier estimates and beyond even the worst official government estimates of last year." Worse, Clinton would have to *raise* taxes to slash the deficit. He quickly reverted to class warfare, lashing out at the 1980s and "the big tax cuts for the wealthy," and promised that 70 percent of his new tax proposals would be paid by those who earned more than $100,000 a year.

The Oval Office address was merely the opening gambit in the bond market strategy. Two days later, he strategically seated Greenspan in the front row of Hillary Clinton's box for his address to Congress. In that speech, he pledged to raise taxes $250 billion over five years while reducing the growth rate of spending by $220 billion. Certain taxes would hit the poor and the middle class—the energy tax, for example—but much of the pain would be inflicted on the wealthy. The top marginal income tax rate would increase to 36 percent from 31 percent for those making more than $115,000, and well-off recipients would have to pay higher taxes on Social Security benefits.

The proposals drew howls of protest from Republicans and
Democrats. But Greenspan appeared to back the proposal, and the
bond market took heed. The interest rate on thirty-year Treasury bonds,
which stood at 7.75 percent in November 1992, had fallen to 7.1 percent
by the time Clinton gave his economic address. In the weeks after the
speech, it quickly plunged to about 6.8 percent. Rubin briefed Clinton
on the bond market nearly every morning, and the president, ever
facile, began using it as a yardstick. "Just yesterday, due to increased
confidence in the plan in the bond market, long-term interest rates fell
to a sixteen-year low," he told the U.S. Chamber of Commerce on
February 23. Throughout the spring, White House staffers watched the
bond market the way they watched the *Washington Post* gossip column,
"The Reliable Source," for mentions of their names in boldface.
Indeed, the Clintonites had endowed the bond market with mythic
powers. "I used to think if there was reincarnation, I wanted to come
back as the president or the pope or a .400 baseball hitter," James
Carville told the *Wall Street Journal*. "But now I want to come back as
the bond market." Carville put his money where his mouth was. As Bob
Woodward reported, the populist consultant had bought some thirty-
year bonds at 8.75 percent for his retirement plan. When the rate
slipped below 7 percent, he sold, netting a substantial gain.

More important, the bond market seemed to be accomplishing
what Clinton couldn't achieve politically. As Clinton's proposed $20
billion stimulus package foundered in Congress, lower interest rates
were performing their magic. Conventional wisdom seemed to hold
that every 0.1 percent (or ten-basis-point, in Fedspeak) reduction in
long-term interest rates was worth $10 billion in stimulus. In his May 22
radio address, Clinton crowed about how millions of Americans had
already refinanced their home mortgages, business loans, and student
loans. "All told, experts estimate that if we can maintain these lower
rates, we can pump another $100 billion into our economy," he said.
The first arcs of the virtuous circle had been traced.

As reasonable as such a strategy later seemed, it was immensely controversial at the time. Even some Republicans saw the alignment with the market as a betrayal of long-standing Democratic principles. "What the bond market likes is a weak economy, the erosion of entitlement programs and tax increases on the middle class," Republican strategist Kevin Phillips said in February 1993. "All those are incompatible with the Democratic campaign promises and the Democratic future." Throughout the spring of 1993, consultants Paul Begala and James Carville continually urged Clinton to return to class warfare, to attack the rich and Wall Street. But the Wall Streeters helped convince Clinton not to pursue that course. At the insistence of Rubin and Altman, a plan pushed by Begala that would have limited the deduction corporations could take for executive salaries was quashed. "Look," Rubin told Begala, "they're running the economy and they make the decisions about the economy. And so if you attack them, you wind up hurting the economy and wind up hurting the president."

In summer 1993, Congress ultimately approved Clinton's controversial deficit reduction package. (Roger Altman was given much of the credit for leading the campaign to pass the bill.) But the budget marked the beginning of the battle rather than the end. As Republicans continued to cry that the tax increase would kill the nascent recovery, the focus shifted to interest rates. Greenspan, of course, was monomaniacal about inflation, and as economic growth picked up throughout 1993—growth for the fourth quarter was a sizzling 7 percent—he began to grow concerned. In January 1994, Greenspan told Clinton and his economic advisers that he might need to raise rates. Rather than jawbone him publicly, Bentsen and Rubin gave their tacit approval. Two weeks later, on February 4, the Fed raised rates twenty-five basis points (0.25 percent), the first upward move in five years. The White House was largely silent. Over the next twelve months, as the economy grew at a 4.6 percent clip and inflation remained under 3 percent, the Fed raised short-term rates six times, from 3.25 percent to 6 percent. The rate hikes angered Greenspan's Democratic critics on Capitol Hill and in the White House. In May 1994, when Lloyd Bentsen said the administration should give the Fed cover by stating that the economy was approaching its "natural" rate of unemployment, Robert Reich was outraged: "Has anybody forgotten? . . . We're Democrats. Even if we are approaching the danger zone where low unemployment might trigger inflation, we should err on the side of more jobs, not higher bond prices." But Reich's proposal that Clinton warn the Fed against further interest rate increases was summarily rejected.

Clinton held his fire, even as, by February 1995, the Fed funds rate had risen by 300 basis points, and hit 6 percent for the first time since May 1991. By then, however, Clinton was in a different position. In November 1994, the Republicans had swept into control of both the House and the Senate, running on a focus group–tested menu of red-meat issues, which included cutting capital-gains taxes and balancing the budget. Clinton was forced into a reflexive Democratic position. The bond market, his friend in 1993, momentarily revealed itself as the enemy. In a February 1995 radio address, Clinton blamed the "unelected Federal Reserve" for having raised rates seven times and for having "added more than $100 billion to our deficit." But as 1995 unfolded, and as Newt Gingrich and his revolutionaries began tossing rhetorical and legislative bombs with abandon, Clinton emerged as the guarantor of stability. Indeed, having reached an uneasy accommodation with the markets in the first congressional session, Clinton would become their protector in the brief Gingrich regnum. For it quickly became clear that the Republicans, in particular the rowdy freshmen, had little interest in the prerogatives of Wall Street.

This new reality became obvious when the Mexican peso crisis exploded in late 1994. In December, the Mexican government let the peso begin to float. In the next several weeks, its value against the dollar plummeted from 3.4 to 6.0. As short-term interest rates spiked above 30 percent, investors began to dump Mexican stocks, and the country's foreign exchange reserves dwindled to dangerously low levels. The currency crisis, coupled with the Zapatista uprising in Chiapas, seemed to have Mexico on the verge of imploding in the early weeks of 1995.

Just days after the Treasury Department and the Federal Reserve Board extended $6 billion in credit to Mexico, Clinton on January 12 formally asked Congress to approve a $40 billion aid package, under which Mexico would use U.S. loan guarantees to replace up to $28 billion in short-term, dollar-indexed bonds with long-term bonds. Meanwhile, the International Monetary Fund (IMF) and the Bank for International Settlement (BIS) would kick in another $12.5 billion. Clinton explicitly drew the link between the difficulties south of the border and the health of the markets in the United States. "We have a strong interest in prosperity and stability in Mexico," he said. "It is in America's economic and strategic interest that Mexico succeeds."

The newly installed Republican congressional leaders, Bob Dole and Newt Gingrich, responsibly signed on. The dispirited core of Democrats—their numbers having dwindled to 204—began to line up behind their president, even though only 102 of the 258 House Democrats had voted for NAFTA in 1993. Liberal stalwart Barney Frank promised up to 130 Democratic votes for the Mexico package. But the GOP freshmen were revolting—in more than one way. Furthermore, some veterans added fuel to the fire. Sen. Phil Gramm, whose home state of Texas would bear the brunt of any economic dislocation in Mexico, took the opportunity to place politics above principle. Seeking to distinguish himself from potential presidential primary opponent Dole, he opposed the plan. (At the time, Gramm was regarded as a serious contender.) Dutifully, Rubin, Secretary of State Warren Christopher, and Alan Greenspan all appeared before the House to drum up support. "If this was strictly about Mexico, I would say there is absolutely no reason" for a federal bailout, said Greenspan. "But it is not just about Mexico."

Nevertheless, the Republican rank and file was intent on refusing to aid the Mexicans and the U.S. investors who owned some $16 billion in

Mexican short-term bonds. Even as former presidents Bush and Ford and dozens of other worthies professed their support for the bailout, the markets continued to slip, and so did Republican support. One GOP congressman told the worried financial types assembled at Davos, Switzerland, that not even 100 House members supported the Clinton proposal. Faced with such opposition, the White House acted unilaterally. In what had become a hallmark of the Clinton administration — the policy all-nighter — Rubin and Greenspan cobbled together a package worth nearly $50 billion. Using discretionary funds controlled by Treasury and the Fed, the United States on January 31 announced it would loan Mexico up to $20 billion from the Exchange Stabilization Fund, a rainy-day fund created by (who else?) FDR. As collateral, Mexico would put up $7 billion in annual oil earnings. The U.S. funds would be complemented by $17.5 billion in IMF loans and $10 billion from the BIS.

The Mexico bailout represented a turning point for Clinton. Having lobbied for NAFTA, Clinton was heavily invested in Mexico's success. Much as the bailout would help big investors and money-center banks that should have known better, he regarded the action as necessary to bring stability to Mexico and the broadening markets. As the Republicans dithered, Clinton embraced what for him had been a rare opportunity to stand up as a responsible, level-headed protector of the markets and the national interest. The government was undertaking the bailout "not because there are large financial interests at stake," he said, "but because there are thousands of jobs, billions of dollars of American exports at stake, and the potential of an even more serious illegal immigration problem."

The bond market strategy and the Mexico bailout allowed Clinton to ingratiate himself with big investors at the institutional level. Meanwhile, he and Al Gore began to reach out to the ultrawealthy on a retail basis. In 1995, the administration initiated the most famous series of coffee klatches in the history of the devil's brew. Of course, the notorious visitors—shady businessman Roger Tamraz and fundraiser John Huang—ultimately garnered the most press. But the gatherings were just as noteworthy because of the legitimate guests who attended— dozens of men and women who had come to occupy preeminent places in Wall Street, the financial services industry, and the democratized 1990s money culture. They included Eli Broad, the proprietor of insurance giant SunAmerica; hedge-fund manager and TheStreet.com founder James Cramer; Wall Street pioneer Muriel Siebert; Sumner Redstone of Viacom; Sanford Weill of Travelers; and the heads of the whitest of the white-shoe investment firms: Jon Corzine of Goldman, Sachs; Stanley Shuman of Allen & Co.; and Alan Patricof of the eponymous venture-capital firm. Democrats all.

Now it was Clinton who pandered. When he spoke before the Business Council, a group of establishment CEOs, in Williamsburg, Virginia, in mid-October 1995, he lamented that in 1993, "I had to raise your taxes more and cut spending less than I wanted to, which made a lot of you furious." At a Houston fundraiser a few weeks later, he delivered a message destined to live in infamy, at least for hard-core Democrats: "Probably there are people in this room still mad at me over that budget because you think I raised your taxes too much. It might surprise you to know that I think I raised them too much, too." So much for eighty years of Democratic dogma on the efficacy of progressive taxation, and so much for punishing those "who speculate in paper."

With such activities and utterances, Clinton explicitly aligned himself with the aspiration of the wealthy and the markets. And he continually stood up to the reckless behavior of the Republicans in Congress. Amid bitter negotiations over a budget, the Republicans churlishly shut down the government twice in November and December 1995. During the fateful shutdowns (Monica Lewinsky gained access to the Oval Office during the second one), citizens were outraged that national parks and passport offices were shuttered. But the real danger was the potential for the shutdown to disrupt the bond market. Lacking the ability to borrow, Robert Rubin saved the day by paying off maturing government bonds from civil servant pension funds. As congressional Republicans played chicken over raising the debt ceiling, the Clinton administration began to suggest that the Republicans were willing to risk anything, even a meltdown in the capital markets, in order to enact their radical program. In late January 1996, Rubin warned Congress that the government would likely be unable to borrow money after March 1. After Clinton's state-of-the-union address, Moody's Investors Service said it was considering lowering the rating for $387 billion in Treasury securities. A crisis was ultimately averted, but these events made the Republicans look reckless and disdainful of investors.

Meanwhile, Clinton continued to align himself with the person most investors deemed the most indispensable protector of the markets, Alan Greenspan. The central banker's term was set to expire in June 1996, and Clinton really had no choice but to reappoint him. Not doing so would have spooked the markets and riled Greenspan's many backers in the Senate; both eventualities would have been election-year no-nos. So on February 22, after publicly toying with the idea of naming investment banker Felix Rohatyn to the post, Clinton reappointed Greenspan, saying he "has inspired confidence, and for good reason." In response to the news, investors pushed the Dow to a record 5,608.

Clinton wasn't the only Democrat who had come to admire the former Ayn Rand acolyte. During the Senate floor debate on Greenspan's reappointment on June 20, Pat Moynihan raved about the "wisdom and the practical knowledge with which Alan Greenspan has conducted his stewardship of our Nation's monetary policies over the last 9 years," calling him a "national treasure." And he offered a rare congratulation to the Clintonites. "Not since the Kennedy-Johnson administrations, in which we had the longest peacetime expansion of 106 months, have monetary and fiscal policy been so well coordinated." Tom Daschle, the ever-loyal minority leader, crossed his fellow Great Plains Democrats to endorse Greenspan. Sure, Greenspan had raised interest rates unnecessarily. But, "on balance, Mr. Greenspan's successful partnership with us in the wake of the 1993 plan merits my support for his reconfirmation. As he himself has noted, the 1993 economic plan 'was an unquestioned factor in contributing to the improvement in economic activity that occurred thereafter.'"

To be sure, there were some dissenting voices, mostly from the prairie populists, for whom wheat prices can never be too high and interest rates can never be too low. "Chairman Greenspan has this long history of focusing solely on inflation to such an extent that all focus on expanding our economy has been lost," said Tom Harkin. Paul Wellstone, the only Washington representative of the Minnesota Farmer-Labor party, complained that "what we have instead is a policy that works great for bondholders, great for Wall Street, but does not work well for families in our country." Nonetheless, on June 20, 1996, Greenspan was approved for an unprecedented third term by a 91 to 7 vote.

Clinton's reappointment of Greenspan helped disarm Republican critics, as did the performance of the economy. By summer 1996, as the presidential campaign kicked into gear, Clinton sported an economic record that bordered on gaudy. Inflation had remained below 3 percent for five years running, and unemployment had fallen to 5.6 percent. In May 1996, the Dow was at a record high, 5,778, up 78 percent since Clinton's inaugural. The willingness of investors to push stocks higher and keep interest rates low proved the financial world had faith in Clinton's stewardship of fiscal policy. As a result, Clinton was running less like FDR in 1936 than Ronald Reagan in 1984. *Putting People First* had been a jeremiad about the declining U.S. economy and the corrosive effects of the market and Wall Street. By contrast, *Between Hope and History*, Clinton's 1996 campaign tome, offered a shining happy take on the American economic situation. To put the nation's economic house in order, "we focused on cutting the deficit in half, bringing interest rates down, spurring private investment to fire up the nation's stagnant economy," Clinton wrote. "The strategy succeeded." (Never mind that

Clinton at first pursued precisely the opposite strategy, pushing to use government-backed stimulus to get the economy going.) He crowed that companies were thriving, interest rates were low, and inflation was at its lowest level "since the Kennedy Administration." In 1994, he hastened to add, the World Economic Forum named the United States the world's most competitive economy. (Take that, Paul Kennedy.) Instead of naming corporate malefactors, as Clinton did back in 1991, Clinton in 1996 singled out companies for praise. He lauded Harley-Davidson for its training efforts, and coffee-chain Starbucks for providing health insurance to workers. CEOs, the corrupt, overpaid exploiters of workers, had morphed into friendly agents for change.

Since the 1994 elections, Republicans had complained with increasing bitterness that Clinton had stolen their rhetoric on responsibility and fiscal restraint. ("The era of big government is over," Clinton proclaimed in his 1995 state-of-the-union address, as if it were he who had proposed eliminating entire cabinet-level departments.) But in 1996, with Clinton having co-opted money, the Republicans began to steal the Democrats' lingo. "Look what's going on in our country, my friends," Pat Buchanan told a New Hampshire audience in early 1996. "When AT&T lops off 40,000 jobs, the executioner that does it, he's a big hero on the cover of one of those magazines and AT&T stock soars." Bob Dole also began to read from the old Democrat playbook. In his campaign book *Trusting the People,* Dole charged that Clinton was "reigning over the first recovery since World War II to leave the American worker behind."

The one event that could have stopped Clinton was a sudden downturn in the markets and the economy. In the first two weeks of July 1996, amid concerns about inflation and corporate profits, the Dow did fall 7 percent. But once again, Alan Greenspan rode to the rescue. On July 18, he told Congress, "There are a number of reasons to expect demands to moderate and economic activity to settle back toward a more sustainable pace in the months ahead." That meant he probably wouldn't have to raise interest rates. His remarks sparked a huge bond rally, sending the rate on the long bond from above 7 percent to 6.92 percent; the Dow rose 87.3 points, or 1.6 percent.

The good news just kept rolling in. In September, when Clinton was campaigning in Florida, the Labor Department reported that unemployment for August had fallen to 5.1 percent, a seven-year low. Like a speedy wide receiver tailed only by 300-pound linemen, Clinton ran for the end zone unharried, seemingly gathering speed. He opened the first debate, October 6, by asking, cheekily, if people were better off than they were four years before, and he chided Dole for his pessimism. "It is not midnight in America, Senator." Whereas Clinton channeled Reagan, Dole and running mate Jack Kemp channeled Walter Mondale. In the vice presidential debate, Kemp, who was supply-side when supply-side wasn't cool, lamented that the "haves are doing well" while "the have-nots are not." On October 28, at University City, Missouri, when Clinton announced that the nation's annual deficit had been reduced by 63 percent during his administration, from $290 billion in 1992 to $107 billion in 1996, the election was all but over. Although Dole still carried the vote of those making $100,000 a year—by a 54 percent to 38 percent margin—Clinton fared better among the wealthy in 1996 than he did in 1992. Clinton boosted his margins in the wealthiest states—Connecticut, New Jersey, and New York.

The alignment with the well-off and the growing army of investors was too much to bear for some of the early Clinton class warriors. "In 1993, Clinton groused that the bond market was turning him into an Eisenhower Republican. By 1996, with the nation prosperous and at peace, with Republicans controlling the Congress, it seemed that Clinton's second term would be even more like Ike's—and he didn't seem to mind," George Stephanopoulos wrote with great disappointment in *All Too Human*. Of course, Stephanopoulos, Clinton's onetime spokesman, followed in Eisenhower's footsteps by taking a job at Columbia University in 1997. He quickly joined the ranks of the nouveau riche, selling his memoirs for $2.85 million and giving speeches for $20,000 a pop to business groups at exclusive country clubs in Connecticut. The proceeds funded an apartment on Riverside Drive, which he had decorated in Ralph Lauren style. As a finishing touch, he unironically sat for a photo spread in that bible of borderline-gauche conspicuous consumption, *Architectural Digest*. The flack-turned-"journalist" had become a New Democrat.

ON AUGUST 5, 1997, as Stephanopoulos was busily penning *All Too Human* and contemplating fabric swatches, his former boss marched out of the White House onto the south lawn, shoulder to broad shoulder with House Speaker Newt Gingrich. As Al Gore and Sen. Frank Lautenberg brought up the rear, a Marine band posted on the White House balcony serenaded the politicos with "God Bless America." Clinton sat down and signed, with great ceremony, the bill that would balance the budget in five years and reduce capital-gains taxes.

Had Ronald Reagan witnessed this event, he would have been understandably confused: a Democratic president signing into a law a measure that included a capital-gains tax cut as Democratic congressional leaders looked on approvingly? For the previous decade and a half, capital gains had been that rare wedge issue that cut *against* the Republicans. Its very definition—money you make while doing nothing but sitting on your rear end—has class implications. Each time Republicans demanded to cut the tax, Democrats tarred their opponents as toadies of the undeserving rich. But in spring 1997, the House Republicans, seeking to recover momentum, pushed for ambitious balanced budget and tax cut bills. Clinton, having fended off a balanced budget amendment, began to dance toward a deal. First he threatened vetoes, saying in early July that the Republicans' plans would benefit the rich at the expense of the poor and the middle class. Having come to accept as inevitable some lowering of capital-gains taxes, Clinton countered with a proposal to cut them for people earning less than

$85,350 to 19.6 percent from 28 percent, and to provide smaller reduc-
tions for the wealthiest. (Those making more than $271,050 would get a
minuscule cut, from 28 percent to 27.72 percent.) Clinton ultimately
gave up on these progressive tax reductions. When the compromise bill
was passed in early August, it cut the capital-gains tax on assets held for
five years from 28 percent to 18 percent, raised cigarette taxes, and
slashed spending another $270 billion over five years. Clinton hailed
the bill as "a triumph for all Americans." There were a few holdouts,
including House Minority Leader Richard Gephardt and forty-two
other House Democrats. But the vast majority of Democrats supported
the measure.

The enactment of capital-gains tax cuts was a function of politics
but also a result of the expansion of the markets and the changing character of the investing public. In 1992, the stock market was something
that Democrats tolerated, at best, and vilified at worst. But by 1996,
being a responsible Democrat, and one interested in prosperity and
opportunity for people at all levels in society, meant being concerned
about the fate of the stock and bond markets. After all, between 1992
and 1996 alone, the number of households with mutual funds rose 42.6
percent, from 25.8 million to 36.8 million. In 1996, the Investment
Company Institute estimated that 63 million Americans owned mutual
fund shares. With the democratization of money, such a posture
became not only mandatory but also a means for Clinton to distinguish
himself from the irresponsible Republicans.

In a sense, Clinton owed much of his success to capital-gains taxes,
because they closed the virtuous circle of falling interest rates and rising
equity values. Each year, more and more money flowed into federal
coffers as more and more people bought and sold stocks. The annual
volume of the New York Stock Exchange tripled between 1993 and
1999. This activity triggered a tremendous and unexpected amount of
capital gains. In 1991, capital-gains taxes provided just $25 billion in
revenues, or 2.3 percent of total government revenues. They rose every

year, to $62 billion in 1996, $79 billion in 1997, and $89 billion for 1998, or 5.6 percent of total federal receipts.

By 1997, America's infatuation with the markets was evident not only in the ratings of CNBC, the circulation of *Smart Money*, or the stock quotes that scrolled across the scoreboard at Shea Stadium. It was also evident in the assets of mutual funds—$4.49 trillion in 1997, up from $2.82 trillion in 1995 and $2.16 trillion in 1994. In the United States in 1997, household equity holdings as a share of disposable income were 143 percent, compared with a 20 percent average for European countries. In other words, for every $100 in disposable income held by Mr. and Mrs. Smith of Anytown, USA, the Smiths had $143 invested in stocks, compared with only $20 for their European counterparts. America had become, as *U.S. News & World Report* put it in a belated 1999 cover story, "401(K) Nation." The "wealth effect"— the degree to which the growth in stock and other asset prices made Americans feel wealthier than they actually were—had entered the economic lingua franca and was spurring what would become the longest peacetime expansion of the century.

Consequently, whenever there was an economic or a political blip, it became immediately important for Clinton to reassure the markets— for political reasons as much as for fiscal reasons. In summer 1998, with the Dow at around 9,000, the economic crisis in Russia rippled through Latin America and Indonesia and ultimately affected the U.S. markets. George Soros's funds suffered $2 billion in losses in Russia, and when hedge fund Long-Term Capital Management imploded, it threatened the stability of the global financial system. Meanwhile, interest rates in Brazil spiked to untenable levels. As they had during the Mexican financial crisis in 1994, the Republicans were content to sit on their hands. After all, they had more important things to do, like impeach the president. Once again, Treasury Secretary Rubin, Deputy Treasury Secretary Lawrence Summers, and Fed chief Greenspan saved the day, reassuring markets and browbeating banks and international lending organizations to shore up the shaky finances of a host of countries. In the breathless description of *Time*'s February 15, 1999, cover story, this trio—two intellectuals and an unassuming arbitrageur—had become "the Committee to Save the World." The anointing of Bill Clinton, the boy governor from Arkansas, and his coterie of left-leaning cronies as the "Superfriends," battling global crises from their Hall of Justice, was surely one of the decade's most unlikely developments.

Perhaps the most astonishing political development of Clinton's second term involved another money issue: Social Security. For much of the twentieth century, policies floated by Democrats were branded by their Republican opponents as radical, disruptive, and economically devastating. These included the measures that created Social Security, the National Labor Relations Board, Medicare, Medicaid, and the Civil Rights Act, all of which became mainstream and were ultimately embraced, in some form, by Republicans. In the 1990s, the process was reversed. Ideas that began life as bastard children of the Republican far right, discussed only in darkened seminar rooms at the Cato Institute, a libertarian think tank, slowly made their way into the mainstream, where they were ultimately embraced, in some form, by Democrats. These included eliminating the budget deficit, promoting free trade, putting time limits on welfare, reducing capital-gains taxes, and, finally, putting Social Security funds to work in the stock market.

The prospect of letting the Social Security safety net flutter in the winds of the equity markets first came to political prominence in the 1996 campaign, and it proved rather unpopular. It didn't help matters that its chief advocate was Steve Forbes, whose eerily focused campaign seemed to consist entirely of the flat tax and Social Security reform. Under his scheme, older Americans would continue to collect benefits under the current system, but younger workers would manage their own retirement savings, with the option of putting the funds to work in the markets. For an extremely wealthy man, who would never have to worry about his or any other family member's retirement, raising this issue was remarkably unopportunistic. Forbes did so because he genuinely believed that the declining ratio of active workers to retirees represented an untenable trend. (Of course, Forbes also genuinely believed that a flat tax, under which he and comparable plutocrats would pay a mere 17 percent of their earnings in taxes, was also a good idea.)

Forbes stuck to his guns, and was hammered for it. Dole blasted Forbes in television advertisements for proposing a "radical, untested plan that would end Social Security as we know it." Coming as it did on the heels of the Republicans' efforts to end welfare and slash Medicaid, the assault on this popular entitlement program played nicely into the hands of Democrats. In 1996, the Clinton campaign mantra had morphed from "It's the economy, stupid," to "We must preserve, protect, and strengthen Medicare, Social Security, education, and the environment." Even as centrist Republicans continued to lambaste Forbes for discussing the reform that dare not speak its name, however, a few Democrats and Republicans supported Forbes in principle. Bob Kerrey and Alan Simpson proposed their own partial Social Security privatization plan, and a forty-member House caucus, headed by Arizona Republican Jim Kolbe and Texas Democrat Charles Stenholm, began studying the issue.

Despite these bipartisan efforts, Social Security reform was still largely championed by Republicans. As such, it engendered a great deal of suspicion. After all, many Republicans had opposed the creation of the Social Security system. "Never in the history of the world has any measure been brought in here so insidiously designed as to prevent business recovery, to enslave workers, and to prevent any possibility of the employers providing work for the people," said Representative John Taber of New York in spring 1935 as the Social Security Act was being debated. Sixty years later, here were the Republicans unironically proclaiming the need to dismantle the system in order to save it. As a result, Democrats were officially cool. In February 1997, Clinton's Council of Economic Advisers released a report saying that reform was still probably too dangerous.

Over the next year and a half, as more and more Republicans began to touch the notorious third rail of American politics and live to tell about it, Democrats began to step forward. In May 1998, a twenty-four-member panel sponsored by the Center for Strategic and International Studies, and led by Kolbe and Stenholm, unanimously agreed that stocks were a viable option for individual investment accounts that could theoretically replace Social Security. By summer 1998, a partial privatization of Social Security was being discussed in earnest by no less a personage than Daniel Patrick Moynihan, perhaps the last of the Great Society Democrats.

Clinton played catch-up. Speaking before the National Council of Senior Citizens in Albuquerque in July 1998, he said that in the near future, Social Security would have to undergo "modest discipline changes" so it would be sound when baby boomers retire. (The president's focus, of course, betrayed the exquisite narcissism of his generational cohort.) Clinton hinted that some funds could be put into the stock market, but he insisted that retirees must be able to rely on their benefits regardless of the vicissitudes of the market. "Not every six years will be as good as the last six years on Wall Street and Main Street," he said.

Throughout the fall of 1998, virtually every candidate for the House or Senate promised to "save" the program, largely because no person with an ounce of common sense could oppose such a stance. And virtually every candidate admitted, conceded, or argued that one approach might be to let some of that money go to work in the stock market. By January 1999, Clinton himself proposed putting a portion of Social Security funds in the stock market. Of course, that strategy offers a cheap way out of the real problem—the imbalance between the program's obligations and its projected assets. The simplest solutions, of course, are the hardest ones: reduce benefits or increase taxes. Because neither course is politically palatable, the option of simply increasing the investment return by shifting from bonds into stocks makes more sense. In some ways, however, the prospect of doing so is still a bit too controversial—even for this nation of investors. By summer 1999, as budget debates degenerated into partisan sniping, the issue of putting Social Security funds into the stock market faded from prominence. Clinton and the Congress slowly hammered out spending bills throughout the fall, paying a great deal of lip service to protecting Social Security. But much of the debate centered around the ways in which various proposals would, or would not, rely on Social Security surpluses to keep the budget in balance. Given such short-term imperatives, the necessity of putting those funds into equities over the long term was no longer part of the discussion. Nevertheless, the issue will certainly resurface eventually.

The most interesting feature of the various Social Security proposals is their potential to take the democratization of money to a new level. Indeed, these proposals would turn every citizen into a stockholder—not only the white-collar workers, union members, and public employees covered by pension funds, but also every man, woman, and teenager who was ever worked on the books. If even a small portion of the $760 billion Social Security trust fund were allocated to equities, the collective holdings would instantly dwarf any mutual fund complex or public pension fund. And if these potential new investors began to vote their shares en masse, they would give activist shareholders like union pension funds a great deal of leverage.

Regardless of the policy outcome, the discussion is a mark of how far things have come. Over the course of the 1990s, as the investor population expanded, as barriers to investing fell and twentysomethings began to cash in with Internet IPOs, the markets became an object of affection rather than one of fear and loathing. The shift in attitude was so great that by the late 1990s many Democrats viewed the markets as sufficiently benevolent to merit the stewardship of their most cherished achievement of the century. When Bill Clinton appeared on the scene in fall 1991, no stock analyst, political pundit, or trendmeister could have predicted that within seven years even this New Democrat would be talking about stowing grandma and grandpa's nest egg in the Den of Thieves.

Of course, putting Social Security funds to work in the markets, as much it would crown an era of tremendous financial democratization, would present a new challenge. A democracy relies for its health upon an educated, literate, active, vigilant populace. This set of requirements applies equally so to a financial democracy. If we're all going to be shareholders, then we all must know the difference between a stock and a bond and understand the workings of Wall Street. Turning all Social Security recipients into active investors would, in effect, impose a new set of civic responsibilities on a society whose citizens aren't particularly adept at handling the few they have—like voting.

A Clinton appointee made this very point at an October 1998 speech at Harvard's John F. Kennedy School of Government. Allowing people to choose where their Social Security funds go could prove to be a moral hazard. "It is likely that giving people the ability to select investment options will provide the unscrupulous with new opportunities to deceive and distort," he said. Diversifying the nation's Social Security portfolio would require more policing and force American citizens to take more personal responsibility. "There is an unacceptable wide gap between financial knowledge and financial responsibilities," he said. "Closing this 'knowledge gap' is among the most important problems we face. It becomes even more of an imperative if Social Security is privatized."

The author of these sensible remarks was Securities and Exchange Commission Chairman Arthur Levitt, an often overlooked and key link in the democratization—and the Democratization—of money. The silver-haired Wall Street veteran has in fact been one of the Clinton administration's most valuable and least appreciated appointees, and only through closer examination of his activities during the 1990s does the extent of the Democratization of money become truly clear.

5

Arthur Levitt and the SEC

Martin Luther King Jr. High School sits on the West Side of Manhattan, just west of Lincoln Center, on 64th Street and Amsterdam Avenue. A living memorial to the slain civil rights leader, the high school is a forbidding hulk, set back on a huge concrete plaza. Once you get past the armed guard at the entrance, the interior is far more welcoming, its wide halls festooned with signs and placards that read "brotherhood" and "civil rights." Along the walls, just under the ceiling, run banners with quotes from King's 1963 "I have a dream" speech. Inside a first-floor classroom is an easel with a black-and-white poster showing King, natty in a fedora, orating fiercely.

The thirty-odd kids who file into the room bear testament to the new America. The students, who attend Martin Luther King and a few other city high schools, are black and Hispanic, with a few Asians thrown in for good measure. The boys wear blue T-shirts, khaki pants, and ties. The girls offer more variety, from sloppy jeans and flannel shirts to sensible business attire. All are members of the National Academy Foundation (NAF), an industry-sponsored group that encourages inner-city kids to pursue careers in finance.

Arthur Levitt Jr., the chairman of the Securities and Exchange Commission, strides confidently into this unlikely setting. Clad in an understated gray suit and light blue shirt, he wears a button on his lapel that reads "Get the facts. It's your money. It's your future." He sits patiently as the principal introduces Frances Navarra, a 1991 graduate of Brooklyn's John Dewey High School and the recipient of an NAF scholarship funded by Citigroup CEO Sanford Weill. Navarra worked her way through St. John's University with a job at Crossland Federal Savings and, after graduating cum laude in 1995, went to work at the SEC as a compliance examiner. Wearing a salmon business suit, she shyly takes the podium but loudly introduces her boss, pronouncing his first name "Awthah."

Levitt, soft-spoken, with one of those patrician yet distinctly New York accents, immediately establishes his bona fides as not just another old white guy come to lecture the kids. "Anybody here from Brooklyn?" he asks. A few hands shoot up. He asks one of the upraised hands which neighborhood he lives in. "Crown Heights," comes the answer, referring to the enclave of impoverished Hasidim and striving Caribbean immigrants. Levitt's eyes light up. "I grew up in Crown Heights," he says, "on President Street. . . . My mother was a public school teacher in Ocean Hill." Levitt doesn't mention that he attended a private high school, Brooklyn Poly Prep, or that he was chairman of the American Stock Exchange for eleven years. He wants these kids to know that he's as Brooklyn as Spike Lee.

Smoothly, he launches into a laconic description of the SEC's role. "Our job is to protect investors," he says. Levitt discusses the vast expansion of the markets and argues that people who commit financial fraud are no less dangerous criminals than those who rob with guns. After describing an Internet scam involving an eel farm, he remarks, with just a touch of sanctimony, "If people are foolish enough to invest in something like that, they almost deserve to lose their money." Next, Levitt leads the students through a series of multiple-choice questions on basic financial concepts, neatly tailored to a multicultural audience. "Monique owns a wide variety of stocks, bonds, and mutual funds to lessen her risk of losing money. This is called: saving, compounding, diversifying, don't know. . . . Carlos has saved some cash and faces three choices. What would be the best thing for him to do? . . . Maria wants to have $100,000 in twenty years . . . ."

The kids raise their hands when he reads the correct multiple-choice answer, and Levitt calls on them to explain. One girl with cornrows describes how investors lose the entire value of their common stock in the event of bankruptcy. Another describes the benefits of diversification. As a group, the students identify stocks as having returned more than bonds or savings accounts over the past seventy years. Levitt cautions them, however, that "common stocks can be very risky on a short term. If you buy a stock today in hopes of making money tomorrow, don't do it." These kids are more financially literate than I was when I arrived for my first day at work as a reporter at Bloomberg Business News, with six years of higher education behind me, and more financially literate than my sixty-year-old parents. It strikes me that this group is David Duke's worst nightmare: urban, smart, black and Hispanic kids, some of them children of immigrants, who have learned the lingo of Wall Street through an internship program sponsored largely by financiers of Jewish extraction.

When he's done, Levitt opens the floor to questions. I'm fascinated by the audacity of these New York City teens as much as by the language they use. "What's a good P/E ratio for a stock?" asks one. "Are Internet stocks overvalued?" pipes up another. Levitt begs off but adds, "I would say that people have been buying Internet stocks using emotion and not using their brains." Kamesha Blake, a junior in a hot-pink business suit, asks about dividend reinvestment plans. "I was curious," asks another, "how do you invest your money?" The kids inch forward on the edge of their seats. "When I came to government," Levitt explains, "they made me sell everything I own and reinvest the proceeds. I could only buy either U.S. government obligations, or I could buy mutual funds. I bought mostly mutual funds that invest in stocks or government bonds. And I guess I have about seventeen of those diversified mutual funds." The kids' eyes light up, impressed. Levitt is plainly impressed, too. He pauses, and seemingly on an impulse, says, "I'm going to have the whole class down to Washington."

The most remarkable aspect of this occasion in the spring of 1999 was its sense of normalcy, as if it were routine that the chairman of the Securities and Exchange Commission, the most white-collar of government agencies, would spend time chatting with inner-city high school juniors about his personal finances. But such events have become routine during Levitt's reign, at seven years the longest tenure of any of the twenty-five chairmen in the agency's seventy-six-year history. Because of such interactions and numerous other initiatives, no government agency has been more crucial to the democratization of money—or the Democratization of money—than the Securities and Exchange Commission.

The SEC was, of course, the creation of Democrats. Between September 1, 1929, and July 1, 1932, the value of all stocks traded on the New York Stock Exchange (NYSE) fell 83 percent, wiping out $74 billion in assets. The capital markets were devastated, and the need for reform was obvious. When he accepted the Democratic presidential nomination, Franklin Roosevelt advocated "letting in the light of day on issues of securities, foreign and domestic, which are offered for sale to the investing public." Soon after the inauguration, Roosevelt and his cadre of New Dealers enacted a slew of ambitious laws that reached as far into the realms of fiscal and financial policy as they did into social reform. Among them was the Glass-Steagall Banking Act, which divorced commercial and investment banks and insured bank deposits, and the Securities Act of 1933, which required greater disclosure by companies and gave the Federal Trade Commission some authority to regulate companies seeking to sell securities.

The momentum for a new agency devoted solely to policing the crippled capital markets built throughout 1933. Predictably, prominent Wall Streeters and other industrialists opposed it. "The Exchange is a perfect institution," said Richard Whitney, the NYSE's aristocratic president. (In 1938, Whitney resigned his post in disgrace when he was charged with embezzlement.) As part of its campaign, the NYSE hired the famous publicists Ivy Lee and Edward Bernays, a nephew of Sigmund Freud, to spread ominous rumors about the proposed agency. As they would do time and again over the next decade, congressional Republicans maliciously trotted out the Red Menace to whip up opposition to a Roosevelt proposal. "The real object of the bill is to Russianize everything worthwhile," said congressman Fred Britten, a Republican from Illinois. The opposition notwithstanding, Congress approved the Securities Exchange Act in spring 1934.

The law called for a five-person commission to be headed by a chairman. Roosevelt proposed forty-six-year-old Joseph P. Kennedy. It was an unorthodox choice. As the *New Republic* put it, "Had Franklin D. Roosevelt's dearest enemy accused him of making so grotesque an appointment as Joseph P. Kennedy to the chairmanship of his Stock Exchange Commission, the charge might have been laid to malice." In retrospect, it was a little like nominating Bill Clinton as a chaperone at a boarding school for promiscuous post-teens. Kennedy had made a financial killing in the 1920s, in part by engaging in shady Wall Street machinations; he had collaborated with Charles Wright and other market manipulators whom the SEC would soon indict. But Kennedy, a major donor to Roosevelt's campaign, was eager for an appointment. Denied a post in the early days of the New Deal, Kennedy cheekily asked that the Democratic party repay a $50,000 "loan." Kennedy stayed at the agency for about a year, and was succeeded by James Landis. Within a few years, the SEC helped the crippled capital markets get back on their feet. The registration process and a new regulatory infrastructure gave shattered investors the soupçon of confidence necessary to begin purchasing public stock offerings.

For the next several decades, the SEC was generally hampered by weak leadership and too-cozy relationships with the very people it was supposed to regulate. During World War II, it suffered the indignity of being removed to Philadelphia. In the 1950s, the neglected agency saw its staffing fall to half the wartime levels, and fraud investigations declined. Throughout the go-go 1960s, despite an infusion of eager Kennedyites, the SEC was frequently overwhelmed by the sheer volume of trading activity.

The agency enjoyed an unlikely renaissance in the 1980s under the leadership of John Shad, a former vice chairman of E. F. Hutton. As might be expected from a Reagan appointee, Shad had a narrow interpretation of the agency's powers. In thrall to the University of Chicago school of economics, he tended to rely on market forces rather than government to regulate industry. Still, Shad promised to come down "on insider trading with hobnailed boots." In the next few years, the SEC garnered headlines for several spectacular busts. In February 1987, federal marshals arrested Robert Freeman, the chief arbitrageur at Goldman, Sachs, and Richard Wigton, a trader at Kidder, Peabody, hauling them off their respective trading floors in handcuffs as if they were common crack dealers. In May 1986, the SEC broke an insider trading ring whose links included investment banker Dennis Levine and arbitrageur Ivan Boesky. (Ironically, both men were invited to participate in roundtable discussions that Shad held with industry figures, even as they were under investigation.)

Shad left the SEC in 1987 to become ambassador to the Netherlands, and was replaced by the more aggressive but equally colorless Richard Breeden. Breeden pursued the trail that led from Levine and Boesky to its logical conclusion: Michael Milken and Drexel Burnham Lambert. The SEC and the U.S. Attorney eventually browbeat Milken and Drexel into a $1.3 billion settlement, and Milken ultimately went to jail. Seeking to repair its reputation, Drexel appointed Shad as its chairman in 1989. But the firm filed for bankruptcy the following February, bringing to a close one of the more triumphant chapters in the SEC's history.

In the 1990s, the SEC's profile as an enforcement agency has declined markedly, in part because of the dearth of truly high-profile criminals. The culprits nailed in the 1980s were among *the* dominant stock market personalities. Imagine if Warren Buffett, Michael Dell, and mutual fund maven Mario Gabelli were arrested today. But the shift away from the "hobnailed boot" stems from the different mentality that Arthur Levitt has brought to the agency. As stocks became among the most widely used consumer products in the 1990s, the federal agency charged with ensuring their safety became an aggressive consumer protection agency. The "Eagle on the Street," as *Washington Post* writers Steve Coll and David Vise described the agency in its 1980s heyday, has become the Nanny on the Street.

Levitt is a perfect exemplar of both the democratization of money and the Democratization of Money. As he pointed out to the students at Martin Luther King High, he was a middle-class Jewish kid from Brooklyn and the son of a public school teacher. He didn't tell the students that his father and namesake, Arthur Levitt Sr., was a legendary Democratic politician. Born in 1900, Arthur Levitt Sr. attended Columbia University and became a prominent civic-minded lawyer in Brooklyn. After Levitt served as president of the New York City Board of Education, Averell Harriman asked him to run for state comptroller on the 1954 Democratic ticket. Reelected five times, Levitt stepped down in 1978 as the longest-serving elected official in the state's history. In his twenty-four years in office, he instituted performance audits of state and local government, zealously watched over the state's pension assets, and earned a reputation for impeccable nonpartisanship and bull-headed integrity. "Two plus two makes four, whether the Comptroller is a Democrat or a Republican," he said. During New York City's 1975 fiscal meltdown, he refused to commit significant pension funds to the bailout operation, even after Mayor Ed Koch publicly argued that Levitt would be responsible if the city went bankrupt. Debt that wasn't sufficiently secure to attract private investors was unsuitable for the retirees of New York, Levitt reasoned.

After graduating from Williams College in 1952, Arthur Jr. worked as a drama critic at the *Berkshire Eagle*. But he eventually returned to New York and made his way to Wall Street. In 1962, Levitt was selling ranches and cattle for Oppenheimer Industries. "One of the people who bought a herd of cattle from me said that if I could sell cows, I could sell securities," he recalled. So he joined Carter Berlind & Weill, where his partners included a group of highly ambitious, street-smart, and, it should be noted, liberal Wall Streeters: Sanford Weill, the future head of Citigroup; Arthur Carter, who would go on to own *The Nation* and found *The New York Observer*; and Marshall Cogan, a future corporate raider. In the 1960s, Levitt was nicknamed "Granny" for what less buttoned-down colleagues viewed as an overweening sense of propriety. But his reputation for responsibility led him to greater positions of authority. In twelve years, Levitt rose from partner to president as the Carter group acquired other firms, including Hayden Stone, where Joseph Kennedy had once worked. (Levitt's firm ultimately metamorphosed into Shearson Loeb Rhoades and was acquired by American Express.) In 1978, Levitt was named chairman of the American Stock Exchange (Amex), a post he held throughout the 1980s.

But politics was never far from his mind. In 1986, Levitt bought *Roll Call*, the tabloid that covers Capitol Hill. In May 1989, he left the Amex to pursue his private business interests, which now included the Broadway magazine *Stagebill,* and to serve as chairman of the New York City Economic Development Corporation. Like the rest of the Democratic establishment, he quickly jumped aboard the Clinton bandwagon in 1992. Levitt was one of a dozen-odd cochairmen of a fall fundraiser that netted Clinton about $3.5 million. After the election, Levitt, who had run a brokerage firm as well as a stock exchange, was seen as a leading candidate to replace the SEC's Richard Breeden, whose five-year term was set to expire in 1993. With the backing of Connecticut Sen. Chris Dodd, he won out over Consuela Washington, an aide to Michigan Rep. John Dingell.

For Levitt, accepting the $123,100-a-year job was tantamount to becoming a dollar-a-year man, as leading industrialists did during World War II. He probably netted more than the SEC annual salary just from director fees. Eager to serve, however, Levitt resigned from the boards, unloaded many of his stockholdings, including more than $1 million of American Express stock, as well as his stake in *Roll Call,* which he sold to *The Economist.* (He gave *Stagebill* to his daughter.) As if to signal his intentions to be an activist, Levitt climbed Mt. Powell, a 13,800-foot Colorado peak, with an Outward Bound group the week before his confirmation hearings were to begin in July 1993. Levitt has an almost masochistic devotion to rough-and-tumble Outward Bound expeditions. (This affection for the outdoors has given his office one of the more unusual decorating motifs in Washington — large posters of Georgia O'Keeffe's eroticized flowers paired with large photographs of whitewater rafting trips.) After being formally approved by the Senate in July 1993, he took up residence in Georgetown.

Levitt entered office with something few of his predecessors possessed: an agenda. "Consumer protection is my mission and passion," he said. Of course, any SEC chairman must proclaim such fealty. But to Levitt the pledge had a greater meaning. Years before the media or most politicians had latched on to the trend, Levitt grasped that with

each passing month, increasing numbers of Americans were viewing
the markets as savings vehicles. This, in and of itself, didn't trouble
him, but he was alarmed by what he saw as a deadly combination of
ignorance on the part of the throngs of new investors and perfidy on the
part of greedy brokers. Levitt cited a November 1993 study showing that
two-thirds of those who bought mutual funds from banks believed
money market funds were federally insured, while 40 percent believed
mutual funds bought from brokers were federally insured.

Almost immediately after his confirmation, Levitt began channel-
ing his mother, the dedicated schoolteacher, and his father, the incor-
ruptible public servant. (The *New York Times* once described Arthur
Levitt Sr. as "polite, even courtly, never ebullient"—a description that
applies just as aptly to the junior Levitt, who inherited his father's strong
tendency to moralistic pronouncements.) Accordingly, Levitt's tenure
proceeded on two tracks. He set out to clean up the behavior of those in
the marketplace through moral example, regulation, and enforcement,
and to arm investors with knowledge and intelligence. But rather than
simply meet behind closed doors with industry worthies, as his predecessors did, Levitt took to the hustings to instruct the benighted public
and dictate new standards of behavior for a marketplace that frequently
followed no other morality than the pursuit of profit.

In some ways, Levitt was similar to another New Yorker who reen-
tered the public stage in 1993: New York City Mayor Rudolph Giuliani.
Both took office intent on improving the quality of life for citizens
within their jurisdiction. Both pursued a kind of "broken windows"
theory that emphasized quality-of-life issues. In Levitt's schema, rogue
brokers were the equivalent of the aggressive squeegee men and pan-
handlers who made life unpleasant for New Yorkers. And Levitt quickly
established himself as something of a scourge, determined to eradicate
unethical practices, one industry sector at a time, block by block.

He started with brokers, the perennial problem children of the
financial services industry. In a speech to the National Association of

Securities Dealers (NASD) in the spring of 1994, Levitt expressed concern about the way corrupt and uneducated brokers sullied all members of the "honorable profession." He was dismayed at the results of an investigation into 161 branch offices of nine of the largest retail brokerages; nearly one-quarter of the offices were referred to enforcement agencies. Worse, two-thirds of the brokers who had been the subject of sales-practice complaints, litigation, or disciplinary actions were still in the industry. Testifying before a congressional committee in fall 1994, Levitt vowed to conduct surprise sweeps of small and midsize brokers to root out problem brokers. "The SEC will be tough on sales-practice abuses," he said. "That means more examinations and more expensive sanctions, which will raise the cost of bad practices." Between December 1994 and November 1995, the SEC conducted 179 examinations at 101 different firms. One-fifth of these examinations resulted in referrals to enforcement.

Broker misbehavior had long been a pet peeve for Levitt. In a 1970s address at Columbia University, he had spoken of the need to raise professional standards in the industry. And Levitt was unrelenting in his rhetorical campaign against rogue brokers. In another speech, he cited a survey in which sales professionals in a number of industries were asked whether they thought honesty was important to their job. Brokers were at the bottom of the list, with only 52 percent responding that honesty was important—below used-car salesmen or real estate brokers. In early 1995, he announced plans to banish unethical brokers from the industry permanently, with the so-called "unqualified bar"—a type of double-secret probation for recidivist stock peddlers. "Any broker applying to the SEC for re-entry into the industry after an unqualified bar can expect the administrative equivalent of climbing Mt. Everest," said the mountain-climbing regulator. Then in July 1995, the SEC mandated that the nation's 485,000 stockbrokers must thereafter undergo three and a half hours of training on regulations and ethics on the second, fifth, and tenth anniversaries of their registration.

Levitt next trained his guns on the municipal bond market, an area of particular interest to him for definite reasons. One, it was dominated by individual investors. In the 1990s, individuals held more than 70 percent of outstanding municipal bonds, either directly or through mutual funds. More important, though, his father had been a giant of public finance.

There had long been fundamental conflicts in public finance, particularly in the practice of bond underwriters making donations to popularly elected officials who made decisions on allocating business. Before Levitt came to Washington, he met with some young municipal bond professionals, and one complained that the only way to get business was to buy tables at political fundraisers. "Lots of people in the securities industry resented the strong-arm tactics used to extort money from them for political purposes," he told me. The practice, known as "pay-to-play," had long been accepted and practiced by even the most prestigious firms, and Levitt, a veteran political fundraiser, was no stranger to it. "I spent a good part of my life in the securities industry, and like many bond lawyers, over the years I found myself attending fundraisers for candidates I didn't know or support, and in some cases couldn't even vote for," he told a legal group in 1997.

Nonetheless, Levitt began a crusade to rid the industry of this practice. Soon after his confirmation, Levitt spoke with Frank Zarb, vice chairman of Primerica Corporation, the parent of Smith Barney Shearson, and suggested a voluntary ban on political donations by firms seeking underwriting business. By December 1993, some forty-two bond underwriters had signed on. In April 1994, the SEC formally approved a rule (G-37) proposed by the Municipal Securities Rulemaking Board, a quasi-governmental body that sets standards for municipal securities dealers. It forbade any investment firm from doing underwriting business with a government entity for twenty-four months after the company or one of its executives made contributions to candidates. Ironically, rule G-37 was far more controversial among elected officials than among interested private-sector parties. Groups ranging from the National Association of State Treasurers to the Republican National Committee expressed dismay at the proposed slaughtering of the cash cow, and pronounced it an unconstitutional infringement on the right to free speech. Brushing aside constitutional challenges, the SEC in March 1996 brought its first proceeding for violation of rule G-37. FAIC Securities, Inc., a Florida-based securities firm owned by the Fanjul sugar family, had to pay penalties and fines of more than $400,000 for having made improper donations to officials in Dade County, Florida.

In the years since, Levitt has tried to expand the ban to other areas of the industry, using equal amounts of shame and bullying. In a June 1997 speech to municipal bond lawyers, he described his audience as "among the most unpopular professionals in our nation today." In order to boost their public profile and regain public esteem, Levitt suggested, lawyers should stop making political donations. He organized a group called the Lawyers Committee to End Pay-to-Play and got New York City's bar association to adopt pay-to-play rules. Initially, the American Bar Association (ABA) was immune to Levitt's charms. "Arthur Levitt should get off his self-righteous horse," said Lawrence Fox, chairman of the ABA ethics committee. But by summer 1999, the committee recommended adoption of a pay-to-play rule.

Levitt in 1998 also asked the SEC's division of investment management to look into the issue of pay-to-play in the public pension area. He wanted to know if the asset-allocation decisions made by popularly elected officials were influenced by campaign donations. "After months of work on the issue, the Division has uncovered strong indications that pay-to-play can be a powerful force in the selection of money managers of public pension plans," Levitt said in a March 1999 speech. "We found allegations of this activity in at least 17 states. The comptroller of a large state raised $1.8 million from pension fund contractors—many of whom are out-of-state." (This last remark was a not-so-veiled reference to the man who sits in his father's chair, Carl McCall.)

Lacking the explicit authority to regulate all the fundraising practices of state comptrollers and the donations made by bond lawyers, Levitt has not succeeded in banning pay-to-play entirely. But his campaign against it illustrated the two methods Levitt has used to get his way: First, he tried to persuade his friends and acquaintances in the industry to see things his way. When that failed, he rolled out the big guns of the federal government and the SEC's regulatory power.

Levitt successfully employed this iron-fist-in-a-velvet-glove technique when he succeeded in changing the behavior of perhaps the most important stock market of the 1990s, the NASDAQ. NASDAQ, which stands for National Association of Securities Dealers Automated Quotation system, was founded in 1971 as an electronic stock exchange and has housed technology stocks like Microsoft and Intel, foreign stocks, and virtually every Internet stock. It operates in a fundamentally different manner from the New York Stock Exchange. At the NYSE, investors—or their surrogates on the floor—trade stocks through the open-auction process. Transactions are done verbally or through the flashing of hand signals. On NASDAQ, so-called market makers post buy-and-sell interest on electronic screens and execute trades on behalf of customers. NASDAQ dealers make their living on the "spread," the difference between the "bid" (the price at which an investor is willing to buy a stock) and the "ask" (the price at which an investor is willing to sell a stock).

In May 1994, Paul H. Schultz and William Christie, professors at Ohio State University and Vanderbilt University, respectively, coauthored a study in which they concluded that NASDAQ dealers colluded to fix prices, kept the spreads artificially high, and thus cost investors billions of dollars each year. In the wake of the study, investors filed lawsuits and government inquiries kicked into high gear. In October 1994, the Justice Department antitrust unit opened an investigation, and the SEC began to look into the oversight efforts of NASD, the governing body of the NASDAQ. NASD responded by appointing a commission led by former Sen. Warren Rudman, which recommended changes. But this wasn't sufficient action for Levitt. In November 1995, he appeared at a NASD meeting and bluntly informed the dealers that the SEC still might bring disciplinary action for their failure to adequately police the market.

In summer 1996, the Justice Department settled with twenty-four NASD firms, which agreed to be monitored more closely, and the SEC censured NASD and forced it to spend $100 million over five years to improve its oversight function. Citing the "singular lack of competition" on NASDAQ, Levitt proposed new rules. One required dealers to display any investor orders that were better for investors than their own quotes, and to post limit orders (stock orders at prespecified prices) for lots between 100 and 10,000 shares. Rather than keep the information on the best prices for stocks private on proprietary systems, NASDAQ was forced to share them with the public.

At first blush, the NASDAQ episode seems rather arcane. But in fact the drive to make the markets more transparent has been an important contribution to the democratization of money. For one thing, as NASDAQ's Web home page notes, spreads have narrowed by 40 percent since the SEC-mandated reforms, saving investors untold billions of dollars. In addition, Levitt's efforts to have NASDAQ share more information with the public has meshed nicely with the second, and perhaps dominant, theme of Levitt's tenure. His most far-reaching efforts, and those that represent his main contribution to the democratization of money, have been in the realm of investor education.

Levitt's radical impulse to educate investors stemmed from his fundamental understanding that people on Wall Street are driven primarily, and almost exclusively, by money, rather than by a desire to do the right thing or by fear of a government regulatory agency. In addition, the SEC's traditional means of remedying malfeasance—forcing companies to settle and disgorge profits—was ultimately ineffective. "Even if you go after somebody in a successful enforcement case, the majority of the time, the money isn't around to get back to an investor," said Nancy Smith, New Mexico's former state securities regulator whom Levitt hired in late 1994 to direct the SEC's Office of Investor Education. So rather than change brokers' behavior through rules, threats, and the occasional hob-nailed boot, Levitt set out to foment a grass-roots revolution. Yes, the SEC could browbeat NASDAQ into offering better prices, and yes, Levitt could politely ask his friends who ran big brokerages to stop rewarding their brokers for pushing house stocks. But if he could teach investors the difference between a stop and a limit order, if he could get them to understand why Merrill Lynch brokers were hawking the underperforming mutual funds owned by the firm and encourage investors to act on that knowledge, powerful market forces would force brokerage houses to reform themselves. If every investor would internalize some of the common sense he had accumulated during his thirty-odd years in the business, enforcement would not be necessary.

Levitt started with cosmetic rearrangement. The Office of Investor Education, which had been something of a passive backwater, was reorganized so that it reported directly to the chairman. In March 1994, he appointed a Consumer Affairs Advisory Committee, composed of consumer advocates, investment group members, and senior citizens' representatives. He also set up a toll-free consumer information line.

But the most effective investor education efforts took place outside Washington. Levitt has a flair for showmanship and an understanding of good public relations. (His son, Arthur Levitt III, is a protégé of Disney's Michael Eisner. He ran the Hard Rock Cafés and now is in charge of adult-themed entertainment at Disney.) In an unprecedented move for an SEC chairman, he hit the road to hold Clintonesque town meetings with small investors. The first was in Cherry Hill, New Jersey, in 1994. By November 1994, he had held sessions with groups in New Jersey, in Chicago, and at Florida Atlantic University in Boca Raton. As time went on, the SEC began to organize events with consumer, investor, and industry groups and with media outlets like the *Los Ange-les Times*, the *Miami Herald*, and CNBC. By December 1999, Levitt had held thirty-four investor town meetings in out-of-the-way locales such as Bangor, Maine; Des Moines, Iowa; and Tulsa, Oklahoma; and had given countless interviews on radio, television, and online.

Levitt lures people to the meetings by offering "the insider's view" of Wall Street. Eschewing the New Age feel-good-about-your-money approach of Suze Orman, or the allegedly foolproof trading schemes of Wade Cook, Levitt has developed a set of very practical tips for investors on the sometimes mysterious workings of the investment world. He tells people how brokers are compensated, how firms use sales contests to promote certain stocks or funds, and how spreads are determined. (It's like tuning into a Fox TV special to hear former magicians reveal secrets of the trade.) "Most people, I've learned, are afraid to ask dumb questions," he said in an interview in his spacious office on the sixth floor of the SEC headquarters. "And by getting a forum such as this, where a lot of people are likely to ask uninformed questions, others come forward and admit to a lack of understanding of things that most people just don't want to talk about."

Levitt's fourteenth town meeting, in Philadelphia, bore all the hall-marks of a school assembly. Accompanied by state securities regulators, Levitt stood on a stage and introduced a group of kids from Valley Forge Middle School who played an investing game. After describing the agency's mission, he fielded questions, and wandered into the audi-ence. Many of the queries were indeed uninformed. One elderly man with a string tie stated his belief that the term "fixed income"—used to describe bonds, which pay fixed incomes—should be banned, because the *prices* of bonds frequently fluctuate. Others used the open-microphone session to vent their spleen at the SEC. One middle-aged man berated Levitt for not responding to a complaint he had made about the Charles Schwab firm: "You have not done your job. I will have to write to the congressional subcommittee to either cut your funds, or shut you down." The democratization of money, like democracy itself, can be a messy matter.

Taking his show on the road has also given Levitt an appreciation of the democratized money culture. As he put it, "Where once we looked out at audiences and saw starched shirts and pinstriped suits, today we also see flannel shirts and denim jeans." One could hardly imagine Joseph Kennedy or John Shad or Richard Breeden going out of his way to interact with a retiree in Bangor who has a question about an annuity. Levitt has also gleaned substantive suggestions from these meetings. At several events, investors complained they couldn't hire a lawyer to represent them in a securities arbitration case. The SEC asked law schools in New York City to start clinics. Pace and Fordham responded and opened arbitration clinics in 1997 and 1998, respectively.

Of course, putting a human face on issues relating to securities can take people only so far. Ironically, the most important investor education initiative undertaken on Levitt's watch was a pure application of technology. The fact that U.S. companies each quarter have to file extremely detailed reports on their operations and finances is an ostensible hallmark of America's transparent markets. Until relatively recently, however, disclosure didn't live up to its promise. For the first several decades of the SEC's existence, companies would prepare massive annual reports or prospectuses for new securities offerings, and file them, in paper form, with the SEC. From, there, however, dissemination was practically Soviet-style in its labyrinthine slowness. Individuals had to hang around the SEC's public reference room to gain free, same-day access to corporate filings. Adjoining it was the press room, a windowless warren where cub reporters fresh out of college and grizzled wire-service veterans would shoot the breeze waiting for a mentally impaired man, who wore a single white glove, to roll a cart into the room and dump forms on the table. Other habitués of the room included couriers from so-called service bureaus, such as Disclosure, who would retrieve documents on specific requests from clients. Anyone interested in seeing older filings, say, last year's 10-K annual report, would have to fill out forms, in pencil, to retrieve microfiche copies. The low-paid civil servants behind the counter, oblivious to deadlines, would sit on documents, misfile or misplace them, or simply lose them.

In the 1990s, the system was ultimately replaced by EDGAR, the Electronic Data Gathering, Analysis, and Retrieval system. Few other public works projects, save New York's West Side Highway, have taken so long to develop. In the 1980s, the SEC began requiring companies to file electronically rather than on paper, and compiled the filings in a database. Throughout the late 1980s and early 1990s, the SEC sold the data to Mead Data, which in turn packaged it and sold it to other information retailers. Clients—mostly Wall Street firms—paid these private firms to access EDGAR.

But Carl Malamud, an info-gadfly who had started the first Internet radio station, set out to displace such contractors. In 1993, a congressional staffer asked if he could put EDGAR on the Internet for free. Malamud believed he could, but found that the SEC's technology specialists weren't interested in working with him, because they viewed EDGAR as a service that catered only to companies. After receiving a grant from the National Science Foundation, Malamud bought the data from Mead and established an Internet site in 1994. Eventually, he added features so that the database was searchable and accessible through the nascent World Wide Web. Quickly, some 50,000 people a day were accessing the site—senior citizen investment clubs, journalists, and Wall Street professionals.

Still, Malamud had trouble convincing the information specialists at the SEC to take over the service. So in August 1995, he posted a notice saying it would terminate in sixty days. A firestorm ensued, as some 10,000 EDGAR users e-mailed letters of protest to the SEC. Ultimately, Malamud bypassed the bureaucrats and took his case to Commissioner Steven Wallman. "Once they realized the potential, they really did move," said Malamud. Several private companies offered quasi-free plans: One would have allowed access for only ten minutes; another would have made users pay to download documents. But Levitt was insistent on having the SEC sponsor the service and having it be free. "EDGAR was paid for with public funds, and it seemed to me that it was a basic service that any investor was entitled to and shouldn't have to pay for," he said. "I want to encourage people who have a very small stake in our economy to learn more about investments." In summer 1995, Levitt announced the SEC would take over the service and offer the corporate filings with the agency's separate Internet service on a single Web page.

Of course, Levitt didn't invent EDGAR any more than Al Gore invented the Internet. But Levitt did make the service a reality. And EDGAR is one of the few examples of how the Internet's promise to revolutionize everything forever has been fulfilled. Indeed, the experience is totally different and seamless. The service is the best source for researching the age of wizened media magnate Sumner Redstone (seventy-five), or how much Donald Trump paid himself for services rendered to his publicly held casino company in 1998 ($1 million), or how much stock *Salon* editor David Talbot has in the newly public Webzine (402,083)—all in a matter of seconds. If you're the sort of person who has the urge to check out the capital structure of General Electric at 3:00 A.M. on a Sunday, then EDGAR is a godsend. It is, in short, immensely empowering. Today, more than a million documents a day are downloaded from EDGAR. The SEC still has a public reference room and a press room. But the outside world no longer relies on their inhabitants for access to crucial information.

With the launch of EDGAR as an SEC service in 1995, the mechanics of disclosure became democratized. But Levitt also believed it was crucial that the *content* of disclosure change, because the documents, laden with boilerplate legalisms and often intentionally obfuscatory prose, were frequently unintelligible to the millions of new investors flooding into the markets. "I was convinced that few people read prospectuses or annual reports, and wanted to do something about it, so I had to start with the language," said Levitt. This state of affairs was particularly pronounced in the mutual fund arena, the first vehicle that drew millions of virgin investors.

At a 1994 National Press Club speech, Levitt read aloud from a jargon-laden prospectus:

> Maturity and duration management decisions are made in the context of an intermediate maturity orientation. The maturity structure of the portfolio is adjusted in anticipation of cyclical interest rate changes. Such adjustments are not made in an effort to capture short-term, day-to-day movements in the market, but instead are implemented in anticipation of longer term, secular shifts in the levels of interest rates (i.e., shifts transcending and/or not inherent to the business cycle).

Levitt had asked Warren Buffett, renowned for turning his annual meetings into informal investment seminars, to translate that paragraph into plain English. Buffett did so as follows:

> We will try to profit by correctly predicting future interest rates. When we have no strong opinion, we will generally hold intermediate-term bonds. But when we expect a major and sustained increase in rates, we will concentrate on short-term issues. And, conversely, if we expect a major shift to lower rates, we will buy long bonds. We will focus on the big picture and won't make moves based on short-term considerations.

Levitt, an English major and a one-time drama critic and newspaper owner, is passionate about clear, concise writing. He proposed a fairly radical change for the companies: "It's my hope to have prospectuses begin to speak a new language—the English language." Levitt asked mutual fund companies to create a "profile prospectus"—a prospectus with a single-page summary. Seven, including Fidelity, Vanguard, and T. Rowe Price, agreed. Encountering little resistance, Levitt pressed to make the profile prospectus a requirement.

In the meantime, William Lutz, a Rutgers University English professor, got in touch with Nancy Smith. For several years, Lutz had moonlighted as a writer and consultant for design firms that produced annual reports. Lutz, who is also a lawyer, suggested the SEC issue a manual for writers of prospectuses and other documents. He started with a list of fifty-eight rules and quickly distilled them into a handbook. The resulting document—A *Plain English Handbook*—is a compendium of home truths about good writing. As Warren Buffett wrote in the preface, "When writing Berkshire Hathaway's annual report, I pretend that I'm talking to my sisters. I have no trouble picturing them. . . . No siblings to write to? Borrow mine: Just begin with 'Dear Doris and Bertie.'" The handbook contains dozens of Hemingwayesque tips on how to write in plain English: Use the active voice and personal pronouns. Keep sentences short. Avoid legal and financial jargon, weak verbs, and superfluous words. Address investors as "you." Substitute terms like "growth" for "capital appreciation." It also includes design suggestions: Serif typefaces are easier to read, and *italics* and **bold** are better than using all-capital letters. Lutz didn't get paid much for his efforts, but he received other compensation. "I had lunch with Warren Buffett and [venerated mutual fund manager] Peter Lynch," he said.

The push for plain English was codified in July 1997, when the SEC formally proposed amendments to mutual fund and securities registration forms and other documents. Rule 498 requires mutual funds to publish a profile, a short-form disclosure document that summarizes crucial data. For example, the Fidelity Short-Term Bond Fund prospectus lays out its objective clearly. It "seeks to obtain a high level of current income consistent with preservation of capital." It lists, in bullets, five investment strategies and highlights in boldface type the risks facing the fund, including interest rate changes and prepayment. A chart on the next page shows returns for the past ten years and compares the performance with that of other bond funds and a Lehman Brothers bond index. Since October 1998, the regulations also have applied to companies issuing stock. As Internet firms hasten to ready

their public offerings, they must take the time to incorporate the word-
ing changes suggested by readers at the SEC.

Some of Levitt's proposals have slipped over the thin line separating
sound policy from gimmickry. In March 1998, for example, he urged
brokerage firms and mutual fund firms to allow first-time investors to
invest without fees. But while it may not capture the imagination of television producers and SEC critics, forcing mutual fund firms to speak in
language that investors can understand is especially important, given
the democratization of money. In January 1997, *Wall Street Journal*
columnist Roger Lowenstein noted that Fidelity had more assets than
there was gold in Fort Knox and the New York Federal Reserve vaults
combined. "This is why the coming Securities and Exchange Commission proposal to redesign and simplify fund prospectuses will have more
practical effect than anything else the SEC does in Arthur Levitt's
tenure as chairman," he wrote. "It may not be literally true that investors
do less research for a fund than they do for a dishwasher, but the
prospectus is still the one and only piece of paper that all of them see."

The growth of the markets in the 1990s would have created a nightmare for anybody involved in oversight. But it posed particular problems for the SEC, whose staff headcount has risen only 3 percent
during Levitt's tenure and whose $320 million budget has barely kept
up with inflation. With stagnant resources, the SEC must monitor the
trading activity of 82 million investors in the 3,114 stocks on the NYSE,
and the 2,429 issues on the combined NASDAQ-Amex—not to mention thousands of thinly traded stocks on the NASDAQ bulletin board.
In 1998, overworked compliance officers had to wade through prospectuses for a record $2.55 trillion in proposed securities offerings, up 76
percent from 1997. The division of corporate finance reviewed only 21
percent of reporting issuers. The random investigations that Levitt
promised are certainly a threat, but they hit only every so often. In 1998,
the SEC inspected investment company complexes at a rate of once
every 4.7 years.

With his emphasis on diction, clean living, and prevention, Levitt is more akin to a community policing officer than a street-crime commando. It's not his style to have guys busted on the trading floor and led away in handcuffs. Enforcement activity has assumed a lower profile under Levitt, though it has been steady since 1994. There were 477 enforcement proceedings initiated in 1998, only slightly below the 1994 level of 487. To be sure, there have been some notable enforcement actions. A sting operation conducted by the FBI, the SEC, and the NASD resulted in forty-six people being charged for illegal kickbacks to brokers for sales of over-the-counter and NASDAQ stocks. In 1998, SEC investigations resulted in sixty-one convictions, and the agency obtained judicial and administrative orders requiring the disgorgement of $426 million. (About 10 percent of that total came from Michael Milken, who forfeited the $42 million in compensation received by an entity he controlled for advising MCI and News Corp. on a 1995 transaction.) The SEC also charged the NYSE in 1999 with failing to stop deals in which groups of independent NYSE floor brokers colluded on trades.

But the SEC has lagged a bit in other areas of enforcement. In 1994, the SEC boasted that "the current level of penny-stock activity is minimal." By 1997, however, regulators estimated that investors lost about $6 billion a year to penny-stock fraud. The Internet has been fertile ground for securities fraud, as Levitt noted in his speech at Martin Luther King High School, but not until 1998 did the SEC establish a two-person office to focus on Internet stock fraud.

Levitt has no more eradicated scams, insider trading, and abusive practices than the FBI has eradicated crime. In fact, because there are so many more investors, including millions of gullible new ones, and because of the anonymity and border-blurring effects of technology and the Internet, there are probably just as many shady stock promoters and flimflam artists out there as ever before. In 1998, the SEC conducted 338 oversight and 308 cause and surveillance examinations of broker-dealers, and found 139 serious violations on issues such as misrepresentations, unsuitable investments, and unauthorized trading. That year, the office of investor education and assistance fielded 51,311 complaints, up 50 percent since 1993. Although the SEC helped investors recover some $1.2 million and referred more than 1,700 complaints to other SEC divisions, these actions are a comparative drop in the bucket. After all, brokerage companies run relatively small risk of getting caught. Most who do get caught up in the maw of the SEC's enforcement unit ultimately settle. And because both sides prefer to avoid a costly trial, the settlement usually includes language indicating that the company in question neither admits nor denies the conduct with which it was charged.

Levitt may not be the toughest cop on the beat, but that shouldn't detract from the success of his tenure. Levitt has been, in some ways, one of the most admirable members of the Clinton administration — quite apart from the fact that he's managed to keep his nose clean. He possesses qualities that so many of the ambitious baby boomers who flocked to Washington in the wake of Clinton's election lacked: gravitas, respect from the private sector, stamina, and an ability to translate strategy into effective action. Like a safe-sex advocate, Levitt doesn't exhort people not to indulge in the gratifying, exciting, and potentially dangerous activity he monitors. Instead, he urges them to be sensible about it, and to take prophylactic measures.

Levitt's populist, consumerist orientation, which is consistent with his Democratic patrimony, will prove to be an important legacy. As the United States has transformed from a nation of savers into a nation of investors, Wall Street has become the new frontier for consumer protection. And consumer protection is an issue that Democrats have traditionally owned. It goes to the heart of how public entities can work to protect citizens from the predations of the private sector.

The introduction of EDGAR, the decrease of NASDAQ spreads, the advent of plain English, and the other developments that occurred under Levitt's watch have helped make Wall Street more democratic. But the SEC's efforts have piggybacked on efforts by other individuals, companies, and forces that have contributed to both the democratization and the Democratization of money. Through their activism and size, institutions representing blue-collar, Democratic workers have proved to be a force in the market. The actions of Wall Street veterans such as Robert Rubin and Arthur Levitt have proved to fellow Democrats that there is ample reason for a Democratic administration to look after the health of the markets. And they have proved to fellow Wall Streeters that Democrats can be effective guardians and regulators of the capital markets.

Indeed, the burgeoning alliance, symbiosis, and mutual-admiration society between Wall Street and the Clinton administration will prove to be one of the more remarkable developments of the decade. The markets grew more democratic in the 1990s, but they also grew more Democratic. A disproportionate number of the most prominent and transformative Wall Street figures of the past decade have been active Democrats. The members of this elite but nonexclusive fraternity—the New Moneycrats—have contributed mightily to their political party. But they have also contributed mightily to the ongoing bull-market party. Their actions in the complementary worlds of money and politics show that there is no inherent conflict between being a financial Democrat and a financial democrat, and that fellow plutocrats and aspiring plutocrats can feel more at home with Bill Clinton's uptown Democrats than with Trent Lott's down-home Republicans.

6

The New Moneycrats

At the end of July 1998, the residents of the eastern end of Long Island were in a tizzy over the imminent arrival of the nation's first couple—and few more so than the region's caterers. Michael Daly, of Southampton's Golden Pear Café, showed up with box lunches at Westhampton's Grabeski Airport, where Air Force One was to land. "The president likes turkey and brie sandwiches, grilled veggie wraps, and we threw in some of our famous chocolumps," he said. At Westhampton, the president boarded the helicopter Marine One, which buzzed eastward over the patchwork of manicured lawns and grand manses toward Easthampton. There, workers at Dreesen's Market were busily cranking out

800 doughnuts for the "First Eater," and star-chef Daniel Boulud's catering company was preparing a quasi–state dinner for sixty. The aerial convoy conveniently flew over the Southampton Full Gospel Church on County Road 39, whose sign featured a pointed biblical quote that could have been directed toward either the president or Republican congressional leaders Robert Livingston and Newt Gingrich: "Whoremongers and adulterers, God will judge." (Hebrews, 13:4.)

On the ground in Easthampton, Clinton immediately paid his respects to the most exalted local potentate. The presidential motorcade proceeded to the home of director Steven Spielberg, where the first couple bunked for the weekend. After relaxing a bit, the Clintons made their way to the 14,000-square-foot oceanside home of investment banker Bruce Wasserstein. Wasserstein, a graduate of the University of Michigan, Harvard Law, and Harvard Business School, began life as a Nader's Raider. In 1972, he coauthored a critique of the U.S. legal system with Mark Green, the future New York City public advocate. After making his bones as a go-go merger specialist at First Boston in the 1980s, he formed a boutique firm, Wasserstein Perella Group Inc. Since 1988, it has been a small but influential force, advising on high-profile deals such as the merger of Dean Witter and Morgan Stanley. True to his Brooklyn heritage, "Bid 'em up Bruce" (the brother of yuppie playwright Wendy Wasserstein) is an active Democrat. He and his wife, Claude, had donated about $80,000 to Democratic campaigns in the previous six years.

The guests assembled in the house, built around a sixteenth-century barn imported from Scotland, included a bevy of Wall Street and media luminaries: venture capitalist Alan Patricof and his wife, Susan, who had given more than $200,000 in soft money—unregulated campaign donations—to Democratic entities in the previous five years and had hosted a $30,000-a-head dinner party for Clinton in Manhattan the previous January; then-Goldman, Sachs chief executive Jon Corzine and his wife; designer Vera Wang and her husband, Arthur Becker, a

Bear Stearns executive; Miramax studio chief Harvey Weinstein; Billy Joel, who arrived by motorcycle; designer Kenneth Cole and his wife, Maria Cuomo Cole; and Roy Furman of investment bank Furman, Selz, and his wife. (Henry and Marie Josee Kravis canceled, allegedly because the Republican buyout baron had been scratched from the president's golf foursome.) For $25,000 a couple—just a skosh more than it costs to eat at caterer Daniel Boulud's outrageously expensive Manhattan restaurant, Daniel—they feasted on fresh Jamison Farms lamb, roasted Montauk tuna wrapped in cured bacon, gratin of zucchini flower filled with eggplant confit, and bittersweet chocolate lemon cake. The proceeds, some $600,000, went to the Democratic National Committee. In what may be one of the most unnecessary sentences ever penned, *New York Observer* columnist Frank DiGiacomo wrote, "The president cleaned his plate."

The next day, Clinton gave his Saturday radio address from the firehouse in neighboring Amagansett, accompanied by congressman Michael Forbes. Then he proceeded to tackle some truly pressing business: golf. In the Hamptons, *the* place to play golf is the Maidstone Club, founded in the 1890s by "genteel, Episcopalian, and rich" summer visitors. In the 1990s, the Maidstone was still dominated by summer visitors who were Episcopalian and rich but not so genteel. Unwilling to host the Arkansas parvenu, the Maidstone claimed its member-guest tournament was scheduled for the day Clinton wanted to play. Rebuffed, Clinton found a newer club, borne of decidedly less genteel (and less Gentile) money: the Atlantic Golf Club in Bridgehampton.

The Atlantic was formed in 1992—year one of the Clinton regnum—by New York moneymen who had either been excluded from the Maidstone or who simply wouldn't feel comfortable there. Its members include Democratic-leaning magnates like George Soros; Edgar Bronfman Jr.; and Steven Roth, the CEO of publicly traded real estate firm Vornado, Inc. (Roth and his wife gave more than $156,000 to Democratic party entities and candidates between 1993 and 1999. But his largest contribution to Democratic political causes may have been when his company bought the Kennedy family's Merchandise Mart real estate holdings in 1998 for $745 million.) In the early 1990s, the founding members bought land on Scuttle Hole Road in Bridgehampton and constructed a beautiful par 72 course. By 1997, the club—referred to as the "Fuck you" club—sported a $210,000 initiation fee and ranked sixty-fifth on Golf.com's list of 100 best courses in the United States. (The Maidstone was thirty-fourth.) At 11:30 A.M., Clinton teed off with Arthur Becker, course designer Rees Jones, and Fred Mack, a real estate executive and major donor. Clinton, who partnered with Jones, reportedly shot an 85. But like his grand jury testimony, the president's reported golf scores are best taken with substantial lumps of salt.

After the golf game, the first family quickly got back to fundraising. Saturday evening, the Clintons attended a cocktail party at the East-hampton farmhouse of composer and conductor Jonathan Scheffer and his partner, Dr. Christopher Barley. This party was less expensive than *l'affaire* Wasserstein—about 100 attendees, including Julie Andrews and Blake Edwards, paid $5,000 each. The hosts expressed sympathy for the president's recent sexual travails. "Gay men and lesbians know what it's like to be vilified, to be stereotyped, to be persecuted," Sheffer said. "I want you to know that today you are among friends." Having hit two of the Hamptons' crucial constituencies—Wall Streeters and artsy types—Clinton proceeded to connect with the third: Hollywood East. From the Scheffer house it was on to the Democratic National Committee's Summer Lawn Party at the Amagansett home of actors Alec Baldwin and Kim Basinger. About 1,000 people paid $250 just to get a glimpse of Clinton from the front yard. Those who paid $1,000 gained entrée to a backyard tent where Hootie and the Blowfish played. For $5,000, donors could enter the house, where Alan Patricof stood by Clinton's side, introducing the president to the likes of Sony Music chieftain Tommy Mottola (the former Mr. Mariah Carey) and public relations guru Dan Klores. On Sunday morning, Clinton strolled down to the Barefoot Contessa with the Spielbergs, ordered coffee, and pressed some of the ample flesh on display. In the afternoon, he headed home.

Presidents, especially those who weren't born to wealth, have always loved rubbing elbows with the rich. After all, they tend to have the best and most commodious vacation homes and access to the finest golf courses. Eisenhower spent more time golfing with a group of wealthy industrialists at Augusta National than he did worrying about the missile gap. Clinton was no different. Eschewing boring Camp David and unhip Arkansas, the First Family spent most of their August vacations among the rich and liberal on Martha's Vineyard—playing golf with Vernon Jordan, sailing with various Kennedys, listening to Carly Simon croon, and swapping bons mots with the likes of *Washington Post* owner Katharine Graham, novelist William Styron, and sainted newsman Walter Cronkite. The president also availed himself of the excellent shopping on the island. On his 1997 trip, he purchased several items for Monica Lewinsky at the Black Dog, the gift shack strategically located just off the ferry dock in Vineyard Haven.

For the first six years of his tenure, Clinton avoided the Hamptons. After all, through their rich 360-year history, the towns collected along Long Island's south fork have been neither very democratic nor very Democratic. The first president to summer there was John Tyler, a Whig (and hence a proto-Republican), who built a house in Easthampton. More recently, in the 1980s, that most Republican of decades, GOPers such as Ron Perelman were the most prominent stars in the Hamptons firmament. The party of the decade, thrown by insurance tycoon Saul Steinberg and his wife, was an over-the-top spectacle that featured naked actors in *tableaux vivants*. The Steinbergs—Saul, short, chubby, grasping, and socially ambitious, and his third wife Gayfryd, skinny, grasping, and socially ambitious—represented all that was putatively awful about the 1980s, right down to their politics. Steinberg had secretly donated $250,000 to Nixon's 1972 reelection campaign.

Of course, there had always been Democrats around these parts, especially in artsy Easthampton. Clinton himself had been a guest umpire at the 1988 Writers and Artists softball game—an annual event held in that parallel celebrity universe in which Mortimer Zuckerman, the real estate magnate who owns the *Atlantic Monthly* and *U.S. News & World Report*, is considered a writer. But the Hamptons changed in the 1990s. These days, many of the biggest and most imposing cottages belong not to Republican industrialists but to Hollywood executives, media all-stars, and Wall Streeters, many of whom are Democrats. And just as the taste in cars shifted from BMWs in the 1980s to Range Rovers in the 1990s, the fashion in politics seems to have turned from Republicans to Democrats. Indeed, so powerful was the Democratic pull that Michael Forbes, the Republican congressman who represents the region, in 1998 became that rare politician to bolt across the aisle from the GOP to the Democrats.

Fleeing the poisonous, scandal-ridden swamp of Washington, the first couple received a warm reception from the equally satisfied and accomplished baby boomers who populate the region. "The people of the Hamptons want desperately for Clinton to be safe," Steven Gaines, author of the best-selling Hamptons Baedeker *Philistines at the Hedgerows*, told the *New York Observer*. "He is the spirit of the bull market." But aside from inducing good vibrations and raising oodles of cash for various Democratic party entities—some $1.75 million on the weekend—the president's visit to the Republic of the Hamptons nailed home a larger point about money and politics in the 1990s. For almost a decade, President Clinton relied on the people he saw in the Hamptons for advice, for crucial campaign funds, and for moral support. The weekend served as a sort of presidential coronation of the Democratic-leaning caste of Wall Street movers and shakers—the New Money-crats—who helped define the decade in finance. This group, "men and women without family connections or social pedigree," as *Washington Post* reporter Brett Fromson put it in 1994, had come to wield substantial influence over the 1990s money culture. Their activism and, in some cases, their business activities substantially abetted the Democratization of money.

The New Moneycrats are a species of the larger genus of *Americanus wealthius*. Their natural habitat is the fertile crescent that carves an arc from suburban New Jersey through Manhattan, Westchester County, and the Berkshires, across to Boston and Martha's Vineyard, and hooks back to terminate in the Hamptons. Many are middle-aged, children of the baby boom — although some are a bit older. Most were raised in modest or comfortable circumstances, usually in the New York area. They think the Great Depression is something cured by a huge dose of Prozac, not by the New Deal. Like the president, they thrived in the East Coast's meritocratic factories. Like the First Lady, they pursued lucrative careers, all the while taking pains to be perceived as individuals concerned with everything *but* wealth and its trappings.

The New Moneycrats have been among the most important contributors to the democratized money culture. For the past decade, the nation's most exalted long-term investor, Warren Buffett, and the proprietor of the most dynamic financial media company, Michael Bloomberg, have been Democrats. The heads of investment banks such as Lazard Freres; Goldman, Sachs; Wasserstein, Perella; and Allen & Co. have all been Democrats. And the list goes on: the chief executives of publicly held real estate companies like Vornado and of money-center banks like Bankers Trust; prominent dealmakers such as Thomas Lee; the traders who lord over major hedge funds like Quantum; the leading lights of online financial news operations such as TheStreet.com — Democrats all. Their escapades, the companies they have built and led, and the deals they have done with one another helped define the decade. Over the course of Clinton's two terms, the president formed a symbiotic relationship with these powerful Democratic executives. Without the Clinton administration's continuing efforts to appease the markets and take strong, frequently unilateral action in times of crisis, it is unlikely these New Moneycrats would have enjoyed such success. In turn, without their financial and moral support, it is unlikely President Clinton and many of his congressional allies would have survived the searing and vicious campaigns of the 1990s.

Indeed, the fingerprints of New Moneycrats can be found almost everywhere in today's financial landscape. The contemporary money culture is defined, in large part, by the growth of financial media and the seemingly insatiable demand for money-related data. In the 1990s, no individual did more to disseminate financial information—or profited more from it—than Michael Bloomberg. The son of an accountant at a dairy, who never made more than $6,000 a year, Bloomberg grew up in blue-collar Medford, Massachusetts. He studied engineering at Johns Hopkins University, attended Harvard Business School, and found his way to Salomon Brothers in 1966. He made partner by the age of thirty. In 1981, when Salomon Brothers merged with Phibro Corporation, Bloomberg received a $10 million payout and was pushed out.

Bloomberg raised $30 million from Merrill Lynch and launched a new financial data and analysis product catering to bond traders. The machine, dubbed "the Bloomberg," began to win a devoted following. In 1990, in an effort to compete head-on with Dow Jones and Reuters, he started his own wire service. He hired reporter Matthew Winkler away from the *Wall Street Journal*, and Winkler built an effective global service with astonishing speed. (The fledgling wire service was so desperate for reporters that it hired me in 1992 for an entry-level position, even though I barely knew the difference between a stock and a bond.)

Anticipating the growing demand for financial information—and seeking opportunities to spread the name of the company—Bloomberg sank the profits from the pricey terminals into his media operations. He provided terminals to newspapers for free, and they began to print Bloomberg news stories. In 1992, he bought New York radio station WNEW for $13 million and converted it into WBBR, an all-news format with a financial tilt. A personal finance magazine, *Bloomberg*

Personal, began to appear in newspapers as a Sunday supplement and was rolled out as a stand-alone monthly. He built television studios and started a financial television station, Bloomberg Information Television, that beamed programming around the country. (If earlier media moguls had felt the same Bloombergian need to plaster their name on their products, we'd be reading the *Sulzberger Times* every morning, plucking *Luce* magazine out of the mail every weekend, and tuning in to the Paley Broadcasting Service.) By the mid-1990s, it was impossible to go anywhere in Manhattan without seeing Bloomberg's name—in big banner ads at Grand Central Station, on the side of billboard trucks inching through midtown traffic, on the electronic "zipper" around Morgan Stanley's headquarters at Forty-fifth Street and Broadway.

Today, Bloomberg's data terminals still drive the company. More than 100,000 are in use, and they bring in revenues of $1.7 billion a year. But Bloomberg gets his juice from his media operations, and he's a refreshing alternative to the faceless bureaucrats who run many media conglomerates. Taken with his own success but mindful of his past, he revels in his increased desirability. "How many single heterosexual billionaires do you think there are, fer Chrissakes?" he asked a journalist. Although the culture at Bloomberg's Park Avenue headquarters is unabashedly authoritarian, it is also strangely democratic. Every employee shares in the profits. There are no titles, no private offices, and remarkably little pretense. Bloomberg draws the same salary as that of the lowest-paid full-time employee. The boss himself—everybody refers to him as "Mike"—is like one of the guys on a trading floor, strolling around the newsroom, checking out female employees and visitors with a certain droit du seigneur. One morning in 1993, as I sat hunched over a computer screen at about 7:00 A.M., I heard a grunt: "Unnhh." I looked up. Mike was standing in front of my desk, checking out the bank of televisions on the wall behind me. One was tuned to an ESPN workout show that featured Amazonian women in bikinis. "How'd you like to have those legs wrapped around you?"

Bloomberg is also a self-described "wealthy Democrat, who has given consistently to my party." Between 1993 and 1999, he gave some $207,000 in soft-money donations to various Democratic entities, compared with just $11,000 in soft money to Republicans. As he wrote in his book, *Bloomberg by Bloomberg,* "I send checks to individual candidates I believe in. I send checks to candidates running under my party's banner even sometimes when I don't really believe they are the best on the ballot. . . . Party allegiance and who's asking are both as important as the individual who's running." For a time, his name was floated as a possible candidate for mayor of New York City in 2001. (If he won, would Gotham be renamed Bloomberg City?)

With his insights into the demand for and mass appeal of financial information, Bloomberg was very much a creature of the 1990s. In his personal style, however, he was a throwback to the 1980s, when swaggering colossi strode the financial scene. But in the more democratic — and Democratic — 1990s, many of the leading investment bankers, merger advisers, and hotshot money managers have deliberately cut a lower profile. Some have even tried to portray themselves as humble, practically middle-class, just "plain folks." Such has been the case with perhaps the leading investment banker of the 1990s: Steven Rattner.

Rattner labored for most of the decade at one of Wall Street's great anomalies: Lazard Freres. An aristocratic, philo-Democratic, French-Anglo-U.S. investment bank, Lazard was founded by the Alsatian Jewish Lazard brothers, who set themselves up as cotton brokers in New Orleans in 1848. Over the years, it evolved into a three-headed firm with offices, or "houses," in Paris, London, and New York. Small but profitable, the New York house alone earned $300 million in 1998. Globally, Lazard ranked fourth among mergers and acquisitions advisers in 1997.

Although it engages in many of the same activities as other investment banks, Lazard has always projected a continental, gentlemanly sophistication. No person embodied this worldliness more than Felix

Rohatyn, the prototypical New Moneycrat and wise-man-cum-party-activist-cum-public-intellectual upon whom Rattner has modeled his career. Born in Vienna in 1927 to a well-off Jewish family, Rohatyn spent much of his youth in a fugue state, fleeing Hitler's advance to Romania, France, Lisbon, Casablanca, Rio de Janeiro, and ultimately New York. After graduating from Middlebury College, he landed a job at Lazard's Zurich office and returned to New York in 1955. In the 1960s, his stature increased as he advised conglomerateurs like Harold Geneen of ITT. But his fame grew in the 1970s as he became involved in public affairs. Rohatyn served as Edmund Muskie's economics adviser in 1972. In 1975, amid New York City's fiscal crisis, he helped create the Municipal Assistance Corporation, which issued bonds backed by the state's credit. After saving the most Democratic city on earth, Rohatyn cemented his reputation among the liberal intelligentsia by contributing articles to the *New York Review of Books* that were critical of Reaganomics. These were assembled in a 1983 book, *The Twenty-Year Century: Essays on Economics and Public Finance.* Even as he maintained his image as an adviser par excellence, the public-minded banker always seemed to have other things in mind. As he put it in 1985, "It's getting more and more difficult for me to do the things we do in dealmaking because in the last analysis I don't think that's what I want on my tombstone."

Lazard in the 1990s become a haven for Democrats who wanted to make big money. Diarist Josh Steiner wound up there after flaming out in Washington. Josh Gotbaum worked at Lazard before serving in several Clinton administration posts, most recently in the Office of Management and Budget. In late 1999, Clinton confidant Vernon Jordan joined the firm. Over the course of the decade, however, Rohatyn and, increasingly, Steven Rattner garnered the biggest headlines. Rattner, the man whom *Vanity Fair* dubbed "the most talked-about investment banker of his generation," is cut from an exceedingly different cloth than Rohatyn. After graduating from Brown University in 1974, Rattner landed a job at the *New York Times* and covered energy policy in the paper's Washington bureau. A rising star, he was shipped off to London in 1981. But Rattner tired of the journalistic rat race and in 1982 signed on with Lehman Brothers, where Roger Altman toiled. He left Lehman in 1984 for Morgan Stanley and ultimately joined Lazard several years later.

Rattner's forte was advising companies on mergers in the converging fields of publishing, cable, and telecommunications. He came to the fore in the epic battle over Paramount Communications, which engulfed many of the players in what came to be known as the "new economy"—Barry Diller, QVC, Comcast Cable, Sumner Redstone's Viacom, CBS, and Cox Communications, among others. (Rattner and Lazard advised Paramount.) Despite his association with highfliers, Rattner was self-consciously low-key. "He doesn't speak any foreign languages. He is not at home—as Rohatyn is—in Europe. He has no panache or flair," as Ed Klein put it in a 1994 *Vanity Fair* article noteworthy for its zeitgeist-defining ambitions. Unlike the greedy characters from the 1980s, Rattner was seemingly uninterested in money. His wife drove a Dodge Caravan. Sure he owned a plane. But it was a two-engine Cessna 421, not a jet, and it was merely a tool that enabled him to get to his second home in Martha's Vineyard more easily. "We don't go to the Caribbean, or, for that matter, the Hamptons," he said. "When I take the boys to school, it is on the M72 bus, even though a car and driver is certainly within our means." He reported that he enjoyed "take-out Chinese food from Shun Lee West far more than Lutece, which I have visited only once, at a client's invitation 10 years ago." (Shun Lee is one of the most expensive Chinese restaurants in the city.) The fair-haired banker, was, in short a democrat. "I often take the subway to and from work, in part because I don't see how one can have a view about the problems of the city without experiencing the city on at least some level as typical people do."

Of course, Rattner wasn't exactly middle class. Later in the *Vanity*

Fair article, *New York Times* heir Arthur Sulzberger reminisced about a scuba-diving trip they had taken in Little Cayman in the Caribbean. At the time, Rattner lived in the Dakota, the legendarily exclusive and expensive Central Park West apartment building whose residents include Diane Sawyer and Yoko Ono. (Rattner has since decamped for Fifth Avenue.) Nor was Rattner quite as guileless as he seemed. Over the course of the 1990s, he challenged, and ultimately vanquished, Felix Rohatyn, both as head of Lazard's New York office and as the Democrats' favorite investment banker.

Rohatyn, of course, had long been a huge Democratic donor. He and his wife contributed nearly a half million dollars in soft and hard money between 1993 and 1999, and he desperately wanted a post in the Clinton administration. His name was frequently bandied about as a potential appointment for a high Federal Reserve post, but he was deemed too liberal by congressional Republicans. In 1997, after he lost an internal power struggle to Rattner, Rohatyn was appointed by Clinton to replace the late Pamela Harriman as ambassador to France.

As the 1990s wore on, Rattner became a significant donor and fundraiser: He and his wife gave more than $280,000 in soft dollars between 1993 and 1998 and supported dozens of other Democratic candidates. Clinton was a regular guest at dinner parties in the Rattner home during the summers in the Vineyard. Like Rohatyn before him, Rattner began to pen op-ed articles in the *New York Times* on fiscal policy and was an easy call for journalists seeking quotations on economic policy. Rattner also championed Democratic candidates like Charles Schumer and forged a strong relationship with president-in-waiting Al Gore. In spring 1999, he hosted a fundraiser for forty people, each of whom promised to raise $35,000 for Gore. That June, he left the distinct impression, as Rohatyn once did, that investment banking was something he could take or leave. When Lazard announced a reorganization that would combine the three autonomous firms in New York, Paris, and London into a single entity, Rattner said he would step down as deputy chief executive of the New York house. Rattner, it seemed, was trying to set himself up as Al Gore's Robert Rubin.

The prospect of a putative Master of the Universe riding a bus—or any public transportation, for that matter—is in itself a commentary on the democratization of money. In the 1980s, an investment banker would have had nothing to gain by trying to appear middle class. Fast living conferred a certain status upon dealmakers. And no event symbolized the high-style living of the 1980s money culture more than Michael Milken's annual junk-bond conference, which came to be known as the Predators' Ball.

In the 1990s, the Predators' Ball was supplanted in the public imagination by two annual investment-oriented events, both of which were the creation of billionaire Democrats. In my opinion, the defining event of the 1990s money culture is the annual meeting of Berkshire-Hathaway, Warren Buffett's publicly held investment vehicle.

In May 1999, some 15,000 Buffett devotees showed up in Omaha, Nebraska, for the annual meeting. Buffett was, as usual, a good sport. As *New York Times* reporter David Barboza put it: "No other American chief executive may be so plain-spoken or so masterful an investor. Nor does any other American chief executive do so many hokey things." Buffett played bridge against a ringer at a local mall. Along with shareholders, he visited the Nebraska Furniture Mart and Borsheim's jewelry store, both of which are owned by Berkshire-Hathaway, and stopped by a Dairy Queen (Buffett owns that too). He dined, family-style, with shareholders at Gorat's steakhouse. Many ordered Buffett's preferred bill of fare: a T-bone steak and hash browns. And they flocked to an Omaha Golden Spikes minor league baseball game at Rosenblatt Stadium, where Buffett threw out the first pitch to Ernie Banks, the Cubs hall-of-famer. (Buffett owns 25 percent of the team.) The tone of the weekend vibes more with a John Cougar Mellenkamp song than with *Lifestyles of the Rich and Famous.*

On Monday, May 3, shareholders lined up as early as 4:30 A.M. outside the Aksarben Auditorium, which holds 14,000 people. During the meeting, Buffett took questions from shareholders for six hours and consumed products made by Berkshire portfolio companies: Cherry Coke, Dairy Queen ice cream bars. Shareholders asked for book recommendations (Buffett liked Katharine Graham's memoirs) and questioned the reason for selling a chunk of McDonald's. Buffett was engagingly self-effacing. "Overall, you would have been better off last year if I had regularly snuck off to the movies during market hours," he conceded. When investors asked why he didn't buy more technology stocks, Buffett remarked that he didn't see value in most of them. "The Dilly Bar is more certain to be around in 10 years than any single software application," he noted.

The whole weekend was like an animated series of Norman Rockwell paintings. And Buffett takes pains to uphold a similarly wholesome image. He doesn't gorge on options, and he takes a small salary — $100,000 in 1998. He lives in the same house he bought in 1958 for $32,000. Instead of running afoul of the SEC, as many 1980s investing stars did, Buffett worked with the agency, helping to produce A Plain English Handbook. And he has turned countless patient shareholders into multimillionaires. Anybody lucky enough to have had $10,000 in Berkshire-Hathaway stock in 1965 would be worth $65 million today.

Buffett not only is a democrat but is also a Democrat. His father, Republican congressman Howard Buffett, was a three-time loser: resolutely opposed to the New Deal, an isolationist, and a member of the John Birch Society. In the early 1960s, Warren Buffett began to read Bertrand Russell, the pacifist philosopher, and was taken with the cause of civil rights. As Roger Lowenstein wrote in his excellent biography of Buffett, "He quit the Omaha Rotary Club specifically because he objected to its racist and elitist policies." Warren Buffett formally broke with Republicans after his father's death in 1964 and proceeded to raise funds for Eugene McCarthy in 1968, back Planned Parenthood, and help bankroll the Washington Monthly. Notoriously unphilanthropic,

Buffett hasn't been a big political donor. In the 1990s, in fact, Jimmy Buffett donated almost as much as Warren. The singer and his wife, Jane, gave $10,000 to the Democratic National Committee (DNC) in 1997 and another $5,000 to Democratic candidates. Between 1993 and 1999, by contrast, Warren Buffett gave just $9,500 to candidates, primarily to Senators Bob Kerrey and Daniel Patrick Moynihan, Rep. Peter Hoagland, and Bill Bradley—Democrats all.

Warren Buffett has regularly attended another annual event, sponsored by an exceedingly wealthy Democrat, that has helped define the 1990s money culture. Each summer, investment banker Herb Allen, the second-generation proprietor of investment bank Allen & Co., hosts a gathering in Sun Valley, Idaho, that is a combination of Bohemian Grove and Renaissance Weekend. Allen graduated from Williams College in 1966 and went to work at Allen & Co., which had been founded by his uncle Charles in 1922. His father, Herbert Allen, joined the firm in 1927. Young Herb's first business coup was in parlaying a $1.5 million 1973 investment in Columbia Pictures into several hundred million when it was sold to Coca-Cola in 1982. By 1996, each Columbia share that he had bought for $4 was worth $2,400 in Coke stock. But the man who ranked 110th on *Forbes'* 1998 list of the wealthiest Americans is another self-effacing New Moneycrat. "I could teach my dog to be an investment banker," he famously said.

As with Rattner, Allen's specialty is advising media companies on mergers and acquisitions. He advised Seagram's Edgar Bronfman Jr. on his $5.7 billion purchase of 80 percent of MCA from Matsushita, for example. In the 1990s, as the worlds of software, hardware, telecommunications, media, and entertainment merged in a blizzard of alliances, Allen's annual gathering assumed an iconic stature. Each July, big hitters from Hollywood, Silicon Valley, and the East Coast media elite flocked to the Sun Valley Lodge outside Ketchum, Idaho. (The lodge was built by Averell Harriman, another fabulously wealthy Democrat.)

Indeed, Allen's gathering has served as an incubator for deals and alliances that were as significant to the 1990s money culture as the transactions consummated by Predators' Ball attendees were to the 1980s. The $19 billion merger of Disney and Capital Cities/ABC was hatched during a Sun Valley golf game between Michael Eisner and Thomas Murphy, CEO of Capital Cities/ABC. In 1996, Allen allowed *Vanity Fair's* Annie Liebovitz to attend the Idaho gathering to shoot photographs for the magazine's annual feature on the New Establishment. The New Establishment is noteworthy, and not only because it provided insight about who *Vanity Fair* editor Graydon Carter believes are the nation's most important businesspeople. In prior generations, such a listing would have included the CEOs of large, progressive manufacturers such as General Motors, Goodyear Tire, and Alcoa, all of whom would have been Republicans. But the New Establishment is somewhat more catholic (and somewhat more Jewish). It usually includes a few captains of industry, like Andrew Grove of chip manufacturer Intel, Louis Gerstner of IBM, and Jack Welch of General Electric, but also named are captains of money, bits, and media. Its ranks counted several Republicans but consisted largely of prominent Democrats: Barry Diller, Jeffrey Katzenberg, Sumner Redstone, Michael Eisner, David Geffen, Edgar Bronfman Jr., and Michael Bloomberg, to name a few.

With each passing year, more and more reporters set up shop around Sun Valley. In 1999, Allen permitted journalists to interview and photograph the guests at the lodge. He also allowed *New Yorker* scribe Ken Auletta, the Boswell of the New Establishment, to chronicle the event. Activities included golf, skeet shooting, white-water rafting for the 300 adults, and ice skating, wagon rides, and pizza parties for the 130 children. The Predators' Ball it isn't. When the banker organized a raft trip for the adults, Auletta reported, "Herb Allen demands an additional accessory—three empty water buckets; he is determined to start a water fight."

Herb Allen is a Democrat. He has given about $100,000 in soft money to the Democrats in the 1990s and smaller donations to about two dozen other Democratic candidates. His right-hand man at Allen & Co. is Stanley Shuman, who has been with the company since the early 1960s. Between 1993 and 1999, Shuman gave at least $165,000 in soft money to the Democratic party and made donations to twenty-one other candidates—all Democrats; he also attended a White House coffee. Not surprisingly, then, the only politicians invited to Allen's ultra-elite Sun Valley gathering in 1999 were Democrats, among them former vice president Walter Mondale and power broker Robert Strauss. On the last day of the weekend, Allen introduced his friend of three decades, presidential candidate Bill Bradley, who spoke about children and family structure—and probably made a subliminal pitch for campaign funds. A cross-check of federal records shows that many of those in Sun Valley donated funds to Bradley, including Mike Bloomberg, Michael Eisner, Barry Diller, Michael Ovitz, and Steve Case of America On-Line.

Like Case, several members of the New Establishment owed their status to the explosion of the Internet. Indeed, many of the most prominent Internet start-ups aimed to capitalize on the growing thirst for financial information and stock-trading services. The proliferation of online brokers like Ameritrade, financial news sites like Marketwatch.com, and Web-based investment banks like Wit Capital contributed substantially to the democratization of money.

Some of the entrepreneurs behind these companies were also New Moneycrats, chief among them James Cramer. In fact, the hedge-fund manager and founder of TheStreet.com has a classic New Moneycrat résumé: middle-class upbringing in suburban Philadelphia; schooling at Harvard, where he worked on the *Crimson*, and Harvard Law; jobs in journalism and at Goldman, Sachs; and a long-standing friendship with *New Republic* owner Martin Peretz, who backed Cramer when he started his own hedge fund. But like other New Moneycrats who preferred not to be marked as merely investment bankers, Cramer had a

powerful urge not to be remembered as just another trader. In the early
1990s, he helped start *Smart Money* and then became personal finance
columnist at *New York* when his buddy Kurt Andersen took over as editor. (The wise Bennett Gould character in Andersen's much-hyped,
little-read novel *Turn of the Century* is plainly a paean to Cramer.)
Throughout the latter half of the decade, Cramer's profile began to rise
as he became a popular guest host on CNBC's *Squawk Box*—where his
manic personality, frizzy hair, and way with a phrase set him singularly
apart from the stammering suits who populate the early morning show.
So too did Cramer's zest for the game, his willingness to acknowledge
losses and crow about wins, and his ability not to take himself or the
markets too seriously.

Cramer's biggest contribution to the money culture was the founding of TheStreet.com, an online financial magazine. Since its launch
in 1997, Cramer has been the leading promoter and writer of the publi-
cation. Acting on the same impulse that led Arthur Levitt to hold town
hall meetings, Cramer aimed to shed light on phenomena that are mys-
teries to average investors. In his columns, zipped off at all hours of the
day, he offers slice-of-life descriptions of a hedge fund. He explains how
professional traders think and act, how after-hours trading works, what
he's buying and selling, and why he believes the old-line brokerages
must change their ways to cater to new investors. His goal: to make
TheStreet.com's 94,000 subscribers—"do-it-yourselfers"—more intelligent investors and traders. TheStreet.com is one of the only forms of
Internet-based content—along with the *Wall Street Journal* interactive
edition—that people have proved willing to pay for. In May 1999, the
company went public at $19 a share, making Cramer's stake worth $64
million.

Cramer is, in many ways, the opposite of Peter Lynch, the calm
buy-and-hold Fidelity mutual fund manager who was featured in the
company's advertisements alongside Don Rickles and Lily Tomlin. (Yet
another example of the democratization of money.) An adherent of the

Church of What Works Today, Cramer is a quick-draw trading artist. In early television advertisements for TheStreet.com, he was shown walking in the deserted mists of Wall Street on a Sunday, in the style of Gary Cooper in *High Noon*. Of course, Cramer is not only a democrat but also a Democrat: He gave $90,000 to the DNC in the 1996 election cycle and attended a White House coffee, where he suggested that downsized workers be given stock options in their erstwhile employers.

The ability of TheStreet.com and scores of other money-losing operations to sell stock to the public has been one of the distinguishing characteristics of the democratized money culture. In the 1980s, the highest aspiration of financiers was to take a company "private"—to use debt to purchase public companies, revamp them, and cash out at some point in the future. In the 1990s, the desideratum for any company was the opposite: to share ownership with public investors. By 1999, firms of all stripes were going public at the rate of three a day. And entities that had assiduously worked to maintain their independence and privacy were opening up their books for all to see.

The event that put an exclamation point on this trend was the May 1999 IPO of Goldman, Sachs, the 130-year-old investment firm. Goldman was the last large partnership on Wall Street, and in many ways its most profitable, most elite, and most mysterious. Unlike its publicly held rivals, Goldman was not required to report quarterly profit and loss statements. The information that did dribble out inevitably inspired awe and envy. In spring 1999, however, the average investor was presented with an opportunity to own a piece of this immensely wealthy firm. Goldman went public on May 3, selling 69 million shares at $53 each. The offering, which raised $3.66 billion, was the second-largest IPO in U.S. history and left the company valued at $29 billion.

Not surprisingly, this iconic firm of the 1990s has a proud Democratic heritage. It was the professional home to Clinton Treasury Secretary Robert Rubin for nearly thirty years. Rubin's successor, Jon Corzine, was also a Democrat, although his life story parallels *Hoosiers* more closely than *Wall Street*. He was born January 1, 1947, in a farm-house in a southern Illinois hamlet called Willie's Station, population fifty, to a wheat farmer and an elementary school teacher. He met his future wife, Joanne, in kindergarten. Together, they attended the University of Illinois, where he was a substitute guard on the basketball team. After serving in the Marines, he moved to Chicago, worked as an analyst at Continental Illinois National Bank by day, and earned his MBA at the University of Chicago by night. In 1975, he joined Goldman's government-bond trading desk. Over the next twenty years, he was given greater responsibility. In 1994, when managing partner Stephen Friedman and thirty-six other partners left in the wake of big trading losses, Corzine was elevated to chief executive.

Like Rattner and Allen, Corzine is yet another humble investment banker. As the *Washington Post* dutifully reported in 1994, he rode in taxis, not limousines, and lived in an "unpretentious house he bought more than a decade ago in Summit, New Jersey." Corzine sported a beard, which on Wall Street is practically the mark of a bohemian. And he commanded the elite troops with a sense of down-home bonhomie. After taking the reins, he set about making Goldman not only a richer but a more complete firm. Responding to the growing ranks of frustrated executives who hadn't made partner, he added a new category of "extended managing directors." He also encouraged employees to volunteer for community projects, "for the soul of the firm."

Corzine's tenure at the top of Goldman was stormy, however. Many of his allies left. The long-debated IPO was pulled in the wake of big losses suffered in the summer 1998 global meltdowns. When hedge-fund Long-Term Capital collapsed, Corzine led a failed effort to buy it out, in concert with Warren Buffett. (In the end, Corzine helped lead a consortium of large investment banks in the bailout.) Within months, a troika composed of Goldman senior partners Henry Paulson Jr., John Thornton, and chief financial officer John Thain conspired against him. On January 11, 1999, Goldman issued a press release saying that

Corzine had given up the title of chief executive officer. Corzine left after the company went public, saying it "marks a logical point for me to move on."

As 1999 wore on, Corzine began to take more of an interest in running for the New Jersey Senate seat to be vacated by Frank Lautenberg in 2000. Long an active Democrat, Corzine had donated $380,000 in soft money in the 1997–1998 election cycle alone. In early 1999, Corzine kicked in $500,000 to establish an exploratory committee. One rival for the Democratic nomination, former governor Tom Florio, called the Corzine boomlet "the equivalent of a hostile Wall Street takeover of the Democratic Party." Despite his lack of political experience, Corzine is an attractive candidate and the odds-on favorite. His longtime association with Goldman has endowed him not only with stunning wealth (about $300 million) but also with a reputation of competency. A fresh face, Corzine will be a great alternative to Florio, who is best remembered for raising taxes and who already lost a statewide race. Finally, and perhaps most important to potential colleagues like Robert Torricelli, the junior senator from New Jersey and chairman of the Democratic Senate Campaign Committee, Corzine can fund his own campaign. That would free up millions for other competitive races.

Throughout the summer and fall, Corzine made tentative forays into retail politics, breakfasting in diners and giving talks to small audiences. But he spoke most loudly with his wallet. Corzine funded advertisements for candidates in the New Jersey Assembly in the 1999 campaign, and the Democrats gained three seats in the election. Grateful, twenty-two of the Assembly's thirty-five Democrats, including Minority Leader Joseph Doria, endorsed Corzine in November 1999. These endorsements—and his large fortune—have helped make the unassuming, shy banker the front-runner.

The fact that the former head of Goldman (or of any other major Wall Street firm) is running as a Democrat for a spot as crucial as the

New Jersey Senate seat is an indication of how far things have come. Wealth and Wall Street experience are no longer liabilities for a Democratic candidate but are assets. Just as remarkable is the fact that the only complaint came from his primary opponent. Besides, Corzine's heart is in the right place. He has given money to guarantee college educations for public school kids. He favors indexing the minimum wage to inflation. In his campaign announcement, Corzine said, "We will fight to improve the lives of working families by focusing on job creation and economic development, protection of Social Security and Medicare, [and] making educational opportunity a reality for every child." He sounded like Paul Wellstone.

If Corzine is elected, he would follow in the worn path that runs from lower Manhattan to Washington. In the 1990s, after all, several Wall Streeters served in the Clinton administration: Robert Rubin, Roger Altman, Ken Brody (a Goldman, Sachs partner named president of the Export-Import Bank), James Wolfensohn (the investment banker who now heads the World Bank), and Jeffrey Garten (a veteran of Lehman Brothers and the Blackstone Group who served as undersecretary of commerce for international trade).

The political leanings of these New Moneycrats are remarkably similar to those of Clinton and Gore circa 1999. They stand for internationalism, free trade, and, above all, less stringent regulation of the securities industry. Many of them invest in U.S. companies that have high labor costs, so they don't express any large measure of sympathy for labor unions. They're for improving public education, although most don't send their children to public schools. They don't believe the rich are overtaxed, and they don't mind paying their fair share. As Michael Bloomberg put it, "Our country gave you the opportunity— now pay back your share and get on with it." During a question-and-answer session at a corporate meeting, Warren Buffett was once asked how he would rewrite the tax code. He responded that he would impose heavy taxes on consumption and inheritance. These men have enough of an appreciation of where they came from and where they are to realize that further reductions of capital-gains and estate taxes are excessive.

On racial issues, the New Moneycrats are putatively liberals, opposed to discrimination and for affirmative action. This stance is perhaps because they have a true knowledge of the degree to which Wall Street and corporate America generally remain bastions of white maledom. But the New Moneycrats don't always practice what they preach. The corporate cultures at Bloomberg, Goldman, Sachs, Bankers Trust, and Lazard are not particularly conducive to women and minorities, despite the fact that these firms' leading lights are Democrats. Many private equity and buyout firms, even those run by Democrats, employ not a single nonwhite professional. Several New Moneycrats, to their credit, have backed programs like Prep for Prep, the New York–based organization that identifies promising inner-city kids, offers them enrichment programs, and then places them in exclusive prep schools. Several others have supported the National Academy Foundation, which helps prepare (mostly minority) high school students for jobs in the financial services industry.

The New Moneycrats have also helped provide jobs for another class of needy people: burned-out Democrats. Historically, Democrats sick of the low pay and long hours in administration or congressional jobs stayed in Washington to become lobbyists or fled to academic posts, whereas Republicans more frequently left town to return to their beloved private sector. After the 1992 Republican loss, for example, several Bush appointees left for high-powered Old Establishment corporate posts. Energy Secretary Samuel Skinner became CEO of Chicago utility Unicom, and Defense Secretary Dick Cheney became CEO of oil-services company Halliburton.

During the Clinton years, some of the most prominent Clintonites fled north to take academic sinecures and to do what they do best: talk. But several Clintonites ended up with investment banks. Richard Holbrooke, the combative diplomat, joined investment bank Credit Suisse First Boston as vice chairman in between diplomatic appointments. Roger Altman returned to New York and started a new buyout firm, Evercore. (Evercore was the adviser on the largest media deal of the decade, the 1999 blockbuster merger between Viacom and CBS.) Rahm Emanuel, the contentious presidential adviser, joined Bruce Wasserstein's gang of merry dealsters. Erskine Bowles, the courtly chief of staff who held his nose through the Lewinsky scandal, became affiliated with buyout firm Forstmann, Little, which is run by the arch-Republican Forstmann brothers.

The Clinton appointee who made the biggest splash on Wall Street in the 1990s was Frank Newman. The chief financial officer of California giant BankAmerica, Newman joined the administration in 1993 as deputy treasury secretary. In 1995, looking to boost his $133,600-a-year salary, he took the top post at Bankers Trust. The large bank had hit a rough spot as customers such as Procter & Gamble had charged it with misleading them in the sale of exotic securities. Newman was an attractive candidate not because of his prior job experience at BankAmerica—CFOs rarely make it to the top spot—but because of his government service. Newman took to the role of New Moneycrat with a vengeance. He spent $3 billion on investment banks Alex. Brown and Wolfensohn & Co. Newman helped organize the May 13, 1996, White House coffee that included the president, Treasury Secretary Robert Rubin, Controller Eugene Ludwig, and the CEOs of a dozen-odd major banks. (Newman later hired Ludwig as vice chairman.) In November 1998, he engineered the $9 billion sale of Bankers Trust to Deutsche Bank. For his troubles, he received a platinum parachute: an annual salary and bonus of at least $11 million until the end of 2003, plus a balloon payment of $14 million. This princely sum didn't seem to anger the man who had appointed Newman and who in 1992 had railed against excessive executive compensation. Perhaps that's the ultimate expression of the Democratization of Money: Even a Democrat can take egregious liberties with the public company he runs and still be regarded as a corporate statesman.

In addition to running for office or taking appointed posts, the New Moneycrats have influenced politics by backing, en masse, certain candidates. One of the main beneficiaries of such support was Charles Schumer, the longtime Brooklyn congressman who in 1998 embarked upon what could have been a career-ending run against Alphonse D'Amato. New York City, a Democratic bastion, had twice elected a Republican mayor, and the state was set to return a Republican governor to office. In D'Amato, Schumer was facing one of the more vicious campaigners and relentless fundraisers around. As chairman of the Senate Banking Committee, D'Amato was responsible for legislation affecting the financial services industry. As such, he was able to make Wall Street executives offers they couldn't refuse. By spring 1998, D'Amato had $10.6 million cash on hand, and he would ultimately raise $27 million for the cycle.

D'Amato may have had the balls of many New Moneycrats in his hands, but Schumer had their hearts and minds, and that ultimately proved to be more important. Schumer, after all, was stamped from the same machine that had produced so many New Moneycrats. A postwar child of middle-class Brooklyn, Schumer was a graduate of Harvard University and Harvard Law. His brother, Robert, is a mergers and acquisitions lawyer with Paul, Weiss, the former home of Democratic legal powerhouse Arthur Liman. The firm's members donated more than $60,000 to Schumer between 1997 and 1999. Furthermore, as a high-ranking member of the House Banking Committee, Schumer had generally voted with the securities industry. Early on in the 1998 campaign cycle, he linked up with the big-time New Moneycrats. "There is no lack of people out there who want to network," said Steve Rattner, an early backer. "But Chuck stands out in a crowd because of his intellect and ideas."

Other Wall Street supporters included James Dimon, the longtime protégé of Sanford Weill. Dimon and his wife gave $8,000 to Schumer between 1995 and 1998 and held a fundraiser for him in fall 1997. This activism was potentially self-destructive, since Dimon was president of Travelers, the financial services conglomerate that had many interests before D'Amato's Senate Banking Committee. "I wanted to do the right thing for my country, not my company," as he put it. (The remark is particularly telling about an era in which people express civic commitment and patriotism by giving their money rather than their time or their lives.) That kind of sentiment may have led to Dimon's departure from Travelers in November 1998, after fifteen years at Weill's side. Others giving Schumer the maximum $2,000 in the 1998 cycle included James Cramer, Alan Patricof, Steven Roth, and Jon Corzine

By spring 1998, Schumer had $8.2 million in the bank, more than four times the combined total of his two rivals, fading icon Geraldine Ferraro and New York City Public Advocate Mark Green. Schumer easily outpolled both in the September primary. Barely pausing for breath, he launched into the fall election season. (Schumer is a political force of nature—I once spent a day with him in his district and needed two days to recover. As we trekked from a street fair in an orthodox Jewish neighborhood in Midwood to the Ancient Order of Hibernians in Gerritsen Beach, Schumer stopped to engage anybody and everybody in conversation, debating everything from Israel's policy toward the PLO to the stench emanating from a waste disposal site.)

Taking his act upstate, Schumer proved an excellent and tireless campaigner. But the real key to his success against D'Amato was his ability to borrow Senator Pothole's tactics: aggressive fundraising, which paid for relentless attack advertisements. In October 1998, New York's airwaves were flooded with reductive, simplistic, and clinically effective negative ads about D'Amato's ethics and his judgment. "Too many lies for too long," read one. Seemingly unable to cope with such an attack, D'Amato contributed to his own demise, referring to Schumer as a "putzhead" in front of a Jewish organization. As the polls began to tilt in Schumer's favor, his campaign received continual boosts from Clinton and the New Moneycrats. The president and the First Lady visited New York several times in fall 1998, helping Schumer gain coverage and funds. On October 13, Clinton came to town for a $10,000-a-head fundraiser at Steven Rattner's place, which was cohosted by Harvey Weinstein, Seagram's heir Matthew Bronfman, investor Dirk Ziff, and *Rolling Stone* founder Jann Wenner, among others. The same night, Clinton appeared at a $1,000-a-head fundraiser for Schumer at the New York Hilton, which attracted 600 people. It wasn't just the money but also the *appearance* of raising money that helped give Schumer's campaign momentum.

Schumer ultimately crushed D'Amato, winning by a 54 percent to 44 percent majority. Interestingly, Schumer won a far larger majority among the well-off electorate. Voters making between $75,000 and $100,000 favored Schumer by a 58-42 margin, and New Yorkers who made more than $100,000 went for Schumer by a stunning 62-37 majority. Schumer's victory rid the Clintons of one of their most shameless and abusive critics. (D'Amato had spearheaded the ultimately fruitless hearings looking into the Clintons' financial affairs.) More important, Schumer's victory gave Clinton another solid anti-impeachment vote in the Senate. A grateful Al Gore came to New York to attend a victory party for Schumer at Jamie Dimon's Park Avenue home. In the end, Schumer was outspent by D'Amato, $27.4 million to $15.5 million. But the fact that Schumer raised that much money to challenge an incumbent, and one that chaired the Senate Banking Committee, was nothing short of astonishing. The securities and investment industry was Schumer's biggest source of funds, providing $1.29 million, compared with $1.75 million for D'Amato.

Schumer's victory put him in a unique position: He was the only person to vote against impeachment in the House during its lame-duck session, and to vote against it in the Senate. Throughout the impeachment process, the captains of the financial industry either remained silent or quietly lent Clinton support. Although it's difficult to prove that this quiescence made a difference in the congressional votes, it was nonetheless important. If the heads of large investment banks, money-center banks, and brokerages had viewed Clinton's travails as a threat to the stability of the markets, they would not have hesitated to make their opinions known. And if these influential individuals, many of whom had supported Clinton, had begun publicly to question the viability of a Clinton presidency, this view would have given a huge boost to the impeachment forces.

Quite the opposite occurred. After all, on Wall Street—as in Holly-wood—alpha males with large sexual appetites are quite common. Those who refuse to do business with executives who have ditched their first wives for airplane stewardesses, or who chase models or fool around with twentysomething women, will quickly find themselves lonely and broke. Most Wall Streeters recognized the spectacle of phi-landerers and serial husbands decrying Clinton's loose morals for what it was: hypocritical partisanship. In fall 1998, amid the growing clamor for impeachment, a full-page advertisement appeared in the *New York Times* that called for censure rather than impeachment. The signers read like the guest list for CNBC's *Power Lunch*: Patricof and Rattner, to name only two. As the impeachment ordeal continued, Clinton time and again turned to the New Moneycrats for support and solace. In August 1998, after the Hamptons extravaganza, Clinton retreated to Martha's Vineyard and attended a dinner party at Rattner's. He returned to New York City frequently for fundraisers. And the reception at the Wall Street project in January 1999 doubtless buoyed the belea-guered president.

The ascendance of the New Moneycrats has produced the series of highly competitive Democratic presidential primaries. At first, it seemed as if Richard Gephardt, the House minority leader and a dyed-in-the-wool Old Democrat, would challenge Gore on precisely the Clinton administration's embrace of the Wall Street agenda. His 1999 book, *An Even Better Place*, was larded with language critical of corporate America. Gephardt aimed to "open a debate about the role businesses play in the world economy," but he lamented that when he and his allies had called on businesses to abide by a code of conduct, the "White House strongly opposed our efforts." The problem? "More so than any other recent Democrat, Bill Clinton has embraced the concerns of business owners and managers." With chapter headings such as "The Tragedy of NAFTA," *An Even Better Place* had all the makings of a fire-and-brimstone Old Democrat campaign manifesto. Indeed, a Gephardt candidacy would have guaranteed an all-out debate over the party's tilt away from some of its historical bases and toward the markets—a battle for the soul of the Democratic party.

In February 1999, Gephardt announced he would forgo a presidential run and focus instead on winning back control of the House. With Gephardt declining to run, Gore faced an unlikely challenge from former New Jersey Senator Bill Bradley—a politician whose political background is remarkably similar to the vice president's. Both contenders are prototypical New Moneycrat candidates: Ivy League–educated creatures of the East Coast meritocracy, comfortable among the New Establishment, conversant with the lingo of technology and free trade. At first it appeared as if Gore would have the New Moneycrats to himself. Ever the diligent student, Gore began early to cultivate high-level Wall Street executives as advisers, contributors, and supporters. He served as the host of many White House coffees. In August 1998, amid the Russian debt crises, he invited a group of Wall Streeters to Washington, among them Steve Rattner, George Soros, Hank Greenberg, CEO of American International Group, and hedge-fund manager David Shaw, a $220,000 soft-money man in the 1998 cycle. Said Shaw: "I was surprised when I met him how much he knew about the economy and finance." In November 1998, about sixty of Wall Street's best and brightest showed up for a Gore fundraising luncheon at the epicenter of Gotham's power grid, the Four Seasons—the Philip

Johnson–designed restaurant in the Seagram Building, owned by
Edgar Bronfman Jr., a New Moneycrat in good standing. (He gave at
least $435,000 in soft money in 1995 and 1996 alone.)

Gore sailed along smoothly for much of 1999, raising $8.9 million
in the first quarter. In a single day in May, he harvested $1.5 million
from New York's rich fishing waters. In addition to relying on veterans
of the Clinton fundraising wars, Gore commissioned new officers, like
Orin Kramer, a hedge-fund manager who had worked on Carter's
domestic-policy staff. Kramer has been a huge soft-money donor—
$315,000 between 1997 and 1999 alone.

But Bradley tapped into the same rich vein of political gold.
Although Gore had a huge head start, the long-legged former senator
quickly gained on the front-runner. Bradley was even more appealing
to some New Moneycrats than Gore. After all, he played college hoops
at Princeton, worked in midtown Manhattan for ten years as a member
of the New York Knicks, and represented New Jersey in the Senate for
three terms. His leading supporters included New Moneycrats such as
Lou Susman, the vice chairman of Salomon Smith Barney, and Len
Riggio, the Brooklyn-born proprietor of Barnes & Noble, who hosted a
fundraiser for Bradley in the Hamptons. With their support, Bradley
elbowed his way into the money race. By December 1999, Bradley
raised $18 million to Gore's $24 million. In the first eight months of
1999, Bradley raised almost $1.6 million from the securities and invest-
ment industry, nearly twice as much as Gore.

In fact, New York—not Iowa or New Hampshire—may have proved
to be the most crucial primary battleground. As John Moore put it in a
National Journal article, "For money, there's no place like New York
City's upper east side, especially zip code 10021, a Golconda of campaign cash for Democratic candidates." In the first half of 1999, Bradley
raised $377,000 in the district bounded by East Sixty-first Street, Fifth
Avenue, East Eightieth Street, and the East River. Gore collected
$323,000 in the same period. George W. Bush, who had out-fundraised

both Democrats by a large margin, reeled in only $267,720 from the so-called silk-stocking district.

The New Moneycrats ensured the vigorous, hard-fought primary between Bradley and Gore. And regardless of who wins, it's likely that an effluence of soft money from Wall Street will continue to flow into the Democrats' coffers. For the money and other support the New Moneycrats have lent to Clinton and his allies is as much a cultural as it is a political statement. Much has been made of the Republicans' remarkable transformation in the 1990s: the explosion from congressional minority to majority, growth in the south and the sunbelt, the party's captivity to fundamentalist voters. These changes have affected the Republicans' policy initiatives, to be sure. But the evolution of the Republican party has had implications for Wall Street and the realm of money as well. As Democrats rose on Wall Street, and in Wall Street's eyes, Republicans retreated.

The leaders of the new Republican party rose to power on the wings of resentment and antipathy for the Northeastern elite and the philosophy and values they represent. Once in power, significant parts of the Republican political elite began to question many of the political and social issues that leading Wall Street figures accepted as gospel. Congressional Republicans took actions that were directly inimical to the interests of investors large and small. As a result, the New Moneycrats, naturally inclined to be Democrats by education and upbringing, have found themselves at odds with the increasingly downscale Republican party. This tilt away from its historical alignment with Wall Street and money has opened up fissures in the Grand Old Party, which have yet to be resolved even by the ascendance of George W. Bush.

7

The Republican Retreat

*P*residential campaign announcements are generally tedious affairs. Surrounded by beaming family members, hangers-on, and rented friends, candidates ascend flag-bedecked podiums, recount their glorious careers, and describe, in painful detail, exactly how they will remedy every social ill befalling the nation, from Alzheimer's to the insidious zebra mussel. To compound matters, candidates in this era of omnimedia regard campaign kickoffs as branding events. To reinforce the fact they are running, they frequently announce more than once. On January 21, 1999, former Vice President Dan Quayle used the celebrity-friendly platform of *Larry King Live* to *announce* that he would be *announcing* his candidacy. "What I am going to announce tonight to you and to your listeners is that I, next week, will file a statement of candidacy for my presidency—my presidential run. On February third, I will have a major announcement in Indianapolis. On February fourth, I have an announcement in Phoenix."

Quayle's announcement process lasted almost as long as his stillborn campaign. (He dropped out in September.) But his conversation with the unctuous septuagenarian was noteworthy for his comments about money. Quayle is, in many ways, the classic rich boy: a scion of a newspaper dynasty whose next private-sector job outside the family business will likely be his first. But here was Quayle, lamenting the growth of income inequality. "If you own stock, if you're a CEO of a company, if you've got stock options, if you've been a corporate officer in a recent merger acquisition, you're fat and happy," he told King. "But I tell you what, if you're out there working every day with your hands, teaching, whatever the case may be, you are having a tough time making it." (Quayle's idea of working with his hands is carrying his own golf bag.)

The exchange that followed was remarkable:

> KING: With that description are you saying Clinton has been good for the Republicans?
>
> QUAYLE: Well, if you describe Republicans as fat cats, but there are a lot of fat-cat Democrats. As a matter of fact, the real rich are Democrats.
>
> KING: Really.
>
> QUAYLE: Oh, sure. The head of Disney, Warren Buffett, all these guys—these are big Democrats. They're not Republicans.

Dan Quayle may not be the best example of anything, save George Bush's poor judgment in choosing a vice president. But his willingness to strike out at the wealthy, and his eagerness to paint the "real rich" as loyal Democrats, highlighted an important trend that gathered strength during the 1990s. Neither the rise of the New Moneycrats nor the profitable alliance between Wall Street and the Democratic party was inevitable. These developments were made possible only by the remarkable transformation of the Republican party and by its retreat from Wall Street.

For much of the twentieth century, the Republican mantle hung about Wall Street as snugly as a shahtoosh scarf caresses the shoulders of a Madison Avenue shopper. Most of the great names on Wall Street were reliable Republicans, from J. P. Morgan on down the line. The Rockefeller Republicans, that august group of Ivy League–educated, moderate establishmentarians, betokened the inherited affiliation of tremendous Wall Street wealth with the party of Lincoln. This group sent its representatives to serve in every post–World War II Republican administration. C. Douglas Dillon, of Dillon Read, was Eisenhower's ambassador to France; Donald Regan, the chief executive officer of Merrill Lynch, became Reagan's treasury secretary and chief of staff; John Whitehead, the cochairman of Goldman from 1976 to 1984, was a deputy secretary of state for Reagan; Nicholas Brady, the onetime chairman of Dillon Read, served as George Bush's treasury secretary.

In the 1980s, a new crop of financial operators arose who considered themselves latter-day Rockefellers—billionaires such as Ron Perelman and Henry Kravis, T. Boone Pickens and the Forstmann brothers. All were Republicans. For most of this century, voting Republican was an activity the wealthy did en masse, like driving Cadillacs and joining country clubs. Through the 1980s, those making more than $75,000 a year—when $75,000 was real money—gave Republican presidential candidates vast majorities. Reagan won 69 percent of this demographic slice in 1984, and Bush garnered 62 percent of it in 1988. As late as 1992, only 32 percent of those making more than $75,000 voted for the Democratic presidential candidate.

But things changed quickly in the 1990s. Stung by being identified with preppy, Northeastern wealth in the 1992 campaign, the Republicans of the 1990s went downscale in a hurry. As the decade wore on, they increasingly defined themselves in opposition to what they viewed as a corrupt Northeastern elite. While Clintonites rocked to the strains of Hootie and the Blowfish, the Republicans went country, trading in Talbot's and Brooks Brothers for Wal-Mart and Garth Brooks, the Hamptons for Hampton Roads, Virginia.

Many Republicans began rooting for the failure of Clinton, a pretender who had failed to gain a true majority, from the chill day of his inauguration. This bias helped tilt the Republicans against Wall Street, because for Clinton to be invalidated, the economy and the markets would have to tumble. As Clinton began to play the bond market, the historical boosters of prosperity began to pray fervently for economic disaster. The apocalyptic rhetoric surrounding Clinton's first budget proposal in 1993 set the tone. Pete Domenici, the otherwise sober-minded Senate Budget Committee chairman, said Clinton's tax increase and budget-deficit reduction package would "devastate the economy." Sen. Phil Gramm, a former Texas A&M economics professor, drew upon his knowledge of America's private sector—a place he visited frequently to raise political funds—and concluded that the Clinton budget would throw the nation into a deep recession and send the stock market into a years-long funk. "I believe this program is going to make the economy weak. I believe hundreds of thousands of people are going to lose their jobs. I believe Bill Clinton will be one of those people," he said. The Gipper himself came out of retirement for one last battle. "The simple truth is that this plan is bad for America," Ronald Reagan wrote in a *New York Times* op-ed piece August 3, just days before the climactic House vote. "And I worry about America's place in the world if our economy falls into the deep doldrums that the program will certainly bring."

On August 5, 1993, the House of Representatives passed the Clinton budget by a single vote, 218-216, with first-termer Marjorie Margolies-Mezvinsky (D-Pennsylvania) providing the margin of victory. All 175 House Republicans voted against it, joined by 41 Democrats. The Senate vote the next day was even closer. The plan was supported by 50 Democrats and opposed by 44 Republicans and 6 Democrats, including Frank Lautenberg and Sam Nunn. Vice President Al Gore had to cast the deciding vote.

Unfortunately for the Republicans, the economic catastrophes they warned about failed to materialize. Instead of a loss of jobs, as Gramm predicted, the economy began to add millions of jobs. Rather than slip into recession within a year, as then-House Minority Leader Newt Gingrich boldly predicted, the country continued to coast along nicely. As quarter after quarter unfolded, interest rates declined, the stock market rose, and employment expanded. And as the markets refused to validate their fears and hopes, Republicans soured on the markets.

Unable to run on Clinton's poor stewardship of the economy in the 1994 congressional elections, the Republicans ran—and ran effectively—against ill-conceived Clinton initiatives such as nationalizing health care, and on their party's focus group–tested "Contract with America." The shocking results of the election would have far-reaching implications for the party's stance toward Wall Street, money, and the New Moneycrats. For the first time since 1954, the Republicans held a majority in the House of Representatives. As they lost ground in the prosperous Northeast, Republicans gained concentration in the poorest areas of the country, areas historically hostile to the center of capital, to meritocratic elitism, to cities populated by various ethnic groups, and to internationalism—the very pillars of Wall Street's New Moneycrat faith.

The revolutionary Republicans of 1994 were of an entirely different stripe from the Clintonites and the New Moneycrats—and from the dwindling numbers of Northeastern Republicans. Born in the backwoods, Bill Clinton relied on a combination of native intelligence, charm, and will to make his way into the establishment. By contrast, the southern Republican leaders of the 1990s were born in the backwoods and apparently possessed neither the brains nor the desire to

escape and have a broader experience. For much of the past thirty
years, many of the best minds and brightest lights of the Republican
party—Henry Kissinger, James Baker, George Shultz, William Kris-
tol—came from Harvard, Yale, and Princeton. But the Republican
leaders of the 1990s were incubated in a vastly different environment.
Gingrich, the self-described CEO of the House, attended Emory and
Tulane and taught at backwaters like West Georgia College. When
searching for a House historian, he trolled the depths of academia and
plucked Christina Jeffery from Kennesaw State in Georgia. "I initially
spent a semester at Vassar but I got C's and hated the whole liberal environment," she said. Gingrich's chief operating officer, Majority Leader
Richard Armey, attended Jamestown College and the University of
Montana, received his Ph.D. from the University of Oklahoma, and
taught at the University of North Texas before being elected to
Congress in 1984. Jon Kasich, the newly installed pork-slaughtering
chairman of the House Budget Committee, got his first job in the state
legislature soon after graduating from Ohio State in 1974 and successfully ran for office three years later. Whereas Democrats were banking
on experienced Wall Streeters like Robert Rubin and Arthur Levitt, the
vast majority of the ascendant congressional Republicans had virtually
no personal, professional, or cultural ties to Wall Street.

Thus it came as no surprise that after the election, the revolutionary
Republicans were unwilling to pay proper obeisance to the Street's pre-
rogatives. When Mexico hit thorny economic difficulty in 1994, the
freshmen's hatred of Clinton and desire for financial mayhem mixed in
a lethal cocktail. Helping Mexico through a rough spot would have
seemed a natural move for most Republicans. After all, the crisis was
threatening the stability of the U.S. stock and bond markets. The
Republican minority had boldly helped push through NAFTA in late
1993. And the Bush administration had been closely identified with
helping bring stability to Latin America. In 1990, Treasury Secretary
Nicholas Brady bestowed his name upon a class of dollar-denominated

bonds, collateralized with U.S. Treasuries, created from pools of non-performing loans that had been made to Latin American governments.

But most of the newly sworn-in freshmen thought Brady bonds probably had something to do with the 1970s TV sitcom. On January 11, 1995, Clinton formally asked Congress to approve a $40 billion package, under which Mexico would use U.S. loan guarantees to replace up to $28 billion in short-term, dollar-indexed bonds with long-term bonds. By forestalling repayment of interest in dollars, which had become very expensive due to the plummeting peso, this action would have given Mexico some breathing room. Senate Majority Leader Bob Dole and Speaker Gingrich signed on, but many Republicans were unwilling to go along. The youngsters ignored the pleas of their elders such as former presidents Bush and Ford. Not even half the Republicans in Congress were willing to come to the rescue of their NAFTA partner, despite the fact that Mexico's collapse had serious implications for Wall Street executives and for individual investors. After all, publicly held banks like J. P. Morgan and Bear Stearns had huge financial exposure to Mexico and Latin America. These were core holdings in many portfolios. Furthermore, mutual funds were stocked with Mexican blue chips such as Telmex.

So while Wall Street waited eagerly for congressional approval, Congress dithered. On January 25, Robert Rubin, Alan Greenspan, and Warren Christopher came to the House to make the case for Clinton's proposal. But their plea fell on deaf ears. It was plain that most Republicans were less favorably disposed to the Mexicans than to the Clinton administration. After all, most prominent Republicans—with the exception of Jack Kemp—had enthusiastically embraced California's Proposition 187, the punitive measure that denied illegal Mexican immigrants various educational and welfare services. Sen. Jesse Helms, the newly installed chairman of the Senate Foreign Relations Committee, drawled, "Maybe it's time to consider a dose of tough love for our neighbor to the south." Phil Gramm, so wrongly pessimistic about the

U.S. economy, had suddenly became a great optimist. Leaving Mexico to its own devices wouldn't be so bad. "Mexico will be forced to restructure . . . They won't have the liquidity bridge they would have had and that will make it harder. But if the restructuring is sound, it will work."

Faced with such opposition, Clinton acted unilaterally at the end of January, coupling credit from the U.S. Exchange Stabilization Fund with funds from the International Monetary Fund that would grant Mexico an amount of credit roughly equivalent to that in Clinton's original proposal. But no sooner had the flames been doused than Republicans rolled out their bellows and started fanning the embers. In March 1995, New York Sen. Alphonse D'Amato proposed limiting loans from the stabilization fund to $5 billion in any twelve-month period. (Like so many of the senator's cockamamie stunts, it failed.) In July 1995, when the United States granted Mexico $2.5 billion more in credit, D'Amato and Dole complained in a letter to Rubin. Later that month, the House voted 254-183 to prohibit the fund from being used to bolster a foreign currency. That vote marked the first time in history that the Republican majority passed a measure drafted by a socialist— Bernard Sanders of Vermont.

Later in 1995, the Republican majority engaged in more behavior that threatened the stability of America's capital markets. The government shutdowns that Newt Gingrich engineered in late 1995 and early 1996 had little effect on Wall Street and the wealthy—other than to shut down passport offices for a few days. But they were fraught with the potential to wreak havoc in the bond market. Interest rates spiked after the first shutdown in November, reaching 6.244 percent on November 24. For the next several weeks, they careened around like a pinball. After the second shutdown in December, bonds and the dollar went south. Interest rates likely would have risen far higher had Robert Rubin not taken action. Over a several-week period, the mild-mannered treasury secretary averted crises by shifting $61.3 billion in two government-employee retirement funds out of Treasury securities and into cash to meet obligations. But his efforts earned him nothing but opprobrium from the Republican Congress. "If he goes much further, without a doubt, that's an impeachable act," said New York Rep. Gerald Solomon on January 4, 1996. Solomon's comments caused the thirty-year bond's yield to rise from 5.95 percent to 6.03 percent. By mid-January, as the second shutdown dragged on, the thirty-year bond spiked again, to 6.14 percent. And when Rubin began to voice concern that the U.S. government might default on its debts, Gingrich dismissed him. The former cochair of Goldman "doesn't have, frankly, very much standing [on Capitol Hill] right now," Gingrich said.

The 1996 presidential campaign provided more evidence that the Republicans could no longer be counted on as reliable allies of Wall Street. As Clinton shifted from the traditional class-warfare rhetoric to Reaganesque optimism, the Republicans began to adopt old-style Democratic politics of resentment. The party of Rockefeller was now particularly self-conscious about its lack of identification with Wall Street. As Republican National Committee Chairman Haley Barbour liked to say, "We're the party of Main Street, not Wall Street, the party of bass boats, not yachts."

To be sure, Republican candidates in 1996 reflexively sang from the Reagan hymnal on the importance of cutting taxes and reducing the capital gains tax. But in some ways, it was the fringe presidential candidates who represented the Republican ancien régime. Morry Taylor was the only true big businessman in the bunch. A genuine midwestern industrialist, he had built Titan International into a $620 million tire manufacturer. Also joining the fray was Steve Forbes, the publisher of *Forbes* magazine, a tractate of the supply-side Talmud. Possessed of an unshakable belief in the power of economics and money to alter human behavior, Forbes may have been the first Marxist to compete actively for the Republican nomination. But Taylor and Forbes ultimately proved marginal. Taylor failed to attract the attention of anybody save the writer Michael Lewis and received less than 1 percent of

the vote. And Forbes, despite spending $37 million of his personal for-
tune, garnered just 1,424,898 votes—or $26 per vote.

Meanwhile, running hard on the legacy of Reagan, for whom he
worked, Pat Buchanan sometimes sounded like Studs Terkel. In March
1996, he proclaimed, "Someone has got to stand up for the working-
men and -women of America who don't have no representatives at
these trade negotiations where they decide what industries are going to
live and what are going to die. It is wrong to negotiate trade deals for the
benefit of transnational corporations that encourage them to shut down
their plants in Toledo and Youngstown and to open up a plant in Sin-
gapore or China because that takes away jobs from American workers
and hollows out our manufacturing base." At the February 15 debate in
New Hampshire, Buchanan, reading either from his crib notes or the
Protocols of the Elders of Zion, lashed out at the economic policies of
"Mr. Greenspan and Mr. Rubin." (When he spoke of perfidious Wall
Street firms, it was always Goldman, Sachs—an obviously Jewish
name—and never Morgan Stanley.) Multinational companies, run by
cosmopolitans, were unpatriotic and treasonous. "Some of the biggest
companies in America don't care about America. They care about profits." Buchanan won New Hampshire and, though generally running
second in subsequent contests, managed to pull more than 21 percent
of the Republican primary vote.

Although his language was less incendiary than that used by
Buchanan, Dole, the eventual nominee, neatly embodied some of the
contradictions within the Republican party. Like most of his congressional colleagues, he had few personal connections to Wall Street. His
idea of big business was Archer Daniels Midland, the grain giant whose
longtime chief executive, Dwayne Andreas, had dispensed numerous
favors to Dole over the years. Like most of the top Republicans in
Congress, Dole had never received a paycheck signed by anyone other
than John Q. Public. He served in the army, attended a public university, became a district attorney, and then ran for elected office. In his

1996 presidential campaign, Dole at first tried to sound the old Republican lines about money and taxes. With "it's your money," he coined one of the more vapid campaign slogans in recent memory. But he continually stepped on his own line. Dole had long exhibited a tendency to class warfare. He had tweaked Bush during the 1988 primary by saying, "I didn't have rich and powerful parents." At one 1996 debate, he turned on Steve Forbes: "I know your problem. You have a lot of money. You want to buy this election. But this election is not for sale." In his acceptance speech, Dole denounced the focus on the economy. "The triumph of this nation lies not in its material wealth but in courage, sacrifice, and honor." At another point, he asked, "Which is more important, wealth or honor?" Dole would ultimately answer that question by going to work as a lobbyist and as a shill for products ranging from VISA to Viagra.

As Clinton trumpeted morning in America, Dole warned that America was in the gloaming. In *Trusting the People*, Dole charged that Clinton was "reigning over the first recovery since World War II to leave the American worker behind." At a speech in Chicago in August, he asked his audience to remember the "forgotten worker" and blasted the Clinton administration's economic stewardship. "The dirty little secret of its middle class-squeeze economy is that the income of the middle class has fallen, even as the rich have gotten richer. . . . Think about it: What Clintonomics means is that the rich are getting richer while the middle class gets left behind." Dole's program—a 15 percent across-the-board tax cut and a reduction in capital-gains taxes by half— was ostensibly a sop to the rich. But the Republicans had been so cowed by the Democrats' prior successful class-warfare rhetoric that they were very sensitive about appearing to ally themselves with big companies, Wall Street, and the wealthy. (When Buchanan wanted to get under Dole's prickly skin, he referred to him as "Beltway Bob of the Business Roundtable." That this label was regarded as a slur was a sign of how things had changed.) Cutting income and capital-gains taxes,

Dole and Kemp noted, "will provide urgently needed fuel to the real engines of job creation—small businesses and aspiring entrepreneurs." They also stated that "over half of the people who pay taxes on capital gains earn less than $50,000 a year." The plan further offered to slash capital gains for those in the lowest tax bracket to a low—very low—7.5 percent. A chart in the Dole-Kemp campaign book, *Trusting the People*, broke down how much the tax cut would save differently situated families. Ended with a hypothetical family that made $100,000; ignored were the top earners putatively in the Republican base.

The attempt to go downscale bore fruit, of sorts. In the 1996 election, Dole received 54 percent of the vote of those making more than $100,000, while Clinton received 40 percent and Perot 5 percent. Among voters making $75,000–$100,000 (the top 16 percent), Dole squeaked by with a 49-44 plurality. These figures represented huge gains for Clinton, who had received only 32 percent of the over-$75,000 voters in 1992. In both 1992 and 1996, Clinton carried Connecticut, New Jersey, and New York—the first time a Democratic candidate had carried all three pockets of wealth since Lyndon Johnson did in 1964. Meanwhile, the Republicans continued to gain ground in the poorer states. After the 1996 campaign, Republicans held an 82-55 edge in congressional seats in the South—36 percent of their caucus hailed from Dixie.

The Republican retreat from the precincts of money continued after the 1996 election. The most significant outcome of Dole's loss was the rise of Trent Lott to the post of Senate majority leader. Like his predecessor, Trent Lott was a private-sector virgin and a stranger to the meritocratic locales frequented by the New Moneycrats. After obtaining his undergraduate and law degrees from the University of Mississippi, he went to work for Rep. William Colmer, one of the more odious segregationists in the House, and was elected to Congress in 1972.

No sooner did Lott become majority leader than he revealed himself to be a man of the nineties—the 1890s. Time and again, he proved himself hostile to the values and issues important to both the New

Moneycrats and, significantly, to big business. As investors came to venerate Alan Greenspan, Lott expressed suspicion of the Federal Reserve Board's independence. Meanwhile, his brother-in-law, a plaintiff's attorney with the Faulknerian name of Richard "Dickie" Scruggs, was growing rich terrorizing Fortune 500 tobacco companies with mass tort actions. As Clinton chatted in Easthampton with well-off gay donors, Lott compared them to criminals. "You should try to show them a way to deal with that problem," he said of gays in June 1998, "just like alcoholism or sex addiction or kleptomania." And as Wall Street and corporate chieftains fell over themselves to embrace the goals of Jesse Jackson's Wall Street Project, Lott described 1950s-era Mississippi—a civilization that bestowed upon the nation such legacies as Sen. Theodore Bilbo, the State Sovereignty Commission, and the murder of Emmett Till—as a "good time for America." Lott also dissembled about his dealings with the Council of Conservative Citizens, a revanchist group of neosegregationists. "The people in this room stand for the right principles and the right philosophy," he told one CCC gathering.

It quickly became clear that Lott's idea of capitalism was a distinctly chicken-fried version. Mississippi, long one of the poorest states in the nation—in 1997 the state's per capita personal income was roughly half that of Connecticut's—had relied on gambling and government-sponsored shipbuilding for much of its growth. Ingalls Shipbuilding, based in Lott's hometown of Pascagoula, is the largest private employer in Mississippi, with 11,300 workers. In an era of relentless budget cutting, Lott took great pains to ensure that Ingalls got more than its fair share of government largesse. In 1999, he crammed $500 million in the military authorization bill to build a $1.5 billion small aircraft-carrier project at Ingalls. Never mind that the House had refused to pass funds for the craft, or that the Navy had never asked for that amount. As Tim Weiner of the *New York Times* noted, "All told, Mississippi military contractors and bases are in line to receive about $8 billion in the coming year."

Lott and Gingrich reigned over a Congress that was increasingly hostile to the markets and to the institutions that helped guarantee their stability. Increasingly suspicious of internationalist organizations, the Republicans began to view them as vehicles for exporting right-wing social policy. In 1997, before the Asian economic crisis hit, Republicans tried to block financing to the International Monetary Fund by linking the package to a provision banning U.S. funds from going to international groups that sponsored or funded agencies that provided family planning or abortion services. They lost the battle, but would find plenty of opportunity to continue the war.

In the wake of the Asian crisis of the summer and fall of 1997, the IMF undertook a drive to increase its capital base by 45 percent, or $285 billion. The United States was to contribute $18 billion—$14.5 billion to replenish the IMF's capital base and $3.5 billion to provide a new line of emergency credit. Like the Mexico bailout, this move was largely supported by the foreign policy establishment, Wall Street, and big business. But the contempt the Republicans had for Clinton and for Wall Street, so apparent in the Mexican economic crisis and the U.S. government shutdown, reared its head again. The Senate approved the contribution by a solidly bipartisan 84-16 margin in early 1998, but the measure stalled in the House.

In February 1998, the National Association of Manufacturers, one of the staunchest allies of congressional Republicans, wrote Gingrich begging him not to withhold the new funds because such action "would only worsen the Asian crisis and risk contagion around the world, severely damaging U.S. economic and security interests." The letter was signed not by Wall Streeters who had attended Clinton coffees and contributed to his coffers but by thirty-three rock-ribbed CEOs such as Donald Fites of Caterpillar, Jack Welch of General Electric, and Chris Galvin of Motorola. The letter had little effect on the House Republican caucus. The members' prevailing opinion was best expressed by House Whip Thomas DeLay, whose personal knowledge of business is limited to the extermination industry: "Our members aren't too thrilled about IMF in the first place." When House Republicans again said they would hold up financing for the IMF and dues owed to the United Nations until the White House agreed to an antiabortion provision, they incurred the wrath of other members of the establishment. "If we fail to act, we'll be sending a message that we're not interested in those markets," said Thomas J. O'Donohue, president of the ur-Republican U.S. Chamber of Commerce. Large U.S. companies such as Boeing, IBM, General Electric, and Motorola pleaded with the Republicans, as did farmers groups and trade associations like the National Foreign Trade Council. Succumbing to the pressure, Gingrich ultimately ironed out a deal with Robert Rubin in spring 1998. The IMF received the funding it needed.

Of course, there is legitimate room for debate about the IMF's role and the wisdom of bailing out large banks that made ill-advised loans. But the Republican opposition to the IMF was not merely intellectual; it was elemental. Remember the gales of laughter and applause that greeted Bob Dole's taunting pronunciation of the name of UN Secretary General Boutros Boutros-Ghali? The same Republicans who found the name funny opposed U.S. intervention in Bosnia and Kosovo, were reluctant to fund the IMF and the UN, and ultimately killed the Test Ban Treaty in 1999. In fact, the largely southern isolationists of the 1990s are heirs to the midwestern isolationists of generations gone by. In the 1910s, Republicans, led by Henry Cabot Lodge, killed the League of Nations treaty and fiddled while Europe burned. Robert Taft, Mr. Republican of the 1940s and 1950s, opposed the creation of not only the IMF but also the World Bank, the Marshall Plan, and NATO for good measure. In short, these modern-day isolationists, more at home with the Council of Conservative Citizens than the Council on Foreign Relations, are content to let the rest of the world go to hell. Richard Armey, the erstwhile intellectual, may have said it best: "I've been to Europe once. I don't have to go again."

Many of the newest Republicans simply couldn't understand the willingness of U.S. executives to regard the IMF funding as a priority. "If there's someone who worries more about a foreign economic crisis than the principle of U.S. taxpayer money going to repeal right-to-life laws, I haven't met them," said John Shadegg, a congressman from Arizona. Obviously, Shadegg had never been to the Hamptons or to the executive suite of the dozens of Fortune 500 companies headquartered in Chicago. Indeed, that's exactly the point. Republican congressmen are no longer interested in playing golf at Pebble Beach with the CEOs of multinational firms. They don't relax with entertainment moguls in Sun Valley. They share so little in terms of background, experience, culture, and worldview with the heads of Wall Street firms that they are literally strangers when it comes to policy. As Charles Mack of the Business-Industry Political Action Committee observed: "We can't figure out where a lot of the Republicans are on a lot of these issues. . . . Communications between the business community and Republicans have become a dialogue of the deaf."

Fully in the thrall of two reactionary southerners, the Republicans in Congress also proved themselves to be out of step with corporate America and Wall Street on issues like free trade and diversity. The Republican caucus, with its lone black member, was trying to dismantle affirmative action in all its forms even as establishment Wall Street firms were making great efforts to promote diversity. One of the grand ironies of the 1990s is that Fortune 500 companies, once among the most regressive of institutions, have emerged as champions of diversity. One J. P. Morgan ad campaign featured a Benetton-like rainbow of employees proclaiming, in various accents, "I work for J. P. Morgan." *Fortune's* annual issue on the best companies for diversity is a big seller. As evidenced by the attendance at the Wall Street Project convention in early 1999, executives like Michael Armstrong of AT&T and Richard Grasso of the New York Stock Exchange are not only comfortable rubbing elbows with Jesse Jackson; they have taken up the banner of Martin Luther King Jr.

Having divorced itself from Wall Street, the Republican party proceeded to make a muck of its marriage to big business. In the first half of 1999, business groups evenly split their donations between Democrats and Republicans; in the previous campaign cycle, Republicans received 61 percent of such donations. It wasn't only corporations that were moving away from Republicans and toward the more responsible Democrats. The rich were deserting the Republicans as well. In 1998, congressional Republicans saw their support among those making more than $100,000 slip to 55 percent from 64 percent in 1994. Among those making more than $75,000 a year, Republican support fell to 53 percent in 1998 from 62 percent in 1994. Meanwhile, Republicans' share of voters earning less than $15,000 rose to 41 percent in 1998 from 38 percent in 1994. By 1998, 82 of the 223 Republican seats—or 36.7 percent of their total—came from the South, up from 26 percent in 1990. The portion of the House Republican caucus hailing from the more prosperous, more moderate East fell from 24.5 percent in 1990 to 17 percent in 1998.

By the late 1990s, the party that once housed the wealthiest family in America—the Rockefellers—and had named an entire wing after them, was marginalizing such people. The only Rockefeller in public life today is Jay Rockefeller, a liberal Democrat from West Virginia. And the southern Republicans have been less than mindful of the remaining Rockefeller Republicans. In April 1998, President Clinton nominated William Weld, the popular governor of Massachusetts, as ambassador to Mexico. Weld was an archetypal Rockefeller Republican—whip-smart, a Harvard graduate, from old money, and socially moderate. But Jesse Helms held up his nomination, absurdly accusing him of being soft on drugs. Senate Majority Leader Trent Lott refused to lift a finger to help Weld, and the nomination was scuttled.

One true heir to the Rockefeller tradition remains in the House: Amory Houghton. The grandson and son of diplomats, and of CEOs of the family business, the Corning Glass Works, Houghton in 1986 ran successfully for Congress after twenty-two years at the helm of Corning.

As the only former CEO of a Fortune 500 company to serve in Congress, Houghton should be a valuable voice on issues ranging from health care to technology transfer, from the minimum wage to global trade. But Amo—as he's universally known—was never invited into Gingrich's inner circle. Worse, he openly questioned the party's antagonism toward international institutions like the IMF and its obsession with social issues over economic ones. As he told *Business Week*, "Businesspeople don't understand what abortion has to do with job creation." So out of step with the majority was Houghton that he openly parted company with them on the issue of President Clinton's impeachment. In early December 1998, he penned an op-ed piece in the *New York Times* calling for a "strong statement of rebuke" instead of impeachment. Houghton was one of four House Republicans to vote no on every count of impeachment.

The impeachment debacle brought some salutary results, including the self-immolations of Newt Gingrich and Robert Livingston. Their departure helped solidify the Republican retreat from money and big business. Gingrich's replacement, Dennis Hastert, though well-meaning and fundamentally decent, is a career teacher and politician with no connection to or experience with Wall Street and the private sector. Not surprisingly, then, congressional Republicans' unwillingness to work with Wall Street and to cater to the needs of big business has spilled over into the Republican presidential primary. During winter 1998 and into spring 1999, ten Republicans cheerfully announced their candidacy, jumping into the campaign waters as if they were actresses splashing into a pool in an Esther Williams musical. With eight years of economic growth and a Dow bumping along between 10,000 and 11,000, it has been morning in America for a long, long time. Thus the ten candidates couldn't offer prescriptions for America's economic woes. Instead, they quickly moved on to other topics: compassionate conservatism (George W. Bush); campaign finance reform (John McCain); an extra X chromosome (Elizabeth Dole); the idea of having ideas (Lamar Alexander); social issues (Steve Forbes, Gary Bauer, Dan Quayle, Orrin Hatch, Alan Keyes, among others); World War II revisionism (Pat Buchanan). Many of the candidates sought to gain the support of the party's core activists by running *against* money and the values of Wall Street and the investor class. Having ceded Talbot's and Nieman-Marcus shoppers to Bush and McCain, the rest of the field began pursuing what Gary Bauer called the Kmart crowd.

Dan Quayle stumbled out of the gate speaking like "an angry middle-aged populist who believes too much of the nation's prosperity is going to investors," as Gail Collins put it in the *New York Times*. Two-time loser Patrick Buchanan entered the race as the Republican tribune of the downtrodden English-speaking working folk left behind by the New Economy. "I will raise my voice on behalf of those Americans who are not being heard, and offer my hand to those who were not allowed to march in the great parade of American prosperity," he said in his announcement speech in New Hampshire on March 2, 1999—and left the party altogether soon thereafter. Gary Bauer also attempted to stake out ground on the far right by going after Wall Street and money. For the conservative policy intellectual, U.S. trade policy toward China was the ultimate symbol of how the nation's great ideals were being sacrificed on the altar of Mammon. In his announcement speech in April 1999, he condemned the "elites of America, in Hollywood, on Wall Street, and in Washington, D.C.," for forgetting that liberty comes from God.

One intriguing development of the early 2000 race was Steve Forbes's efforts to march out from his policy bunker—tax and money issues—onto the murky ground of morals. In 1996, Forbes staked whatever claim he had on America's attention by virtue of his status as a centimillionaire and a true-believing supply-sider. In subsequent years, Forbes clumsily branched out into an increasingly strident moralism. Out went the Robert Mapplethorpe pictures on the family yacht. In the prelude to the campaign, the once plausibly pro-choice candidate favored a proposal before the Republican National Committee to deny campaign funds to pro-choice candidates. By fall 1999, Forbes was tacking hard to the right, an exercise he must find particularly excruciating because he is not a natural campaigner. The closest he's come to a Kmart is in viewing the one near his Manhattan corporate headquarters through the tinted windows of a Town Car. On October 15, a day the Dow fell 266.9 points on fears of higher interest rates, Forbes posted the following on his Web site: "President Clinton and Fed Chairman Alan Greenspan are responsible for the turbulence in the markets. Their misguided policies are putting the American economy at risk. . . . The first to get hurt will be families, farmers, young people and minorities." For much of the past decade, as Greenspan oversaw a 500 percent rise in the Dow and the longest peacetime expansion in U.S. history, Forbes had kind words for the Fed chairman. But when the Dow dropped a few percentage points in campaign season, it was cause for condemnation. *Et tu*, Steve?

The Republican ambivalence toward money and Wall Street has been further complicated by the rise of George W. Bush. Bush entered the campaign similarly downplaying the importance of economics. Indeed, a candidate seeking the mantle of the party whose 1996 mantra was "it's your money," and whose father won a campaign by vowing "no new taxes," wanted to talk about everything *but* money and lower taxes. At one of his many campaign announcements, in Cedar Rapids, Iowa, on June 12, Bush said: "I'm running because our country must be prosperous. . . . But prosperity alone is simple materialism. Prosperity must have a greater purpose. The success of America has never been proven by cities of gold, but by citizens of character." To be sure, Bush toed the line on red-meat Republican issues. "I believe we should cut taxes to stimulate economic growth," he said in a July speech. But he continually undermined his own discourse to make the case for compassionate conservatism—which, as far as I can tell, means saying nice things about the poor and minorities. "Yet I know that economic growth is not the solution to every problem. A rising tide lifts many boats—but not all. Many prosper in a bull market—but not everyone."

Like Steve Forbes, Bush is an ambivalent product of the world for which his party has developed so much antagonism. A graduate of Yale who doesn't read books, a graduate of the Harvard Business School who largely failed in business, George W. Bush has been a classic under-achiever. Pitched into some rather competitive pools, he has remained afloat only because of the substantial ballast provided by the family name. A self-described C student—and an obvious beneficiary of affir-mative action for the wealthy and connected—Bush started his first oil company, inauspiciously named Arbusto Energy, in 1977. After it nearly went *el busto*, he changed its name, merged it with another firm, and finally sold it to Harken Energy Corporation in 1986. Bush sold most of his Harken stock in June 1990, just days before it announced a disas-trous quarterly loss; the stock quickly sank below $1 a share. In 1989, Bush used the only commercial asset he had—his name—to help bro-ker the deal for the financiers who bought the Texas Rangers baseball team. In exchange for contributing $500,000 (borrowed) to the $86 million purchase price and lending his connections to the purchase effort, Bush ultimately received an equity interest in the team and was named general partner. When the Rangers were sold in 1998 to Tom Hicks for $250 million, Bush's share came to $14.9 million. Fortunate son, indeed. He was born at home plate (my apologies to Ann Richards) and thinks he hit an inside-the-park home run.

Bush is plainly trying to reach an accommodation with money. His demand for "prosperity with purpose" is a rebuke of those who would argue that Republicans can return to glory by emphasizing only eco-nomics and taxes. But he has distanced himself from the Kmart candi-dates by issuing the appropriate utterances on free trade, China, and the early reappointment of Alan Greenspan. In turn, money seems to be reaching an accommodation with Bush, if only by virtue of his stunning fundraising record—$67 million in 1999. The numbers are certainly impressive but are easily given too much weight. Republican donors have a long tradition of lining up behind the heir apparent. Factor in a booming economy and eight years of consistently escalating hatred of Clinton, and any sod anointed by the Republicans as the front-runner would have put up great numbers. Besides, Bush's money is coming more from good old boys than from New Moneycrats. The vast majority of Bush's campaign lucre has come from outside New York, New Jersey, and Connecticut, the Democrats' most fertile fishing grounds. Indeed, Bush raised just 5 percent of his total from New York. To be sure, several prominent New Moneycrats have tossed $1,000 into George W.'s pot, including Steven Roth of Vornado. For them, however, this amount—equal to half the maximum donation—is chump change, limousine fare, an efficient hedge.

Bush has the pedigree and the policies to recapture the ground his party has lost among the wealthy. But he may have more difficulty recapturing the ground his party has lost among the investor class. To restore the party's reach, he—or any other candidate—will have to do more than pay the appropriate respect to Alan Greenspan. Over the past decade, the terrain underlying the relationship between money and politics has shifted in some unalterable ways. And the new politics of personal finance will provide opportunities and challenges for candidates of all stripes.

8

The New Politics
of Personal Finance

*F*or much of the past century, the major parties' use of
money and the markets has adhered to a familiar pattern. Democrats, or rare reform-minded Republicans
like Theodore Roosevelt, condemned "malefactors of
great wealth," railed against the disconnect between
Wall Street and Main Street, and laid the blame for
social woes at the feet of the rich. For their part, Republicans, depending on the state of the economy, adopt
postures ranging from defensiveness to admirable can-
dor about their identification with the rich and business.
As Calvin Coolidge put it, "This is a business country
. . . and it wants a business government."

With the determination of drunken stockbrokers

hitting on single women at a Thursday night happy hour, Silent Cal's heirs have stuck to the premise that if we just give companies and the rich a freer rein, their ingenuity and virtue will carry everyone along with them, that "a rising tide lifts all boats." (In yet another great irony of the interplay between money and politics, the author of that supply-side mantra was John F. Kennedy, the last Democratic president before Clinton to cut the capital-gains tax.) So the Republicans have advocated a series of policy initiatives intended to benefit the rich: lower taxes, less regulation, and low interest rates. Of course, the data from the past decade has proved that fiscal discipline and low interest rates *can* produce broad-based prosperity. It was the Republicans' hard luck that their candidates were too inarticulate to take advantage of these developments in 1996.

The most immediate effect of the Democratization of Money is that class warfare—a tested and, in my mind, wholly honorable political tactic—as previously practiced is outdated. Yes, we are a country still divided along class and income lines. Indeed, the pernicious trend of income inequality (or perhaps more accurately, *asset* inequality) has not abated in the Clinton years. But the old polarities of haves and have-nots, rich and poor, Wall Street and Main Street, don't have the same clarity they once had: Not when David Bronner in Alabama is a more significant investor than Ron Perelman. Not when Carl McCall controls more equities than the hedge-fund giant Julian Robertson. Not when a union can rally fellow shareholders to defeat a measure proposed by the billionaires who run Marriott. Not when an up-from-the-bootstraps Democrat from Brooklyn and Clinton's former treasury secretary run Citigroup. Not when half the families earning $25,000–$50,000 own equities, either directly or indirectly. Not when the *Wall Street Journal's* editorial page rhapsodizes about "Worker Capitalists." In 2000, when we speak about the ownership of companies, we're no longer talking exclusively about the Rockefellers and the members of the Trilateral Commission. Rather, we're talking about the Smiths and the members of the Huntsville (Alabama) All-Star Bowling League.

In an era when one household in thirty has assets of more than $1 million, and a substantial percentage of the other twenty-nine are trading and saving their way to that lofty aerie, the usefulness of running against the rich may be declining. The authors of the surprise bestseller *The Millionaire Next Door* note that the typical millionaire lives more like Joe Sixpack than Robin Leach. Just so, pointing to the dichotomy between the performance of Wall Street and the travails of the middle class—as Michael Dukakis did in 1988, Bill Clinton did in 1992, Bob Dole did in 1996, and Dan Quayle (among others) did in 1999—is no longer a viable tactic without further explanation. Running against the markets is a recipe for disaster. Anybody who tries to spook them, or who revels in a 300-point drop in the Dow, would be branded a traitor to the vast investor class. In 2000, no mainstream politician, save Pat Buchanan, is standing astride the roaring market and trying to tame it. The choice for the rest is to embrace the new era—to run with the jubilant bulls—or to lumber around with the grumpy bears.

The age of rational exuberance calls for a more nuanced brand of class warfare—one that centers on the issues discussed in the previous chapters. Now that the personal *finance* has become the political, controversies over investments and the markets inevitably take on a political tinge. In the absence of war, economic crisis, and pressing social issues, these matters will assume greater prominence in upcoming elections. As Jack Kemp put it in 1996, "Democratic capitalism is not just the hope of wealth, but it's the hope of justice." Today, the world can be divided between those who strive for justice and those who commit injustice, between those who *get* the democratization of money and those who don't. Many executives have embraced the new era by making the world safe for investors, and understand that being involved with a public company means being party to a democracy. Others rig the system to reap more than they deserve, and routinely elevate their interests over those of the public. Sapping a public company of its strength and resources is a violation of public trust—no less serious than that of a politician who reneges on a campaign promise or prostitutes his office for private gain.

In 2000 and beyond, therefore, the armies of class warfare should line up not along lines of capital versus labor but in the trenches that separate two often competing *kinds* of capital: humble capital and arrogant capital. This distinction refers not only to means of the people behind the capital but also to the attitudes of the managers. Humble capitalists— managers of public pension funds, union pension funds, and TIAA-CREF, and many executives—take seriously their role as fiduciaries for millions of investors. Arrogant capitalists regard their responsibilities cynically and use their positions essentially to cheat. With apologies to Lenny Bruce: Hotel workers are humble capital. Bill Marriott is arrogant capital. David Bronner is humble capital. Robert Rubin is humble capital. Companies that want to charge for access to SEC documents are arrogant capital. John Bogle, founder of the Vanguard funds, is humble capital. Reckless hedge-fund manager's like John Meriweather are arrogant capital. Offering options to all employees, as Starbucks does, is humble capital. Repricing options for top executives is arrogant capital. No-load mutual funds are humble capital. Internet trades for $8.95 at Ameritrade are humble capital. Commissions of $200 for 500-share transactions at Merrill Lynch are arrogant capital. Arthur Levitt's town hall meetings are humble capital. Millionaire politicians like Steve Forbes who advocate tax cuts that benefit the rich disproportionately are arrogant capital.

Until recently, the terms of art that define the stock market have been confined to newspaper business sections and cable networks. Now that they've burst onto the front page and into the nation's consciousness, it is perfectly reasonable—even mandatory—for politicians to talk about them. In an era when the discussion of putting Social Security funds in the stock markets is commonplace, candidates may increasingly be asked to discuss P/E ratios, and could be forced to bone up on the prices of stocks the way they were once forced to memorize the price of a gallon of milk. Poor George W. Bush: He not only has to memorize the unpronounceable names of leaders of obscure outposts like Chechnya and Pakistan, but he also has to know the difference between a 401(K) and a SEP-IRA.

Indeed, issues that were once relegated to the darkest recesses of *Kiplinger's* are now being plastered on the front page. The arcane world of pensions is a prime example. Along with George Will's columns, pension reform is one of the most potent cures for insomnia. The very mention of the dread term can induce glaze in the eyes of even the most ardent policy wonks. But with astonishing speed in fall 1999, a savings vehicle known as the "cash-balance pension" entered the political arena. Under traditional defined-contribution plans, pensions were determined by formulas based on age and years of service. Contributions escalated with years of service, and companies made the largest contributions in employees' final years of work. Under so-called "cash-balance" plans, approved by the IRS in 1985, companies make monthly contributions based on a percentage of an employee's pay. That allows younger employees to amass larger savings in their first years of employment. Cash-balance plans are more suited to the new economy, since they are more easily portable. As important, they're cheaper for companies to administer.

In the past fifteen years, more than 300 of America's largest companies have adopted cash-balance plans, but the change has stirred controversy. When companies switch, older employees frequently find that the large contributions they expected under defined-contribution plans evaporate, making their pensions worth substantially less than projected. In summer 1999, older IBM employees, angered by that company's conversion, began to protest loudly. Workers at a plant in Vermont found a sympathetic ear in the person of Representative

Bernie Sanders. Vermont Senator James Jeffords, the Republican chairman of the Senate Health, Education, Labor, and Pensions Committee, scheduled hearings. And the IRS and the Equal Employment
Opportunity Commission announced their intention to boost their
scrutiny of cash-balance plans.

Seeking to head off controversy and political action, IBM in
September said it would let employees over age forty with ten years of
service opt to remain in the traditional plan. But the issue continued to
spill into political debate. Democratic senators like Pat Leahy and
Edward Kennedy said they would introduce legislation to regulate such
conversions. In November 1999, Al Gore proposed that companies
switching to cash-balance plans essentially guarantee the value of the
benefits under the old plans, and that older employees with fifteen
years of service be allowed to stay in existing plans. The issue poses
more complexity than most political reporters can unravel, so it probably won't get much play on *Meet the Press*. But as candidates traverse
the nation and chat with voters at town hall meetings, they are likely to
face as many questions about cash-balance pensions as they are about
missile-defense systems and welfare reform.

Given the changing mind-set of the electorate, there are several less
complicated money- and investment-related issues and positions that
candidates can make use of in the 2000 elections and beyond—at the
House, Senate, or presidential level. Together, these topics constitute a
manual for class warfare in the age of rational exuberance, a sort of
"Contract with Investing America." And though it might be easy for
Democrats to pick up these two-by-fours and brain their Republican
opponents with them, there's no reason Republicans could not, or
should not, pound them into their platforms as well.

Executive Compensation

One of the most easily identifiable aspects of arrogant capital is excessive executive compensation. CEOs love to yammer about perfor-

mance. When a division doesn't perform up to snuff, they jettison it. When a manager doesn't meet his or her numbers, it's bye-bye. But they have a curious blind spot when it comes to their own compensation, which by and large bears absolutely no correlation to their performance. Between 1990 and 1998, average CEO pay at the nation's largest companies rose from $1.8 million to $10.6 million—17 times the pace at which workers' wages rose. CEOs receive huge pay raises and option grants when their companies and stocks do well. And they get huge pay raises and option grants when their companies and stocks do poorly. CEOs frequently justify a company's poor performance—and hence their lack of responsibility for it—by blaming the market or the industry or the sector. If they trail the S&P 500 by 80 percent, then it was simply a difficult or challenging year. On the other hand, when they keep pace with the market, they're geniuses, worthy of Michael Jordan–esque remuneration.

Being a CEO is a tough, highly demanding job. And for some executives, the top job is the culmination of decades of exceedingly hard work; for example, Ivan Seidenberg, the CEO of Bell Atlantic, started as a line installer. As a society of investors, we should not as a matter of principle begrudge CEOs the high salaries they earn. On the other hand, there is something rotten about the whole system of executive compensation. Generally, the putatively independent members of the board of directors' compensation committee are beholden to the CEO for their directorships, and frequently rely on them for consulting, investment banking, or legal business. Executive-compensation consultants, who advise boards on how to structure salaries and other benefits, are in the pockets of the companies. The process is, in essence, an undemocratic sham. And the size of many salaries is downright obscene—especially for a group of people who cavil against raising the minimum wage. The recent salary history of Disney's Michael Eisner has proved to be one of the more grotesque examples of the divergence between pay and performance. But there are dozens of others.

Representatives of humble capital have been trying to put a crimp in executive pay. Responsible Wealth, a Boston-based group composed of 400 *vieux riches*, has been filing proxy resolutions seeking to cap executive pay at companies like BankBoston. The Louisiana Teachers Retirement System, a public pension fund, filed proxy resolutions with Occidental Petroleum protesting its executive-pay practices. In the previous five years, the company's CEO, Ray Irani, had been paid about $100 million while Occidental's stock underperformed the S&P 500 by half. Under fire from institutional investors to tie Irani's compensation more closely to performance, Occidental bought out his existing contract in fall 1997 for a stratospheric $95 million and took a $54 million charge against earnings.

Back in 1992, candidate Clinton argued that companies shouldn't be allowed to deduct more than $1 million of CEOs' salaries from taxable income, and said shareholders should determine the compensation of top executives. Eight years later, neither proposal has much chance of becoming law. Still, a politician of any stripe could score some points by calling attention to examples of egregious executive pay and by calling for boards of directors to mend the error of their ways. It's not envious or socialistic to insist that millionaires and billionaires earn their paychecks, just as is required of welfare mothers and minimum-wage workers. In this investor nation, when seemingly everybody tracks the performance of stocks, there's nothing wrong with making public examples of avaricious CEOs who break faith with the public by taking compensation they don't deserve. It's a matter of *responsibility* and *accountability*—words that resonate with compassionate conservatives as much as they do with New Democrats.

Options

Stock options are the cocaine of the 1990s—thrown around by the rich with reckless abandon and without regard for the way they erode values. Just as with its chemical analogue, the options epidemic merits public discussion. On the one hand, the prevalence of options seems to betoken a heartening trend to link executive pay to performance. After all, between 1992 and 1997, the percentage of CEOs' pay that came from salary and bonus fell from 45 percent in 1992 to 24 percent in 1997, whereas the percentage coming from stock options rose from 37 per-cent to 64 percent, according to *Executive Compensation Reports*. But research suggests that there is no correlation between the existence of large option grants and performance. Alfred Rappaport of L.E.K. Con-sulting reported that of the stock options given over the past six years to CEOs of companies in the Dow Jones industrial average, 60 percent went to bosses whose companies lagged their industry competitors, while 68 percent went to those whose firms lagged the S&P 500.

There's more to the story. Each option granted gives the owner the ability to buy a share at a lower price. When exercised, these options add shares to the number of shares outstanding—that is, the "float." By issuing options, in other words, a company is selling pieces of itself for bargain-basement prices, and allowing executives and employees then to make money by selling the optioned shares at the market price. The government doesn't require companies to record such option grants as expenses, but they can have a substantial cost to shareholders. Accord-ing to the *Analyst's Accounting Observer*, sixty-five of the S&P 500 com-panies have options outstanding equal to more than 10 percent of basic shares outstanding, while another forty-one have between 5 percent and 10 percent outstanding. These include well-known and widely held companies like Dell. If a substantial portion of these options were exer-cised at any of these firms, existing shares held by the public would drop in value.

Options are designed to carry risk. They have value *if and only if* the stock rises above the target, or strike, price. That's why CEOs sitting on huge option grants—like General Electric's Jack Welch—work fever-ishly to ensure that their stocks rise consistently. For the past several years, as the market has risen as if fueled by Viagra, pumping up stock prices has been a relatively easy task for most CEOs. But when stocks slump, options are generally the first casualty. In a matter of days, CEOs' and managers' massive option grants can plunge in value from millions to worthless. That's how options are *designed* to work.

But in a trend that undermines shareholder democracy, and gives the lie to pay-for-performance, companies simply have taken to repricing existing options at lower strike prices. Voilà! They're in the money again. There is a certain strategic rationale in the maneuver. Employers rightly fear that employees with worthless options may be more eager to jump ship. Executives and computer programmers alike have wrongly come to view options as entitlements rather than incentives. This sensibility has frequently led companies to reprice options prematurely. In summer 1998, Ciena Corporation's share plummeted from the 80s to the low teens after the telecommunications equipment company botched some major orders and a merger was canceled. To keep employees and managers from bolting, Ciena that fall repriced employee stock options to $12^3/_8$. Ciena's CEO, Patrick Nettles, called the move "a critical element in helping us retain our team." In the next year, the company's fortunes improved, and Ciena's stock more than quadrupled, topping 50 in November 1999. The repricing turned out to be an enormous gift to employees at the expense of shareholders.

Frequently, the beneficiaries of such actions aren't low-level techies but top-level executives. The SEC requires disclosure of option repricings only for the top five executives. According to the Investor Responsibility Research Center, 231 of the 1,800 largest companies announced option repricings for their top five employees in 1998 or 1999. The large-scale granting of options was meant to ensure that top executives, middle managers, and shareholders all ride in the same boat, floating or sinking together. But option repricings make the reality more like the situation on the *Titanic*, on which the first-class passengers and favored staffers filled up the lifeboats while the rest were left to fend for themselves.

What to do? The State of Wisconsin Investment Board has been pushing for companies to amend their bylaws to make option repricings subject to shareholder votes. That's a good start. But such reforms should go a step further. What about banning option repricings for CEOs? CEOs who build companies from the ground up are unlikely to jump ship for a competitor. And with options on millions rather than thousands of shares, they have far more incentive to stick around for the long term in hopes of a recovery. Besides, top executives have figured out dozens of ways to extract money from the companies they run — from interest-free loans to massive unnecessary pensions. Forbidding the richest of the rich from defining performance down wouldn't exactly be controversial.

Public Stewardship

Conservative virtuecrats such as William Bennett have been quick to denounce the loose morals of Hollywood, the president, single mothers, abortion providers, gays, and pretty much everybody else they find objectionable. Of course, they are generally silent about the loose virtues of people who undermine confidence in the public markets by treating publicly held companies like private piggy banks. The management of publicly held companies is likely to find its way into politics more and more in the coming years. After all, the Republican frontrunner's involvement with an ill-fated public firm led to an SEC investigation. (George W. Bush was ultimately cleared.) And Donald Trump, whom some news producers seem to take seriously as a presidential candidate, has been involved with several public companies.

In 1995, Trump took his casino company, Trump Casino Hotel and Resorts, public at $14. In the years since, its stock has fallen hard, to about $3 in 1999. (According to *Fortune*, the company ranked 469th out of 469 firms surveyed for its tally of the most admired companies.) Trump, of course, owns 42 percent of the company. But the Donald has found manifold ways to wrest money from the pockets of his public shareholders. Between 1996 and 1998, years in which the stock fell sharply, Trump, who sits on the company's compensation committee, received at least $8 million in direct compensation. It gets worse. In the second half of 1998, Trump took no less than $26 million out of the company, including a $24.5 million loan and a $1.5 million advance on his 1999 salary. The investors who own 58 percent of Trump Hotels apparently did what no sane banker would do—they floated cash to Trump for personal uses at the same interest rate Chase Manhattan extends to its prime customers. Those customers, unlike Trump, do not have a history of stiffing bondholders and bank lenders. And this is the man who announced an interest in the *Reform* Party nomination!

The insult and pain of holding such stocks are frequently compounded by the arrogance of the managers. Richard Snyder, the publisher who was booted from his roost at Simon & Schuster in 1994, plotted his comeback by taking over Golden Books Family Entertainment in 1996. In the ensuing three years, Snyder tried to transform the publisher of children's books like *Pat the Bunny* into a full-fledged adult publishing house, and moved most of the offices from Racine, Wisconsin, to New York. "Racine is a place you cannot get to," he told *Vanity Fair.* "And I was not, at my age, with two little kids, going to spend all my time making air connections to Racine." Over the next three years, he earned more than any other publishing executive save the CEOs of far larger firms such as Barnes & Noble and McGraw-Hill, while leading Golden Books straight into bankruptcy. The stock fell from $12 in early 1998 to a few cents in 1999. "Don't forget, buying stock doesn't mean you make money," Snyder said. True. But shareholders also don't expect to have the CEO destroy virtually the entire $400 million value of a company in two years while pocketing millions in salary and benefits.

The litany could go on. It would be easier to swallow such self-dealing and poor performance if these men expressed some contrition for their awful stewardship of public capital. After all, entrepreneurs who voluntarily sell shares of their companies to the public are nominating themselves for a form of public office. There should be consequences when they don't live up to their duties. This is one area of business where Japanese business culture is far ahead of us. Just imagine seeing a CEO of a U.S. company whose stock blows up because of a botched acquisition call a press conference and symbolically impale himself upon a six-foot pike. But almost to a man, the executives who fail miserably take no responsibility for their actions. Erecting a public stockade for those who by their inane actions, greed, and bullheadedness imperil the savings of millions of Americans might be a good start. Bill Clinton had the audacity to name names in 1991, singling out Salomon Brothers as a bad actor. Why not use the bully pulpit to shame executives into being better stewards of public capital? It's something Democrats *and* Republicans could carry off with aplomb.

Heroes

Class warfare in 2000 is a matter not only of criticizing bad managers but also of publicly identifying and rewarding the good ones. Sure, CEOs of companies get plenty of validation, from puff-job cover stories to the obeisance of fawning employees. But there are some genuine stockholders' heroes out there, and they deserve recognition. This concept goes in the cheap category. Associating oneself with popular chief executives who have made investors rich doesn't exactly demand a high profile in courage. Besides, some of them happen to be Democrats— like the sainted Warren Buffett, who has made millionaires out of hundreds of people who did nothing more than buy a few shares of his stock and hold on to them. In return, he takes little compensation.

There's nothing wrong with becoming a billionaire in this country, especially if you're carrying people along with you, and if your wealth stems almost entirely from the appreciation of common stock, which increases at the same rate as that of the investor who has 100 shares socked away in a retirement account. Bill Gates's Croesus-like wealth is easier to swallow, despite his occasionally unsavory business practices, because Microsoft's stockholders share in his wealth—his gazillions come from actual stock ownership, not options. Any value Gates adds to his kids' trust funds is also added proportionately to the fund of the middle manager in Iowa with 100 Microsoft shares socked away in a 401(K). The *Wall Street Journal* in June 1999 ran a front-page story about Fred Housel, a commercial photographer without a college degree, who bought 150 shares of Microsoft in 1987 and held on as the stock rose, split, and then rose and split again. Over the years, he occasionally sold a few shares, using the proceeds to buy a second home, or bought a few more. By 1999, he had some 14,000 shares worth $1.2 million.

Well-run companies that pay attention to their stockholders can make people's dreams come true. There are dozens of other examples: Wal-Mart, General Electric, Home Depot, America On-Line, Cisco Systems, among others. Why not invite the founders and proprietors of these firms to the White House for a summit? Or call them to Capitol Hill to testify on the glories of shareholding, the risks of options, the perils of excessive executive compensation, or other important issues? Or create Medals of Honor for executives who have created billions of dollars in value for their shareholders? This is such a cheap and easy means of showing appreciation that even President Clinton could have carried it off.

Preserve, Protect, and Strengthen the SEC

Just because the SEC is a nonpartisan agency doesn't mean more can't be made of its successes. Arthur Levitt Jr. is an admirable, effective public servant, who deserves more attention than he gets. In a decade in which congressional leaders spoke of eliminating entire cabinet departments, the SEC quietly proved its worth in spades. It has presided over a vast expansion of the markets while enacting significant changes that affect the lives of individual investors. Understaffed, underpaid, and frequently outgunned, the SEC's policemen and policewomen are helping to make the streets, and the Street, safe for investors. The democratization of money would have been impossible without people's confidence in the markets. In an era when the most popular and revered federal appointees have been the guardians of the bull market—former Treasury Secretary Robert Rubin and Federal Reserve Chairman Alan Greenspan—it makes sense to promote the good work done by the SEC.

Plus, the institution could use some help. After all, it is arguably the most important consumer protection agency in the government. But turnover has been high, because salaries of government jobs severely lag those paid in the private sector. Top SEC officials, veterans in their forties and fifties, earn about what a fourth-year associate at a midsized Manhattan law firm does. Also, because of the vast expansion of the mutual fund industry, there is a great demand for lawyers and other professionals who know their way around the SEC. Indeed, the revolving door is part of the allure of working for the agency. Levitt has made a practice of rewarding staffers by acting as an outplacement agent. In the week before his reconfirmation hearings in March 1998, Levitt asked Congress for an extra $7 million to pay bonuses to SEC staffers. He was turned down. "We didn't get it, and I'm asking for it again," Levitt said.

In 1999, Clinton proposed budgeting $341.1 million for the SEC, and it ultimately received $351.3 million. That's an improvement from 1993, when its budget was $253 million. But the SEC's staff hasn't increased since 1996. Requesting more money for the SEC is another cheap action, because the agency takes in far more money than it spends. In 1998, the SEC collected $1.78 billion in fees—the sixteenth consecutive year it collected fees greater than its operating expenses. As one of the few government agencies that turns a profit without inhibiting the expansion of the industry it oversees, the SEC deserves more funding. That would allow the agency to hire more compliance and enforcement officers, invest in the necessary technology, and raise salaries. Fighting stock fraud is no less a social imperative than fighting crime. And unlike most violent crime, financial crimes fall within the federal government's jurisdiction. The Clinton administration has long crowed about its efforts to put 100,000 new cops on the street. The next administration should call for more cops on Wall Street.

Encourage Shareholder Democracy

One of Arthur Levitt's signal contributions has been to consistently encourage the American public to become intelligent consumers of financial services products. This is a lesson politicians can teach as well. Instead of ignoring the markets' success over the past several years, politicians, especially Democratic ones, should embrace it. It behooves Al Gore to tout how well the markets have performed under the Clinton-Gore administration, about how many new investors have entered the markets and done reasonably well, about how the financial services industry has made great efforts to serve humble capital. The American dream now includes a brokerage account stocked with GM and AOL. There's no reason a poor white kid in Hope, Arkansas, can't aspire to that lofty goal, any less than he can aspire to become president.

So politicians should encourage people to invest, and to invest smartly. Yes, there's a hazard to this, especially if the markets slump for a long period. But there exist thousands of different types of investments—index funds, bond funds, international funds. Most are diversified and relatively conservative. From dividend reinvestment plans to mutual funds that bear a $250 fund minimum, from IRAs to state-administered college savings plans, there are dozens of vehicles for even the most modest of investors to choose from. The expansion of such instruments should be encouraged.

In his 1994 book *Arrogant Capital*, Kevin Phillips denounced the notion that companies are run primarily for their shareholders' benefit as "financialization"—a socially destructive force. The logical conclusion of financialization, of course, is the democratization of money. Companies *should* be run for their shareholders, but for *all* their shareholders—for the founding CEO who owns 15 million shares, for the mutual fund that owns 2 million shares, for the young accountant who has stowed 100 shares in an IRA, for the teamster whose pension fund holds several hundred thousand shares. Once people invest, they should be encouraged to participate in the ownership of their companies and mutual funds. Politicians should encourage people to read their prospectuses and proxy statements and to vote their shares. Mutual funds and pension funds should be given further inducements to render accounts of their activities in plain English. And companies should be forced to highlight executive pay and examples of self-dealing more plainly. All these efforts can help make stockholders experience their ownership. With apologies to all those who revere John F. Kennedy's memory: Ask not what you can do for your corporation; ask what your corporation can do for you!

Read My Lips: No New Across-the-Board Tax Cuts
Throughout the 1990s, the Republicans kept clanging the tax-cut bell that rang so harmoniously in the 1980s. But the vibe is gone. And that's why Democrats should stand firm in opposing broad-based cuts in payroll or capital-gains taxes. It's good fiscal policy, and it's better class-war policy. Despite all the positive news of the past decade—seven years of economic growth, 8,000 points on the Dow, the swinging of the budget from a $292 billion annual deficit to annual surplus—many Republicans still believe that high taxes are holding this country down. Never mind the longest peacetime expansion and the largest legal accumulation of wealth in world history. If we just cut that 39.6 percent marginal tax rate, then we'd really see some growth.

Such inanities are generally confined to the *Wall Street Journal* editorial page and Cato Institute press releases. But the thesis exerts a remarkably powerful hold on the conservative mind. In the mid-1990s, Larry Kudlow, the smooth-talking market pundit and Reagan administration budget official, experienced a harrowing and embarrassingly public bout of addiction to cocaine that cost him his job as chief economist at Bear Stearns. He checked into Hazelden (a rehabilitation center in Minnesota), converted from Judaism to Catholicism, landed a new job, and is, by all accounts, a changed man. The introduction in his book of collected columns is larded with New Age homilies about his "journey." Kudlow has shed his 1980s skin entirely—except for his adherence to supply-side economics. (Perhaps there's a different twelve-step program for the unfortunates saddled with that addiction.) In early 1999, he claimed that the Republicans, who were put on this earth to cut taxes, had been "snookered" into helping Mr. Clinton defend big government, adding "it is not moral to deny tax relief to ordinary people."

Set aside for the moment Kudlow's credibility as a moral arbiter. The problem with virtually any dramatic effort to cut taxes is that ordinary people frequently do not benefit. And the American people, in their wisdom, know it. In early 1999, congressman Jon Kasich, seeking to jump-start one of the many Republican presidential campaigns without any visible means of support, floated the idea of a 10 percent across-the-board tax cut. Senate Majority Leader Trent Lott, lacking any original ideas, latched onto it. The proposal, which had about as many legs as Kasich's candidacy, quickly fell prey to some good old-fashioned class warfare. Citizens for Tax Justice, a liberal research outfit, issued a report contending that 62 percent of the proposed tax cuts would go to the wealthiest one-tenth of all taxpayers. The House and Senate Joint Tax Committee—which somehow didn't get the message that it was supposed to cook the books in the Republicans' favor—prepared a study saying that about 48 million taxpayers would get no relief whatsoever from the initiative. Most of those people, of course, were American families earning less than $30,000 and already paying no income taxes due to various credits. By definition, their federal income taxes *can't* be cut. As if on cue, Democratic stalwart Charles Rangel rode in from stage left, brandishing a mace. "To call this a tax cut for all Americans insults the nearly 50 million families who pay taxes and do not get a penny," he told the *Wall Street Journal*.

It stands to reason that the wealthy will benefit disproportionately from this—or any—tax cut. That's largely because they pay a disproportionately large share of taxes. As Heritage Foundation economist Daniel Mitchell noted, the top 1 percent of income earners pay more than 30 percent of the total income tax burden, while the wealthiest 10 percent of earners pay more than 60 percent. By contrast, the lower half account for less than 5 percent of federal tax revenues. In 1997, the highest-ranking 111,000 of the 120 million tax returns filed received 19.9 percent of all reported household income, up from 14.6 percent in 1994. In the same years, the share of all household income taxes paid by the top earners rose to 37.2 percent from 29.9 percent. As the Congressional Budget Office put it, "The more unevenly income is distributed, the higher the effective tax rate will be." The rich *are* different from you and me. They pay more taxes—which is as it should be.

The fact that the rich carry the largest tax burden shows that our system of progressive taxation works exactly as intended. It's why the benefits of any broad-based tax reduction will appear *de minimus* to the vast majority of middle-income Americans, especially compared with the windfalls reaped by their richer countrymen. It also explains why repeated Republican attempts to cut taxes have failed to catch fire. In summer 1999, beleaguered congressional Republicans, seeking to reclaim the political high ground, proposed a tax-cut package worth nearly $800 billion. Clinton brushed it off as easily as Newt Gingrich does the shackles of marriage. By that fall, Republicans had internalized the anticipated criticism. In December 1999, when George W. Bush announced a five-year, $483 billion across-the-board tax-cut plan, he described it as a way to "make life better for average men and women and children." Bush proposed slashing the top marginal rates from 39.6 percent and 36 percent to 33 percent. But he also called for reducing rates for the lower brackets even more severely, from 15 percent to 10 percent—a 33 percent cut.

In theory, Bush's proposal wasn't as skewed to the rich as previous Republican proposals were. But the figures, at least as calculated by Citizens for Tax Justice, shook out almost exactly the same. The group concluded that under Bush's proposal, the top 1 percent of earners, or those making $301,000 or more, would receive 36.9 percent of all reductions, while the top 10 percent, those with incomes of more than $89,000, would receive 61.6 percent of the cuts. The bottom 60 percent, those making below $38,200, would receive only 11 percent of the benefits. And guess what? Because of income inequality and progressive taxation, virtually any proposal that seeks to cut all marginal rates will produce similar results.

In the United States, the wealthy are worshiped, venerated, and admired. Well and good. But does anybody—save a few of the tone-deaf ultrarich—seriously feel the upper crust is overtaxed? We accept, without bitterness, the fact that Bill Gates is worth $85 billion. We likewise accept, with a smidgen of bitterness, that Steve Forbes and his brothers have several hundred million dollars at their disposal, simply because they went to the trouble of being born. Just so, nobody sheds a tear about the capital-gains taxes Gates must pay when he sells 500,000 shares of Microsoft to get some walking-around money. And something tells me the day trader who bought Amazon.com at 20 and sold it at 150 three months later isn't letting the capital-gains tax stop her from jumping back into the market. Nonetheless, the Republican party seems wedded to the notion that taxes are too high, and that they're particularly too high on the rich. As Democrats sound the Klaxons of class warfare, they would do well to remind their adversaries that the dread expression "soak the rich" has a proud Republican pedigree. On March

10, 1932, Fiorello LaGuardia, the Republican congressman from East Harlem, took to the House floor to denounce a flat-tax proposal. Arguing that Congress should instead boost taxes on luxuries, he bellowed, "I am simply going to say 'soak the rich.'"

LaGuardia was speaking in a time of great upheaval, when long-held notions of the natural order of things were being questioned. The state of affairs today is more stable than it was in the 1930s. But it is still more than a little confused. The sharp lines drawn between Republican revolutionaries and Democratic reactionaries as recently as 1994 have blurred. In the 2000 presidential campaign, it was the Republicans who started running too soon, and whose field was filled with a dozen-odd fringe and unviable candidates lining up in a circular firing squad. Meanwhile, the battle for the Democratic nomination quickly narrowed to a contest between two similarly moderate establishmentarians. And sometimes it's hard to distinguish the compassionate conservatives from the practical idealists. George W. Bush, striving to carry the standard for a party that expended a great deal of political capital bashing immigrants, lapses into Spanish the way Catskills comedian Myron Cohen used to revert to Yiddish. And when Al Gore announced his candidacy June 16, he sounded like the Gipper. "I want to keep our prosperity going, and I know how to do it. . . . Seven years ago, we needed to put America back to work, and we did."

The same situation holds for money issues. In 1999, Steve Forbes, the publisher of a magazine that is nicknamed "capitalist tool," sought to curry favor with Republican voters by lambasting Alan Greenspan as a threat to economic good times. Al Gore, who in the early 1990s had identified the internal combustion engine as one of the great threats to mankind, gave the Fed chairman the superlative grade of "A plus plus." In 2000, the one Rockefeller in public life is a Democrat, and the financial disclosures of several Republican members of the House read more like those of Money Store clients. A Democratic administration has emerged as the guardian of global financial markets, while Republicans have continually sought to undermine the shaky international financial architecture. Rightly or wrongly, the Clinton administration and its appointees—the list includes Alan Greenspan—have been given credit for the performance of the economy and the markets in the 1990s. Meanwhile, many congressional Republicans seem to have tired of the ravages of the markets and are increasingly skeptical of free trade. All of these factors present challenges and opportunities for anyone seeking elected office.

Politicians, be they Democrats or Republicans, should not shy away from wealth and money in the 2000 elections. They should encourage Americans to amass capital but not abase themselves before it, to love wealth but not the arrogant wealthy. George Bush was right about one thing in that disastrous 1992 debate. Just because a politician "has means" doesn't mean he can't identify with the aspirations and needs of people who are not as fortunate. FDR, the greatest Democrat of the past century, proved that. What matters is the *attitude* toward those means, and the way those means are employed.

The 2000 presidential election will assuredly come down to a choice between two millionaires. The one who doesn't understand the distinction between humble and arrogant capital, and the need to ally himself with the former against the latter, may suffer the same fate as Bush the Elder. It's still morning in America. And the opening bell on another trading day is about to ring.

Sources

For details and quotes on virtually all of the events and individuals described in this book, I relied on coverage in the *New York Times*, *Wall Street Journal*, *New York Daily News*, and *Business Week*. Government sources consulted for events and figures include the *Congressional Record*, and the Web sites of the Bureau of Economic Analysis, the Bureau of Labor Statistics, and the Federal Reserve Board. The annual reports and Web sites of the following organizations and trade groups provided a great deal of information on investors and investing: Securities Industry Association, New York Stock Exchange, Investment Company Institute, NASDAQ, and the Securities and Exchange Commission. All campaign donation figures came from the Center for Responsive Politics' Web site, www.crp.org.

CHAPTER ONE: THE DEMOCRATIZATION OF MONEY

Books used for this chapter included Beardstown Ladies Investment Club with Leslie Whitaker, *The Beardstown Ladies' Common Sense*

Investment Guide (New York: Hyperion, 1994); Haynes Johnson, *Sleepwalking Through History: America in the Reagan Years* (New York: W. W. Norton, 1991); Bryan Burrough and John Helyar, *Barbarians at the Gate: The Fall of RJR Nabisco* (New York: Harper-Perennial, 1990); Connie Bruck, *The Predator's Ball: The Junk-bond Raiders and the Man Who Staked Them* (New York: Simon & Schuster, 1988); William Jennings Bryan, *The Cross of Gold: Speech Delivered before the National Democratic Convention at Chicago, July 9, 1896* (Lincoln: University of Nebraska Press, 1997); and David Anderson, *William Jennings Bryan* (Boston: Twayne Publishing, 1981). The material on Greenspan was drawn in part from Stephen Beckner's *Back from the Brink: The Greenspan Years* (New York: John Wiley & Sons, 1996).

CHAPTER TWO: PUBLIC EMPLOYEE PENSION FUNDS
Much of the material on the Retirement Systems of Alabama was drawn from interviews with David Bronner and members of his staff. Bronner also gave me access to his extensive archival collection, which included back issues of *The Adviser*, RSA Annual reports, and hundreds of articles from Alabama and national newspapers and magazines. Material on the relationship between buy-out firms and public pension funds came from George Anders, *Merchants of Debt: KKR and the Mortgaging of American Business* (New York: Basic Books, 1992); Sarah Bartlett, *Money Machine: How KKR Manufactured Profits* (New York: Warner Books, 1991); and George David Smith and George Baker, *The New Financial Capitalists: Kohlberg Kravis Roberts and the Creation of Corporate Value* (Cambridge, UK: Cambridge University Press, 1998). Information on CALPERS and NYPERS came from those institutions' annual reports and Web sites.

CHAPTER THREE: PROLETARIAN INVESTORS AND UNWITTING MILLIONAIRES
Books used in this chapter included Theodore Lowi, *The End of Liberalism* (New York: Norton, 1969); Joseph Nocera, *A Piece of the Action: How the Middle Class Joined the Money Class* (New York: Simon & Schuster, 1994); Arthur A. Sloane, *Hoffa* (Cambridge: MIT Press, 1991); and Peter Drucker, *The Unseen Revolution: How Pension Fund Socialism Came to America* (New York: Harper & Row, 1976).

Tom Pinto of TIAA-CREF supplied me with annual reports, prospectuses, and a copy of William C. Greenough's *Its My Retirement Money; Take Good Care of It: The TIAA-CREF Story* (Boston, MA: Irwin, 1990). TIAA-CREF's annual reports and Web site also contained much valuable information.

Some of the material for this chapter came from interviews with Matthew Walker, Richard Ferlauto, Douglas Dial, and Peter Clapman. I also relied on several excellent articles on union shareholder activism in *Institutional Investor,* including Barry

Rehfeld's "The Man Who Would Save Union Pensions," December 1997, and "A Suite Victory for Shareholders," July 1998. Material on Thomas Jones came from "#2 at the World's Largest Retirement Fund," *Black Enterprise*, June 1994; "A Century at Cornell," *Cornell Daily Sun*, 1981, and the *Cornell Daily Sun*, April 19, 1999. Other important magazine articles included "Five Investing Lessons from America's Top Pension Fund," *Money*, January 1998, and "Teachers Expands its Curriculum," *Chief Executive*, November 1998.

CHAPTER FOUR: BILL CLINTON AND MONEY

The Wall Street Project provided tapes of the 1998 Wall Street Project conference. For data and accounts of events in the campaigns of 1992 and 1996, and the Clinton years, I relied on a host of books: Bill Clinton, *Putting People First* (New York: Times Books, 1992) and *Between Hope and History: Meeting America's Challenge for the 21ˢᵗ Century*, (New York: Times Books, 1996); Bob Woodward, *The Agenda: Inside the Clinton White House* (New York: Simon & Schuster, 1994) and *The Choice* (New York: Simon & Schuster, 1996); Robert Reich, *Locked in the Cabinet* (New York: Alfred A. Knopf, 1997); George Stephanopoulos, *All Too Human: A Political Education* (Boston: Little Brown, 1999); Elizabeth Drew, *On the Edge: The Clinton Presidency* (New York: Simon & Schuster, 1994), *Showdown: The Struggle Between the Gingrich Congress and the Clinton White House* (New York: Simon & Schuster, 1996), and *Whatever It Takes: The Real Struggle for Political Power in America* (New York: Viking, 1997); Stephen Beckner, *Back From the Brink*; E. J. Dionne, *They Only Look Dead* (New York: Simon & Schuster, 1996); Dick Morris, *Behind the Oval Office: Winning the Presidency in the 1990s* (New York: Random House, 1997); John Hohenberg, *Reelecting Bill Clinton: Why America Chose a New Democrat* (Syracuse: Syracuse University Press, 1997); Jack Germond and Jules Witcover, *Mad as Hell: Revolt at the Ballot Box* (New York: Warner Books, 1993); Jeffrey Birnbaum, *Madhouse: The Private Turmoil of Working for the President* (New York: Times Books, 1996); Michael Lewis, *Trail Fever* (New York: Alfred A. Knopf, 1997); Peter Goldman et. al., *Quest for the Presidency*, 1992 (College Station: Texas A&M University Press, 1994); Mary Matalin and James Carville (with Peter Knobler), *All's Fair: Love, War, and Running for President* (New York: Random House, 1994); *Almanac of American Politics*, 1992–1998.

CHAPTER FIVE: ARTHUR LEVITT AND THE SEC

The SEC's Web site—www.sec.gov—contains many of Levitt's speeches, public appearances, and enforcement activities. Chris Ullmann of the SEC's public affairs office provided me with the SEC's annual reports and Fiscal 200 Budget Estimate, as well as videotapes of an investor's town meeting, and set up my interviews with Arthur

Levitt Jr. and Nancy Smith. I also interviewed Carl Malamud and William Lutz. For Levitt's early career, I relied on Judith Ramsey Ehrlich and Barry J. Rehfeld, *The New Crowd: The Changing of the Jewish Guard on Wall Street* (New York: Little Brown, 1989). For the SEC's history, the best useful sources were Joel Seligman, *The Transformation of Wall Street: A History of the Securities and Exchange Commission* (Boston: Houghton Mifflin, 1982); John Brooks, *Once in Golconda: A True Drama of Wall Street, 1920–1938* (New York: Harper & Row, 1969); Arthur M. Schlesinger Jr., *The Age of Roosevelt* (Boston: Houghton Mifflin, 1957–1968); David A. Vise and Steve Coll, *Eagle on the Street* (New York: Scribner's, 1991); and James Stewart, *Den of Thieves* (New York: Simon & Schuster, 1991).

CHAPTER SIX: THE NEW MONEYCRATS
For coverage of Clinton's visit to the Hamptons I relied on several local newspapers, including *Dan's Papers*, *The Southampton Press*, *Easthampton Star*, and *Easthampton Independent*. Ehrlich and Rehfeld's *The New Crowd* contained a great deal of background on Felix Rohatyn and other Wall Street executives. Other books I used included Stephen Gaines, *Philistines at the Hedgerow: Passion and Property in the Hamptons* (Boston: Little Brown, 1998); Michael Bloomberg with Matthew Winkler, *Bloomberg by Bloomberg* (New York: John Wiley & Sons, 1997); Roger Lowenstein, *Buffett: The Making of an American Capitalist* (New York: Random House, 1995); Richard Gephardt, *An Even Better Place: America in the 21ˢᵗ Century* (New York: Public-Affairs, 1999); Felix Rohatyn, *The Twenty-Year Century: Essays on Economics and Public Finance* (New York: Random House, 1983); Daniel F. Burton Jr., Victor Gotbaum, and Felix Rohatyn, editors, *Vision for the 1990s: U.S. Strategy and the Global Economy* (Cambridge, Mass.: Ballinger Publishing Co., 1989); and Bruce Wasserstein, *Big Deal: The Battle for Control of America's Leading Corporations* (New York: Warner Books, 1998).

Key magazine articles included "Paramount Player," *Vanity Fair*, January 1994; "Wild on TheStreet.com," *Vanity Fair*, June 1999; and "Al Gore's Money Problem," *New York Times Magazine*, May 9, 1999.

CHAPTER SEVEN: THE REPUBLICAN RETREAT
The account of the Republicans' relationship with money and the markets in the 1990s drew from virtually all the sources cited in Chapter Four and a few other books: Bob Dole and Jack Kemp, *Trusting the People* (New York: HarperCollins, 1996); *Contract With America: The Bold Plan by Rep. Newt Gingrich, Rep. Dick Armey and the House Republicans to Change the Nation*, edited by Ed Gillespie and Bob Schellhas (New York: Times Books, 1994); Newt Gingrich, *To Renew America* (New York: Harper-

Collins, 1995); *America Votes* (Washington, DC: Elections Research Center, *Congressional Quarterly*, Vols. 20–23); Cary Reich, *The Life of Nelson A. Rockefeller: Worlds to Conquer, 1908–1958* (New York: Doubleday, 1996); Patrick Buchanan, *A Republic Not an Empire* (Washington, DC: Regnery, 1999); Steve Forbes, *A New Birth of Freedom* (Washington, DC: Regnery, 1999).

CHAPTER EIGHT: THE NEW POLITICS OF PERSONAL FINANCE

In addition to drawing upon many of the books cited previously, I relied on Kevin Phillips, *Arrogant Capital: Washington, Wall Street and the Frustrations of American Politics* (New York: Little Brown, 1994); Thomas J. Stanley and William D. Danko, *The Millionaire Next Door: The Surprising Secrets of Today's Wealthy* (New York: Longstreet Press, 1996); and Thomas Kessner, *Fiorello H. LaGuardia and the Making of Modern New York* (New York: McGraw-Hill, 1989). Significant magazine articles included "Dick Snyder's Tarnished Crown," *Vanity Fair*, May 1999.

Acknowledgments

Over the last three years, as *Bull Run* evolved from an undeveloped set of ideas into a finished book, many people at a variety of institutions have patiently endured my frequents runs of bull.

My agent, Sloan Harris, of ICM, helped shape my proposal, and prodded me to pursue it into a new and more incisive direction. I am grateful for his patience and counsel, and for the aid of his assistant, Teri Steinberg.

At PublicAffairs, Geoff Shandler and Peter Osnos decided to take a chance on this book. Geoff's gentle yet insistent editing has improved the manuscript in ways too numerous to count. Managing Editor Robert Kimzey expertly shepherded the project to completion,

Ida May B. Norton was a diligent copy editor, and Evan Gaffney and Mark McGarry were creative jacket and page designers, respectively. I'm also grateful to Publicity Director Gene Taft for all his hard work.

Ben Soskis was an excellent and efficient research assistant. Several editors allowed me to air bits and pieces of this book in their pages. My thanks to Bob Kolasky at *Intellectualcapital.com*, Glenn Coleman and Marlene Star at *Investment News*, and Alexander Star at *Lingua Franca*.

Over the last several years, many friends and colleagues have suggested sources, served as sounding boards, sent clippings, and provided havens on my trips to Washington. They include Larry Arnold, Glenn Coleman, Adam Lashinsky, Jonathan Rosenberg, Michael Santoli, David Shuster, and George David Smith. Tempting as it is to blame them for any mistakes that appear in the following pages, I alone am responsible for the contents of this book.

My two brothers, Michael and Leon Gross, both of whom work on Wall Street, have provided me with valuable perspective and background, cleared up misconceptions, and steered me away from mistakes. Needless to say, they did not provide any information on the institutions where they work.

My wife, Candice Savin, has lived with this project since its inception. Her constant love, good humor, and encouragement have sustained me throughout these last several years. Our daughter, Aliza, who provided me with a reason to take a break from writing every fifteen minutes, is a source of unending joy.

This book is dedicated to the two people who have had the greatest influence on my life. Through patient example—never didactic lecturing—my parents have taught me a number of immensely valuable lessons on everything from parenting to politics. Most important, they taught me that reading and writing can not only be great joys but the stuff of a life's work.

Index

PublicAffairs is a new nonfiction publishing house and a tribute to the standards, values, and flair of three persons who have served as mentors to countless reporters, writers, editors, and book people of all kinds, including me.

I. F. STONE, proprietor of *I. F. Stone's Weekly*, combined a commitment to the First Amendment with entrepreneurial zeal and reporting skill and became one of the great independent journalists in American history. At the age of eighty, Izzy published *The Trial of Socrates*, which was a national bestseller. He wrote the book after he taught himself ancient Greek.

BENJAMIN C. BRADLEE was for nearly thirty years the charismatic editorial leader of *The Washington Post*. It was Ben who gave the *Post* the range and courage to pursue such historic issues as Watergate. He supported his reporters with a tenacity that made them fearless and it is no accident that so many became authors of influential, best-selling books.

ROBERT L. BERNSTEIN, the chief executive of Random House for more than a quarter century, guided one of the nation's premier publishing houses. Bob was personally responsible for many books of political dissent and argument that challenged tyranny around the globe. He is also the founder and longtime chair of Human Rights Watch, one of the most respected human rights organizations in the world.

———

For fifty years, the banner of Public Affairs Press was carried by its owner, Morris B. Schnapper, who published Gandhi, Nasser, Toynbee, Truman, and about 1,500 other authors. In 1983, Schnapper was described by *The Washington Post* as "a redoubtable gadfly." His legacy will endure in the books to come.

Peter Osnos, *Publisher*